MEXICAN NATIONAL CINEMA

Mexican National Cinema offers an account of the development of Mexican cinema from the intense cultural nationalism in the aftermath of the Mexican Revolution, through the 'Golden Age' of the 1940s and the *Nuevo Cine* of the 1960s, to the renaissance in Mexican cinema in the 1990s.

The book moves from broad historical and theoretical contexts, particularly theories of nation, emergent discourses of 'mexicanidad' and the establishment and development of the Mexican industry, towards readings of key film texts and genres. Films considered include:

- *Y tu mamá también*
- *¡Que viva México!*
- *La mujer del puerto*
- *El castillo de la pureza.*

In each case, Andrea Noble considers the representation of nation inherent in these films and genres placing an emphasis on the ways in which they intersect with debates in cultural history, particularly Mexico's quest for modernity.

Mexican National Cinema provides and thorough and detailed account of the vital and complex relationship between cinema and national identity in Mexico.

Andrea Noble is reader in Latin American Visual Studies at the University of Durham. She is the author of *Tina Modotti: Image, Texture, Photography* (2000) and co-editor of *Phototextualities: Intersections of Photography and Narrative* (2003).

NATIONAL CINEMAS SERIES
Series Editor: Susan Hayward

MEXICAN NATIONAL CINEMA

Andrea Noble

Routledge
Taylor & Francis Group

LONDON AND NEW YORK

First published 2005 by Routledge
2 Park Square, Milton Park, Abingdon, Oxon OX14 4RN

Simultaneously published in the USA and Canada
by Taylor & Francis Inc
270 Madison Ave, New York, NY 10016

Routledge is an imprint of the Taylor & Francis Group

Typeset in Galliard by
Keystroke, Jacaranda Lodge, Wolverhampton
Printed and bound in Great Britain by
The Cromwell Press, Trowbridge, Wiltshire

British Library Cataloguing in Publication Data
A catalogue record for this book is available from the British Library

Library of Congress Cataloging in Publication Data
Noble, Andrea.
  Mexican national cinema / Andrea Noble.
    p. cm. – (National cinemas)
  Includes bibliographical references and index.
1. Motion pictures—Mexico. I. Title. II. Series: National cinemas series.
  PN1993.5.M4N63 2005
  791.43′0972—dc22   2005005097

ISBN10: 0–415–23009–8 ISBN13: 9–78–0–415–23009–4 (hbk)
ISBN10: 0–415–23010–1 ISBN13: 9–78–0–415–23010–0 (pbk)

CONTENTS

LIST OF ILLUSTRATIONS

ACKNOWLEDGEMENTS

This book exists thanks to the intellectual stimulation and support provided by many individuals and organisations. Forgoing the kind of narrative that conventionally accompanies acknowledgements, I'd simply like to list the colleagues, friends and family members who in different ways either provided advice and guidance, took the time to read and comment on drafts, opened my eyes to new ways of seeing things, or showed exceptional kindness and patience during some of the more difficult moments of the book's production. These people include: Katie Grant, John King, Ian Macdonald, Alex Hughes, Jonathan Long, Ed Welch, Claire Lindsay, Nuala Finnegan, Paul Julian Smith, Jo Labanyi, Antonio Sánchez, Jens Andermann, Chris Perriam, Ignacio Durán (the UK is exceptionally lucky to have such a dynamic and generous cultural attaché at the Mexican embassy), Patricia Torres San Martín, staff at the Filmoteca de la UNAM in Mexico City, especially Antonia Rojas, at IMCINE, especially Guadalupe Ferrer, and the CIEC in Guadalajara, César Avilés Icedo, Julia Tuñón, John Mraz, Seth Fein, Susan Hayward, Miriam Haddu, students on my Mexican film courses at Durham – especially Tom Rowson and Alexia Richardson, Heather Fenwick, Denise Ward. And of course, Lalo and Alma.

Books don't get researched and written without funding and I would like to acknowledge three institutions for their generous financial support of this project: The Arts and Humanities Research Board and the Secretaría de Relaciones Exteriores for research visits to film archives in Mexico and the Leverhulme Trust for a year's research fellowship during which most of the book was drafted.

I would especially like to thank the Trustees and Jean Cater of Leverhulme for their exceptional sensitivity at a difficult moment.

For the same reason, everyone at Routledge has been more than kind and patient; in particular, I would like to thank Aileen Irwin, Katherine Sheppard and Sandra Jones.

Finally, although they are no longer here, I thank my mother, Joyce and my grandmother, Phyllis.

INTRODUCTION

Para su público, los 'mitos' del cine nacional son puentes de entendi-
miento, rostros y figuras privilegiadas que asumen la biografía colectiva,
encarnaciones de experiencias pasadas y presentes.

For its audience, the 'myths' of the national cinema are bridges of
understanding, privileged faces and figures that stand in for collective
biography, embodiments of past and present experiences.

(Monsiváis 1990: 39)

Ask an urbanite Mexican to make a selection of the classic moments and key
protagonists – the myths – that evoke and emblematise Mexican cinema in the
contemporary popular imagination and chances are they would not struggle to
do so. As one of Latin America's most commercially successful film industries, the
institutions that constitute Mexican cinema have generated a panoply of movies,
directors and stars which occupy a privileged position in the popular imagination
both within the Republic itself, and across the Spanish-speaking world and those
parts of the United States with a high density of Latinos. For the Mexican film
buff, the list might include, in no particular order, some of the following:
archetypal couples – Tito Guízar and Esther Fernández in *Allá en el Rancho
Grande* (Over at the Big Ranch, Fernando de Fuentes, 1936); Dolores del Río
and Pedro Armendáriz in *María Candelaria* (Emilio Fernández, 1943), Pedro
Infante and Blanca Estela Pavón in *Nosotros los pobres* (We the Poor, Ismael
Rodríguez, 1948) and its sequels.

The inventory might incorporate iconic landscapes both rural and urban. The
central plateau of the Bajío region with its sculptural cacti and infinite skies as
captured by the lens of cinematographer Gabriel Figueroa and inhabited by proud
and picturesque Indians. The working-class *barrios* of the nation's metropolises
and particularly its capital, with their sleazy cabarets populated with exotic dancers
such as the Cubans Ninón Sevilla or María Antonieta Pons, or the starkly realistic
urban environment of *Los olvidados* (The Young and the Damned, Luis Buñuel,
1950).

The inventory would certainly include the working-class comic heroes: the northern *pachuco* (zoot-suiter) Germán Valdés 'Tin Tan', and the *pelado* (or working-class) Mario Moreno 'Cantinflas', whose verbal dexterity has officially passed into the Spanish language in the form of the verb '*cantinflear*', meaning 'to speak nonsense'.[1] It would undoubtedly be an oversight to omit the host of wrestlers, clad in tights and lamé masks, who enjoyed a period of celluloid popularity of some thirty years from the 1950s, and whose most celebrated representative was the mythical El Santo. Any inventory would be incomplete without signalling the presence of a host of stars who are purported to incarnate 'authentically Mexican' values, especially those who emerged during so-called Golden Age of the 1940s: the indomitable María Félix; the people's idol, Pedro Infante; *charro* or singing cowboy, Jorge Negrete; Dolores del Río; Pedro Armendáriz; etc.

Finally – and arguably more familiar to a contemporary, English-speaking audience – the Mexican cinema might be evoked in a number of successful films of recent years that have gained exhibition and critical acclaim in an international arena: *Danzón* (María Novaro, 1991), *Como agua para chocolate* (Like Water for Chocolate, Alfonso Arau, 1992), *Amores perros* (Love's a Bitch, Alejandro González Iñárritu, 2000), *Y tu mamá también* (And Your Mother Too, Alfonso Cuarón, 2001), or the controversial *El crimen del padre Amaro* (The Crime of Father Amaro, Carlos Carrera, 2002).[2]

This necessarily selective inventory, with its inevitable, yet not exclusive, emphasis on film culture of the 1940s, is not simply meant to whet the reader's appetite with a tantalising array of movies, stars and themes that point to Mexico's diverse and fascinating film culture. To the degree that it excludes more than it includes, it serves a purpose that is at once thematic and methodological and opens avenues of exploration that will be developed in this introduction and the chapters that follow. On the one hand, it invokes a cinema that enjoyed a nostalgically depicted Golden Age which coincided with a moment of national confidence and optimism; an era that is recalled with longing, and to which, recent international blockbusters notwithstanding, return has been elusive. It is also meant to signal a national cinema that is regarded with affection and whose myths and icons occupy a privileged position in cultural memory, a collection of fragments which in their diversity coalesce to signify Mexican identity at a moment of heightened nationalism.

In fact, the list and its idiom of nostalgia are not an invention. In 1990, the prestigious cultural magazine *Artes de México* devoted a special issue to a revision of the Mexican cinema. Based on an exhibition to commemorate national cinema, held at the equally influential Palacio de Bellas Artes (Palace of Fine Arts) in the heart of Mexico City, this particular issue is a lavishly illustrated celebration of iconic still images selected from the nation's cinematic patrimony. In addition to the stills, it contains the results of a survey devised to elicit an impressionistic sense of what remains of the Mexican cinema in the hearts and minds of some of its most devoted fans, the directors, scriptwriters, cinematographers, cultural critics and writers who, collectively, have produced this cultural institution. As Alberto Ruy Sánchez explains in the introduction: 'Intencionalmente hemos evitado en estas páginas el recuento global del cine mexicano. Nuestra aventura tiene el fragmento como material: la fotografía, el episodio memorable, el instante de intensidad estética' / 'We have intentionally avoided a global account of Mexican cinema in these pages. The fragment is the material of our adventure: photography, memorable episodes, and instants of aesthetic intensity' (Ruy Sánchez 1990: 23).

At the same time, the fragmentary, emblematic quality of the inventory, its allusive focus on that which endows the Mexican cinema with its peculiar 'Mexicanness', serves as a model for the organising principle of this book. *Mexican National Cinema* does not aim to present an all-inclusive chronological survey of the development of the Mexican cinema from its inception in 1896 through to the present day. Instead it is selective: it offers a series of case studies, exploring thematically oriented and methodologically inflected lines of inquiry that intersect with important debates in Mexican cultural history and issues in Latin American and Euro-American film studies. In brief, these include: the quest for modernity; the legacy of the Mexican revolution; the audience, movie theatres and spectatorship; melodrama, masculinity and the patriarchal state; the representation of indigenous Mexico; and the role of the US–Mexico border in the southern cultural imaginary. In each instance, the theme of the case study has been selected precisely because it seems to evoke and emblematise the 'Mexicanness' of this national cinema, where 'Mexicanness' is understood not as a reified and static concept, but rather a dynamic and fluid construct closely linked to patterns and changes in cultural and historical developments. To this end, the volume is organised as a series of diachronic case studies which precisely seek to reveal movement and flow. And yet, if this book eschews chronological survey in favour of diachronic case studies, this is not to suggest that the former approach lacks validity or relevance. Rather it is because the Mexican cinema is now admirably archived and well documented in Spanish and, increasingly, in English. Indeed, according to Eduardo de la Vega (1994: 22), a scholar who has been actively engaged in the process, it may be one of the most studied national film cultures in the world.

ON MEXICAN FILM STUDIES

Claims such as De la Vega's might prove difficult to substantiate. As a rhetorical gesture, nevertheless, it points to the fact that the Mexican cinema has generated considerable scholarly interest and engendered an extensive critical literature both in Mexico and, more recently, beyond, which testifies to the importance of this cinema's regional and international status.[3] In Mexico itself, publications devoted to the national cinema are prolific and diverse, ranging from non-academic magazines and coffee-table style books, to serious scholarly endeavours emanating from the established and highly respected centres for the study of cinema: the Filmoteca de la UNAM in the capital, and the Centro de Investigación y Enseñanza

Cinematográfica (CIEC) Guadalajara, amongst others. Of the former category, for example, are *Somos* (with issues dedicated to charting the lives and careers of a range of Mexican stars), or Editorial Clío's lavishly illustrated series devoted to periods and themes, such as the Golden Age, new cinemas and movie theatres. Available for purchase from news-stands and targeted at a non-specialist readership as collectors' items, both *Somos* and the Clío series testify to enduring popular interest in and nostalgia for the national film industry.

At the academic end of the market, Mexican film scholarship has a long and distinguished trajectory and its particular strengths lie in the rigorous socio-historical documentation of the national cinema. Perhaps unsurprisingly, the first steps towards preserving and documenting the nation's cinematic patrimony coincided with the fervour that surrounded the increased cinematic production of the Golden Age. Under the auspices of the Secretaría de Educación Pública, Mexico's first *filmoteca* was established in 1942, charged with the task of con-serving all state-produced films. Shortly afterwards in 1944, the pioneering film journalist José María Sánchez García made the first serious attempt to offer a more or less systematic chronicle of the Mexican cinema in a series of articles published in the newspaper *Novedades*. And finally, in the 1950s, the first encyclopaedias dedicated to the Mexican cinema appeared.

The 1960s, however, marked a watershed decade in Mexican cinema scholar-ship. Coinciding with developments in the cinema itself, namely the activities and initiatives associated with the *Nuevo Cine* or New Cinema group, the 1960s saw the emergence of a new generation of film and cultural scholars who shaped the direction of film scholarship to this day. First, the late Emilio García Riera, himself a key member of the *Nuevo Cine* group, started work on what would become the monumental, seventeen-volume series *Historia documental del cine mexicano* (Documentary History of the Mexican Cinema) which traces its development from 1929 to 1976. This series, the product of a three-decade labour of love, is an essential resource for Spanish-speaking scholars in the field. It provides a wealth of invaluable detail, including credits and synopses for over 5,000 films produced in the period surveyed, and also contextual information regarding cinematic legislation and policy, critical evaluations and more than a little dry wit. Charting the years 1929–37, the first volume was originally published in 1969 by Ediciones Era. Subsequent volumes, chronicling busier periods in cinematic history, tend to focus on spans of no more than two years.

Another landmark text in the history of Mexican film scholarship, Jorge Ayala Blanco's *La aventura del cine mexicano* (The Adventure of the Mexican cinema), was originally published in 1968 and covers cinematic production from 1931 to 1967. In contrast to the affectionate, but critically acute idiom that characterises García Riera's work, Ayala Blanco is renowned for his polemical style, which does not fight shy of vitriolic and openly hostile critical evaluations. Organised thematically, *La aventura del cine mexicano* subsequently gave rise to an on-going series of books, covering ensuing periods in film history, each taking its title from the following letter of the alphabet. Thus the series runs: *La búsqueda del cine mexicano* (The search of the Mexican Cinema, 1974); *La condición del cine mexicano* (Condition of the Mexican Cinema, 1986); *La disolvencia del cine mexicano* (Dissolution of the Mexican Cinema, 1991); *La eficacia del cine mexicano* (Efficacy of the Mexican Cinema, 1994); and most recently *La fugacidad del cine mexicano* (Fleetingness of the Mexican Cinema, 2001). As the titles indicate, with their downward spiral, after the optimism of '*aventura*', Ayala Blanco's provocative and caustic brand of film criticism has, if anything, become more acute over time.

Like film industries the world over, Mexico's film heritage of the early period is the most difficult to access, owing to a combination of erratic archival practices and outright neglect. Nevertheless, the work of Aurelio de los Reyes has done much to rescue the early period from obscurity and offers an incisive and historically rigorous insight into the first years of film practice. Based on painstaking research in public and private collections, the two volumes of *Cine y sociedad en México* (Cinema and Society in Mexico, 1981) cover the years 1896–1920 and 1920–24 and are an invaluable resource for scholars with an interest in early cinema.

To be sure, the work of García Riera, Ayala Blanco and De los Reyes focuses on a range of historical periods and each project is propelled by a different critical and personal agenda. The motor that drives each, however, is the impulse to document and chronicle the Mexican cinema: an impulse that is complemented by a range of more narrowly focused approaches to the study of national film culture. These include books that analyse the work of individual directors such as De la Vega's 'bio-filmographic' work on Juan Orol (1987), Alberto Gout (1988), Raúl de Anda (1989), Arcady Boytler (1992), José Bohr (1992) amongst others; Carlos Monsiváis's chronicles of cinema as popular culture;[4] or the 'Testimonios del cine mexicano' series (Testimonies of the Mexican Cinema), in which protagonists of the national cinema are interviewed by established critics about their work. These include directors Felipe Cazals (García Tsao 1994), Arturo Ripstein (García Riera 1988) and cinematographer Gabriel Figueroa (Isaac 1993). There is also a large body of scholarly and popular biographies of the major stars, including Dolores del Río (De los Reyes 1996b), María Félix (Taibo 1991), Pedro Infante (García, G. 1994a) and so on.

Until recently, the Mexican cinema was largely uncharted territory for those who do not read Spanish. However, this situation has changed dramatically, especially since the 1990s, a decade that marked the start of an on-going upsurge in interest in this national cinema in the English-speaking world. In this field, an early precursor, Carl J. Mora's *Mexican Cinema: Reflections of a Society* was originally published in 1982 and constitutes a comprehensive introduction to the industrial development of the Mexican cinema.[5] Ordered chronologically, each chapter provides detailed plot summaries of key films which are simultaneously framed within a discussion of the growth and decline of the industrial base, socio-historical events and parallel developments in both Latin American and Hollywood film production. Although a general history of Latin American cinema, John King's ambitious *Magical Reels* (1990/2000) is also in its second edition and contains important sections on Mexican cinema. A ground-breaking text that has been instrumental in mapping the terrain of Latin American film scholarship, King's book sets up a historical framework in which to understand the cinemas of the region and, moreover, pays careful attention to the links between these cinemas.

Following in the established, chronological mould, in 1996, the British Film Institute, in association with the Instituto Mexicano de Cinematografía (IMCINE) and the Consejo Nacional para la Cultura y las Artes, published *Mexican Cinema* to coincide with the centenary of this national cinema.[6] Edited by the Paris-based Brazilian critic Paulo Antonio Paranaguá, *Mexican Cinema* combines historical with thematic essays, and includes a lengthy introductory section detailing important political and cultural events alongside a chronology of film production; a history of the Mexican film industry from the silent cinema, through to 1991; sections on currents, structures and genres; a section on directors – including Emilio Fernández, Roberto Galvadón, Luis Buñuel; and finally a 'dictionary' section, featuring film synopses, filmographies organised by stars and directors and a substantial bibliography. Not only is Paranaguá's volume comprehensive, it is also noteworthy insofar as it introduces an English-language readership to the work of an impressive range of important Mexican film scholars, including some already mentioned in the present context: De los Reyes, García Riera and De la Vega – as well as Tomás Pérez Turrent, Carlos Monsiváis, Julia Tuñón, Leonardo García Tsao and Ariel Zúñiga. This trend towards showcasing Mexican film scholarship is continued in the volume edited by Joanne Hershfield and David Maciel, *Mexico's Cinema: A Century of Film and Filmmakers* (1999) which, as its title indicates, is also structured chronologically and includes thematic and survey-style essays by Mexican and US-based scholars of Mexican cinema.

In addition to these wide-ranging, general surveys, a growing number of English-language monographs have started to appear, centred on specific periods and themes. These draw, to a greater or lesser degree, on methodological approaches and preoccupations that have emerged in film studies as it is practised as an academic discipline in the Euro-American academy.[7] Thus Charles Ramírez Berg's *Cinema of Solitude* (1992) focuses on film production in the period 1967–83, probing issues of gender, state and the family. Joanne Hershfield's *Mexican Cinema/Mexican Woman, 1940–1950* (1996) explores six woman-centred melodramas of the 1940s in relation to prevalent culturally specific myths of femininity and sexual relations; whilst her *The Invention of Dolores del Río* (2000) draws on studies of performance, race and feminism to offer a detailed analysis of Del Río's star persona. Two recent, incisive additions to the English-language corpus continue the trend for scholarly interest in issues of gender with careful attention to socio-political context: Elissa J. Rashkin's *Women Filmmakers in Mexico* (2001) offers a historical overview of women's filmmaking from the 1930s and detailed analysis of the work of five contemporary directors, whilst Susan Dever's *Celluloid Nationalism and Other Melodramas* (2003) is transnational in focus (its subtitle is 'From Post-Revolutionary Mexico to *Fin de Siglo*

Mexamérica) and acutely sensitive to the role of gender in its discussion of this ubiquitous film mode.

To offer a detailed overview and in-depth critical analysis of the state of play in film scholarship related to the Mexican cinema would be a book-length project in itself. The foregoing snapshot serves to give a sense of the ways in which Mexican and, more recently, English-language scholarship have developed in the form of some of its most important monographs. In a nutshell, the former tradition has strong socio-historical affinities, concerned with documenting and chronicling the national cinema; it has remained largely, although not completely, impervious to the kinds of issues that have emerged in Euro-American film studies over the past thirty years. (The work of Julia Tuñón on gender and Patricia Torres on questions of reception, for instance, is exemplary of an emerging critical tradition in Mexican scholarship that attempts to marry national cinema with a culturally specific attention to developments in Euro-American film studies and theory.) The latter corpus of English-language studies, which has gained ground over the past ten to fifteen years, now offers a number of indispensable surveys and increasingly seeks to engage Euro-American film studies in dialogue with themes, debates and issues in Mexican film history and culture.

Mexican National Cinema, as will become clear in the pages and chapters that follow, acknowledges a profound debt to and draws widely on both Mexican and Anglophone scholarship. At the same time, it eschews chronological survey in favour of diachronically structured case studies, on one level and simply stated, because such monographs and anthologies already exist in abundance. On another level, however, it seeks to avoid an, albeit understandable, pitfall associated with the chronological survey, namely the lack of close audio-visual analysis, which invariably is sacrificed to the panoramic overview. In adopting a case-study-centred, close analytical approach, *Mexican National Cinema* is not, however, bereft of panoramic contexts that serve to anchor its analyses. Rather, in what remains of this introduction, I seek to frame the exegeses that are the subjects of the main body of this book in the light of two crucially important contextual settings. On the one hand, drawing on insights from Mexican history, particularly the work of Alan Knight, and with an emphasis on the first half of the twentieth century, I offer a general introduction to the events that gave rise to this period of heightened cultural nationalism.[8] On the other, having sketched the themes in cultural history that will inform the analyses that follow, I then provide an overview of the growth of the industrial bases of Mexican cinema, signalling the key developments, particularly the avatars of the relationship between state and cinema. In adopting this broad-brush approach, I aim to provide in condensed, synoptic form a backdrop to the films, themes and methodologies examined in the main body of this book.

ON MEXICAN CULTURAL HISTORY

In an important essay titled 'The Peculiarities of Mexican History: Mexico Compared to Latin America, 1892–1992', Knight sets out to 'offer some explanations of the distinctiveness (as well as commonality) of Mexico's history, compared to the history of Latin America, in the national period'. Observing, in a footnote, that it is not difficult to find claims for the distinctiveness of other Latin American countries, Knight (1992: 99) nevertheless provocatively suggests that 'Mexico – or Mexican history – is particularly distinct, peculiarly peculiar' for reasons that he elaborates in the body of the essay. Briefly, his point is that, ideological contradictions notwithstanding, the enormously complex 1910 revolution and the regime that it bequeathed conferred on Mexico a level of political stability and historical continuity that render it if not unique, then certainly uncommon in the region.

Mexico, like the rest of Latin America and the Spanish-speaking Caribbean, is the product of European expansionist ambitions in the fifteenth century which inaugurated the rise of (European) modernity understood as historical category and which established some three centuries of colonial rule.[9] Unlike other, later European colonial enterprises, the Spanish (and Portuguese) encounter with the so-called New World engendered significant miscegenation between native Amerindians, imported African slaves and European invaders, producing a hybrid colonial body politic that was as highly stratified and hierarchised as it was complex and ambiguous.[10] Mexico, like most Spanish-American countries, achieved independence from European domination in the early decades of the nineteenth century. The notion of 'independence' at a regional level, however, should be approached with a degree of caution. Whilst engendering the conditions for the production of the various polities that would come to form the republics of Spanish America, liberation from Spain did not give rise to clear-cut national entities. The historian and anthropologist Claudio Lomnitz describes this phenomenon in the following terms:

> Like many peripheral nations, Mexico emerged as the result of the collapse of an empire more than because of an overwhelmingly popular desire for national independence. Nationalism was thus not widely shared at the time of the national revolutions. Moreover, like most Spanish-American countries, Mexico achieved statehood long before its territory was bound together in a 'national market' or by a 'national bourgeoisie.' As a result, the territorial consolidation of the country was a long, conflict-ridden process involving secessions, annexations, civil wars, and foreign interventions.
>
> (Lomnitz 2001: 126)

Mexico's historical trajectory in the nineteenth century was, then, to mirror that of other Latin American nations to some degree. In broad terms, the century witnessed a search for national roots as the newly liberated republics cast around for cultural, social and political constructs to encapsulate their independent identities. Political turmoil and upheaval were, however, the order of the day for a significant proportion of the century. In concrete terms, turmoil in Mexico involved *inter alia* the Mexican-American war of 1846 in which US troops captured Mexico City; the loss of significant tracts of territory to the United States in 1848; and the ill-fated French intervention which installed Maximilian of Hapsburg as emperor in 1864.

Nevertheless, the 1910 Mexican revolution marked a moment of profound rupture that set the agenda of national development throughout the twentieth century, taking the Republic on a path that would distinguish it from the historical trajectories of other countries of the region. In 1910, with the celebrations to commemorate the centenary of independence from Spain barely over, Francisco Madero, a wealthy landowner from the northern state of Coahuila, drafted the Plan de San Luis de Potosí, calling for the nation to rise in revolution. The ensuing civil war was violent and protracted. Lasting 10 years, with a death toll of some 1.5 to 2 million, the revolution was hailed as Latin America's first social revolution and was to shape the course of Mexican history.[11] It swept aside the thirty-three-year presidential reign of Porfirio Díaz, during which Mexico experienced unprecedented peace and order after the political chaos of the post-independence years. During this period the country underwent a process of rapid and dramatic modernisation and urbanisation, which in turn brought about economic and material progress.[12] Despite this progress, the territory demarcated by the national boundaries still lacked a coherent, cohesive identity. Knight (1986, vol. 1: 2) describes the country during the *Porfiriato* (as the period was known after the dictator) as 'less a nation than a geographical expression, a mosaic of regions and communities, introverted and jealous, ethnically and physically fragmented, and lacking common national sentiments'. Largely unconcerned with the means by which these fragments were to cohere, President Díaz was nevertheless keen that they should adhere to the centre. Ensconced in Mexico City, Díaz allowed political abuse and endemic corruption in the provinces to go unchecked (or even encouraged it) in the name of tightening central control. Wealth in the form of land remained in the hands of a few privileged families, whilst great pockets of the population subsisted in abject poverty. French culture was *à la mode* amongst the Mexican aristocracy: one of the major thoroughfares in Mexico City, the Paseo de la Reforma, underwent a 'make-over' to make it look like the Champs Elysées; and French cuisine was *de rigueur* in the capital. Meanwhile sanitation and diet amongst the masses was so poor that average life expectancy was estimated at around thirty years.

The one undisputed achievement of the conflict was, then, the toppling of Díaz. Many of the other achievements, however, are rather less easy to define, for the revolution was not a clear-cut struggle between liberators and oppressors. Instead, it was a bitter factional strife of shifting allegiances and political agendas, in which the chief protagonists – Francisco Madero, Emiliano Zapata, Francisco Villa,

Venustiano Carranza and Alvaro Obregón –became the victims of political assassination at the behest of their rivals.[13] Riven with internecine conflict, the revolution
ultimately saw the triumph of the middle-class, conservative Constitutionalists, led
by Carranza and Obregón, who fell heir to the project of taking the revolution
forward, setting in motion the process of national reconstruction. This was
no simple task. The Mexican nation had been a fragmented, mosaic-like entity in
the century since independence. If anything, as a highly factionalised and bitter
civil war, the revolution simply compounded this state of affairs. What is more,
the regimes that carried out the project of national reconstruction, the so-called
institutional phase of the revolution (1920–40), had to face up to the second
indisputable achievement of the conflict: the birth of the *pueblo* not as an elite,
bourgeois concept, as it had been up until this point, but a popular construct
embodied in the masses.

Indeed, the deposal of Díaz and the subsequent struggles to define the future
direction of the revolution had involved a level of mass mobilisation unheard
of in Latin American history. And with it 'came new popular forces, manifested
in social banditry, guerrilla and conventional armies, sindicatos and mutualist
societies, peasant leagues and embryonic political parties of both Right and Left'
(Knight 1994: 393). Even as the revolution gave rise to unprecedented mass
mobilisation, it also engendered an authoritarian political culture and party of
state – which would become the oxymoronically titled Partido Institucional
Revolucionario (Party of the Institutional Revolution, PRI) – that was to govern
Mexico uninterrupted for seventy-one years.[14] This new, self-perpetuating political class – the presidency passed on to anointed successors in six-yearly terms,
or *sexenios* – harboured few illusions as to what was in the best interests of the
masses.[15] In the eyes of its representatives, the unleashed power of the masses
needed to be harnessed to the strongly centralist project of nation-state. The
masses required education. They needed to be secularised and to learn to identify
with the 'nation', whose manifestations, in turn, had to reflect the masses back to
themselves. Furthermore, the masses had to leave their traditional practices and
allegiances in the local community behind and to be inducted into the ways of
the modern nation in pursuit of capitalist development with its associated social
forms. In short, they had to be *modernised*. Perhaps these last points are the
ultimate paradoxes underpinning the outcome of the revolution, paradoxes that
historians Gil Joseph and Daniel Nugent (1994: 15) put in the following terms:
'Understanding how such a regulated set of social forms of life – i.e. capitalism
– emerged in so strong a form in Mexico is not an easy task, particularly since
that historical outcome is frequently masqueraded as the result of a popular,
peasant war.'

The revolution, then, gave way to a new form of mass participation and politics
(although as Knight (1994: 400) cautions, *not* liberal-democratic politics). With
capitalist development, Mexican society also experienced radical change and rapid
transformation in the post-revolutionary period associated with accelerated
processes of modernisation. It would be wrong, however, to claim that the drive

towards modernisation conceived as a path of progress and civilisation was a uniquely twentieth-century phenomenon. 'State projects of "modernization" – embracing education, anticlericalism, nationalism, and "developmentalism" – were nothing new in Mexican history. They can be traced back to the [colonial regime of the eighteenth-century] Bourbons at least' (Knight 1994: 396). Modernisation was also certainly high on the political agenda of President Díaz and his advisers who, for example, oversaw the dramatic expansion of the railroad system. Nevertheless, as Schelling (2000: 10) points out, in Latin America more generally, 'What occurred [. . .] was the partial modernisation of infrastructure without the social modernisation implicit in, for instance, the formation of a nation-state of citizens.'

Social modernisation – or more to the point, 'the combination and simultaneity of modern and pre-modern modes of production and ways of life' (Schelling 2000: 7) that characterise Latin American modernity more generally – arrived in Mexico in the first half of the twentieth century with the vertiginous changes that began to transform lived human experience. The very fabric of traditional family life had been ripped asunder during the armed struggle, with huge sections of the population literally on the move, and the high death toll left widows and orphans in its wake. After the conflict, these changes persisted with mass migration, as Mexico became increasingly industrialised and made the transition from a predominantly rural to urban entity. Those who flocked to the cities not only had to learn to adapt to different social mores and customs that came with the loosened family bond which wrought profound changes, particularly in the sphere of gender relations. They also encountered the accelerated speed of modern life as trams and automobiles replaced non-mechanised modes of transport, cityscapes were transformed, and movie theatres took the place of *carpas* (makeshift vaudeville theatre tents) as the most popular form of entertainment.

Indeed, as mass migration to the urban centres required the citizens of the modernising nation to alter their geographical, cultural and moral co-ordinates, these changes were reflected and refracted in the shifts in sensory perception that came about as a result of the advent of the mass media. For, of course, the emergence of the *pueblo* in the wake of the mass mobilisation of the revolution and the accelerated pace of life that came with modernisation also coincided with the rise of the mass media. Indeed, by the mid 1930s, tabloid newspapers, women's magazines, comic books, radio and increasingly cinema began to insinuate themselves into everyday Mexican experience. In fact, culture, in its broadest sense, played no small role in the project to mould a new modern polity. In addition to the mass media, official commemorations, monuments, civic rituals, photography, the plastic arts (notably muralism), and music all had a role to play in the processes of national 'imagining', whereby a series of disparate stereotypes started to coalesce around notions of *lo mexicano* (Mexican-ness).[16] What is more, the status and significance of the cultural sphere in national development arguably represent another factor that contributes to the peculiarity of Mexican history. Indeed, historian Mary Kay Vaughan (2001: 471) goes so far as to claim that in the

11

twentieth century, 'no other state in the Western Hemisphere invested as much in the creation of a national culture as the Mexican central government'.

The significance of the role of the state in the post-revolutionary creation of a national culture cannot be overstated. As Roger Bartra (2002: 4) warns, however, 'this does not mean that the writers and artists themselves are the official spokespeople of government culture'. Similarly, it is equally important not to over-exaggerate the notion that culture is a top-down hegemonic construct imposed on the masses from above. Instead, as much recent scholarship on Mexican cultural history has stressed, these relationships must be understood in terms of accom-modations and negotiations between the various sectors in society. Or, in the words of Anne Rubenstein:

> The comparative calm that has prevailed is not an artifact of a completely repressive police state, but the achievement of a government that has more or less controlled the course of events in Mexico, while still allow-ing an adequate space for dissent and maintaining enough flexibility to respond, at times, to those voices. In large part, the success of the Mexican state is attributable to its cultural politics.
>
> (Rubenstein 1998a: 4)

In such a socio-political climate, popular participation in the arena of cultural politics can be both hegemonic and resistant and sometimes both at the same time. One thing for certain, though, is that such accommodations between state and society have made the eruption of civil unrest and the need for violent repression the exception rather than the rule. This is not to suggest that Mexico has remained immune from political repression and violence. As Dever (2003: 6) observes, the 1950s marked the onset of an ultraconservative era and an increasingly paranoid anti-communism culminating in 1968, when government-backed paramilitaries were sent in to suppress student demonstrations in the Plaza de las Cuatro Culturas. Similarly, 1994 is another watershed year in which the Ejército Zapatista de Liberación Nacional (EZLN, Zapatista Army of National Liberation) took the nation by surprise, staging an uprising in the southernmost state of Chiapas, forcefully placing indigenous rights on the national agenda.

Nevertheless, these events simply do not register on the same scale as the violence unleashed during the various military dictatorships in countries of the Southern Cone in the 1970s, or the right-wing paramilitary squads that terrorised indigenous communities in Central America in the 1980s.[17] Indeed, thanks to its ambiguous stability and relative democracy, Mexico has acted as a safe haven for a range of political exiles fleeing violence and persecution: from refugees from the Spanish Civil War in the late 1930s – a significant number of whom were to enter the national film industry as actors, directors, set designers etc. – to Chileans and Argentines in the 1970s.[18] It is in these ways that the course of Mexican history has diverged significantly from other areas in the region, and is that which endows it with its exceptionality.

ON THE MEXICAN CINEMA'S INDUSTRIAL CONTEXTS

If we accept that the course of Mexican history in the twentieth century deviates from that of other countries in the region, this particular model – we might, following Knight, call it the 'peculiarist' model – also serves to illuminate the development of the national cinematic industry. On the one hand, this is because regional developments in terms of competitors and audiences are an essential point of comparison for an understanding of the Mexican cinema's position in the pan-national Spanish-speaking market.[19] On the other hand, thanks to its unique geo-political position, at key moments the development of national cinema, like Mexican history, diverges in important ways from regional trends. Or as Ana López (1994: 7) puts it in the opening of her influential essay 'A Cinema for the Continent': 'Mexico has always played a crucial role within Latin America, yet in the twentieth century it has also always been asynchronous to the other major countries of the continent.'

At the same time, however, it would be short-sighted to limit the points of comparison to the Spanish-speaking world for, of course, it is impossible to ignore the global impact of Hollywood cinema, which as is well known was already firmly established by the 1920s. Indeed, in the first volume of his indispensable *Historia documental del cine mexicano*, García Riera produces some illuminating comparative statistics about the Mexican and Hollywood cinemas that speak volumes about the relationship between the two. Thus, he notes that in the 1920s, Hollywood was already producing some 600 features annually; by contrast, between 1916 and 1929, Mexico produced a total of ninety, or an average of six per year (García Riera 1987: 11). López summarises the impact that Hollywood's 'profoundly international' presence in world cinema markets in the following stark terms:

> One way or another, all other nations aspiring to produce a 'national' cinema have always had to deal with Hollywood's presence [. . .] Perceived as the industrial 'vanguard', Hollywood always seems to lead the way in technology, capital investments, and pleasure-producing innovations. Yet paradoxically, 'Hollywood' and everything it stands for have also been the nemesis of national cinemas throughout the world: the seductive polish, production values and constant presence of Hollywood films invariably precluded or prejudiced the industrial development of indigenous production.
>
> (López 2000a: 419)

Dealing with Hollywood is about acknowledging how the narrative logic of its products – continuity editing, narrative causality and the construction of time–space coherence that have traditionally characterised this cinema's mode of filmmaking – has had a profound influence on the kinds of expectations audiences bring to the film-viewing experience. It means facing up to the way Hollywood products dominate international circuits of film distribution and exhibition.

In this respect at least, the Mexican cinema, like other national cinemas across the subcontinent, has grown up in the shadow of the powerful presence of its northern neighbour. A cursory glance at some of the literature on Latin American cinema will turn up a series of watchwords that seem to characterise the development of the industry across the region: 'in crisis', 'discontinuous', 'uneven', 'in decline'. Thus, for example, Alberto Ruy Sánchez (1981: 9) opens *Mitología de un cine en crisis* (Mythology of a Cinema in Crisis) with the following unequivocal statement: 'El cine mexicano – para variar – está en crisis. Ahora nos lo dicen hasta los mismos funcionarios cuyo trabajo consiste únicamente en que no lo esté.' / 'Mexican cinema – just for a change – is in crisis. And now those very officials charged with it not being in crisis are telling us that it is.'

These negative watchwords stand in opposition to the brief periods in which various cinemas across the subcontinent started to show signs of flourishing. That is, the key cinemas of the region – those of Argentina, Brazil and Mexico – have enjoyed periods of popular success during which, if not competing with Hollywood on equal terms, then they have certainly managed to win a greater share of their national and regional markets. Thus, the Argentine cinema prospered in the 1930s, when tango singer Carlos Gardel in particular found favour with audiences throughout the region. Similarly, in Brazil, in the same decade, a rush to establish up-to-date studios and a sound technical base witnessed the rise of the *chanchada*, or musical comedy, which would capture the popular sectors of the national audience.[20] Of all cinemas of the region, however, the Mexican cinema has arguably known the greatest popular, commercial and critical success.

Like its regional counterparts, Mexican cinema, as anything nearing an industrial entity, only really started to solidify in the late 1930s. It was only by this third decade of the twentieth century that the kind of technical and financial base that could support a continuous rather than erratic supply of new films came into existence. This is not to say that the 1930s were devoid of industrial progress or commercially viable films. From the nadir of 1931, in which only two features were made, production figures rose steadily throughout the decade, peaking at an unprecedented fifty-seven features in 1938. Furthermore, the state started to take a keener interest in the cinema as an aesthetic form that could promote national values by, for example, subsidising the new CLASA studios (Cinematográfico Latino Americana, SA), which were inaugurated in 1935 and equipped with the most up-to-date equipment. In fact, 1936 proved a watershed in national cinema history, for it was the year in which Fernando de Fuentes produced Mexico's first truly international hit, the *comedia ranchera* or rural comedy, *Allá en el Rancho Grande*. With its focus on rural life and stock popular characters and music, it struck a chord with audiences across Latin America, eager for films that reflected local colour and folklore.[21]

If the foundations for a credible industrial base were laid in the 1930s, it was in the following decade that Mexican cinema took off to such an extent that cinema became the sixth most important industry in the country (García Riera 1998: 123). As we have noted, the period became retrospectively and nostalgically evoked as a Golden Age, although critical opinion varies considerably as to the duration of this boom period. Carl Mora, for example, states that the Golden Age coincided with the economic growth and prosperity of Miguel Alemán's presidential term (1946–52); on the other hand, for Carlos Monsiváis (1993: 142), the Golden Age spans the years 1935 to 1955 'more or less'. García Riera (1998: 120) is possibly the most circumspect of all: 'Suele hablarse de una época de oro del cine mexicano con más nostalgia que precisión cronológica. Si esa época existió, fue la de los años de la segunda guerra mundial: 1941–1945.' / 'It is common to talk of a golden age of Mexican cinema with more nostalgia than chronological accuracy. If the period existed at all, it was during the years of the Second World War: 1941–1945.'

There are possibly as many periodisations of the Golden Age as there are critics of the Mexican cinema. One thing is for sure, however: film production certainly increased significantly throughout the 1940s, rising from thirty-eight features in 1941 to eighty-two in 1945, and reaching a record 123 in 1950. And yet, the flourishing of the Mexican cinema during the war years was no simple coincidence. Mexico was the only major film-producing country in the Spanish-speaking world that could boast both an industrial base *and* an alliance to the United States. Both Spain and Argentina remained neutral, whilst displaying decidedly pro-Axis tendencies, a position that was to cost the latter dearly in cinematic terms. Under the direction of Nelson Rockefeller, the US Office of the Coordinator for Inter-American Affairs (OCIAA) offered the Mexican industry technical, financial and material assistance.[22] With celluloid in scarce supply, and an allied Mexico receiving preferential treatment, Argentine production plummeted from forty-seven features in 1941 (compared to Mexico's thirty-eight), to twenty-three in 1945 (as opposed to Mexico's eighty-two). Hollywood and, it goes without saying, European competition declined during the war years, creating a more favourable environment for Mexican production to flourish. What is more, Hollywood films tended to be dominated by war propaganda, which held less appeal for Latin American audiences.

Aside from increased production figures, what are the defining features of the Golden Age? On one level, as noted, a number of important figures – amongst them, Cantinflas, María Félix, Arturo de Córdova, Dolores del Río, Pedro Arméndariz and Jorge Negrete – began to gain popular recognition. The growing appeal of these figures would make of them the Spanish-speaking cinema's first conglomeration of authentic stars, competing with their Hollywood counterparts for the affection and admiration of audiences across the Hispanic world. These stars' contribution to the national industry gained official recognition with the foundation of the Academia Mexicana de Ciencias y Artes Cinematográficas (Mexican Academy for the Cinematographic Arts and Sciences) in 1946, which inaugurated an annual prize-giving ceremony to present the national industry's own award, the Ariel.[23] One director in particular, namely Emilio Fernández, enjoyed an especially gilt-edged Golden Age, his films garnering acclaim at international festivals.

Behind the effervescence of the 1940s and the glitter of stardom, economic factors also boosted the national cinema. Most significantly, on 14 April 1942, the Banco Cinematográfico was created with the sole purpose of financing national film production and distribution. This unique institution – no other national cinema has created a bank given over to financing film – extended credit to production companies. In this way, these companies were liberated from the, until then, common practice of selling land to finance business, and production was thereby placed on a firmer footing. Established originally as a private institution, the bank was nationalised in 1947, becoming the Banco Nacional Cinematográfico, setting the pattern of film financing for the foreseeable future, in which state and private initiatives combined to offer funding. An index of the industry's solidity and success, by 1945, some 4,000 people were employed in the industry, all of whom were affiliated to the Sindicato de Trabajadores de la Industria Cinematográfica (STIC, Workers Union of the Film Industry) (García Riera 1998: 122).[24]

The war over, in numerical terms, Mexican feature production did not decline. Indeed as we have seen, it increased. For most scholars of Mexican cinema, however, whilst recognising the on-going popular success of the nation's films – Pedro Infante's star status, for example, became stratospheric – the second half of the 1940s also saw the onset of a decline that would turn into crisis.[25] On the one hand, Hollywood began to regain a hold over its Latin American markets, accompanied in Mexico by the withdrawal of the financial and technological support that it had provided during the war years (De la Vega 1999: 165). On the other hand, by 1949, William O. Jenkins, a North American businessman resident in Puebla, in conjunction with Mexican business associates, managed to extend his exhibition monopoly to some 80 per cent of the republic's movie theatres and in so doing exerted considerable influence over production values. Finally, during the war years, the industry had witnessed an influx of workers that were not only protected by union rights, but also continued to demand high salaries. García Riera (1998: 151), for example, notes that Mexican stars of the period earned twice as much as their Argentine and Spanish counterparts. Furthermore, in legal terms, it was impossible to lay off staff; the only alternative was therefore to cut production costs by reducing filming from a previous minimum of five weeks to three weeks or fewer.[26]

The result was increasingly formulaic films that were rapidly churned out, earning the name *churros*. 'Viewers began to refer to many movies made in Mexico as *churros* as early as 1950, comparing them to the machine-made crullers [ring-shaped, deep-fried cake] for sale on many city street corners: Like *churros*, Mexican movies were not nourishing, rapidly made, soon forgotten, identical to one another and cheap' (Rubenstein 2000: 665). Amongst the most successful and popular formula movies of the period were brothel melodramas set in the city's seedier districts, family melodramas, and comedies starring Tin Tan, Cantinflas,

Adalberto Martínez Resortes and others. At the same time, and surely another of the key peculiarities of the Mexican cinema, it became increasingly difficult for new directors to break into the industry. Such were the closed-shop policies of the directors' section of the STIC, whose principal aim was to protect the interests of already established directors, that it became impossible for new directors with the potential to inject innovation to break into the national industry.

These problems were compounded in Mexico, as in nations of the (semi) industrialised world over, with the arrival of the television, which launched its first transmission on 26 July 1950. Ownership of a television set at first was rare, the preserve of the wealthy; however, from as early as 1955 even fairly humble households were starting to possess their own set (García Riera 1998: 210). In time, the television undoubtedly became an important showcase for Mexican cinema and a contributing factor to the aura of nostalgia that surrounds the Golden Age as audiences had the opportunity to see their favourite movies and stars in endless repeats. Nevertheless, the advent of the television signalled major competition for the cinema, which had to devise strategies to retain the dwindling audience for national products. At an official level, the new head of the Banco Cinematográfico, Eduardo Garduño, an appointee of the incoming president Adolfo Ruiz Cortines, devised the Plan Garduño in an attempt to promote 'quality' cinema. The Plan was controversial, plagued by problems and ultimately ineffective. It sought to wrest power away from the distributors, whose on-going monopoly produced the effect known as *enlatamiento* (literally 'canning'), whereby the screening of national films got held up in the exhibition schedules. The Plan also attempted to limit the importation of foreign films to some 150 per year and, whereas the Banco Cinematográfico had previously offered finance of some 10 per cent of production costs, this was increased from 60 to 85 per cent. In short, throughout the 1950s, the state became increasingly interested in all areas of activity, from production, through to distribution and exhibition.

In Mexico, as elsewhere, attempts were made to win audiences back to the cinema by offering formats that television, constrained not only by technical but also moral considerations, could not replicate. Thus more films were made in colour and CinemaScope. And ironically, despite an atmosphere of heightened austerity and conservatism that prevailed during Ruiz Cortines's administration, the era gave rise to increasingly risqué displays of female nudity in those films with an adults-only classification. Ultimately, however, whilst the 1950s did not witness a drop in quantity, with the national industry maintaining an average of some 100 films per year, the decade did see a decline in quality. Mora sums this up in the following terms:

> The basic problem was that as films became costlier and had to be produced on an assembly-line basis, there was ever-greater reliance on 'formulas' – comedias rancheras; films based on dance fads – cha-cha, charleston, rock and roll; comedies; lacrimogenic melodramas; horror vehicles à la Hollywood; American style westerns' and 'super-hero'

17

adventures in which masked cowboys or wrestlers took on a variety of evildoers and monsters. Quality plummeted but production increased.

(Mora 1989: 99)

By the 1960s, then, audiences were losing their appetite for *churros* and were staying away from the national cinema in droves. In the late 1950s, some of the nation's most important studios – Tepeyac, CLASA and Azteca – had ceased to function. And with the revolution of 1959 inaugurating a politically committed Cuban film culture, the Mexican cinema lost another traditionally important audience. In the words of García Riera (1998: 210): 'A fines de los años cincuenta, la crisis del cine mexicano no era sólo advertible para quienes conocían sus problemas económicos; la delataba el tono mismo de un cine cansado, rutinario, y vulgar, carente de inventiva e imaginación.' / 'Towards the end of the 1950s, the Mexican cinema's crisis was not only noticeable to those who knew its economic problems; the very tone of a tired, ordinary and vulgar cinema, lacking in inventiveness and imagination gave it away.'

Without doubt, the sector of Mexican society that gave national cinema the widest berth in this crisis-ridden period was the educated middle classes. This sector, however, also provided the impetus behind the development of a more critical and politically engaged cinema culture. Influenced by currents in French New Wave cinema and theory and Italian neorealism, the *Grupo Nuevo Cine* was formed, whose membership included aspiring young critics, writers and filmmakers, amongst them Carlos Monsiváis, Emilio García Riera, Jomi García Ascot, Salvador Elizondo and Paul Leduc. The *Grupo Nuevo Cine* edited the short-lived journal of the same name as well as publishing articles in a number of important places – *México en la cultura, Revista de la Universidad, Novedades* – to promote radical change for Mexican cinema based on a politics of authorship. At the same time, an important film club movement started to flourish at the Universidad Nacional Autónoma de Mexico (UNAM) which also opened the republic's first film school – the Centro Universitario de Estudios Cinematográficos – in 1963. A combination of these developments gave rise in 1965 to the first Concurso de Cine Experimental (Experimental Film Competition), which as its name suggests, was designed to promote and reward innovative filmmaking practice.

These movements, with their leftist political charge, were in no sense limited to the Mexican cinema; indeed, far from it. Rather, they were part of wider, regional developments transforming cinematic practice and theory across the Americas, which in turn spearheaded the international phenomenon of Third Cinema theory and filmmaking practice. If anything, developments in Mexico were on a smaller scale than parallel events taking place elsewhere across the region. Indeed, the Cuban revolution not only deprived the Mexican cinema of an audience; at the epicentre of radical politics in the Americas, it brought to life a cinematic culture on an island with a surprisingly large number of cinema-goers, but with little in the way of film production.[27] It also defined the radical political cultural climate of the time, which saw the production of films and the publication of a series of manifestoes by filmmakers and critics that together constitute what is known as New Latin American Cinema. Spearheaded primarily by filmmakers based in Argentina, Brazil and Cuba, those involved in the New Latin American Cinema conceived of film as a form of oppositional practice, a potent political tool that could be deployed to denounce the region's underdevelopment, economic dependence and imperialism emanating from the United States. At the same time, as a movement that was simultaneously nationalist and internationalist in its outlook, New Latin American Cinema was based on the concept of film as a medium that could transform social practice through its radical appeal to its audience.[28]

In short, the New Latin American Cinema developed in response to the radical social and political transformations that define the era, particularly the 1960s. Given the relative quiescence and political stability, on a surface level at least, these transformations made their impact slightly later in Mexico. Nevertheless, by the late 1960s, as we have noted, political and social unrest had started to permeate the multiple layers of Mexico's social fabric, reaching crisis point in the demonstrations of 1968, when students, peasants and workers united, calling for an end to state corruption and the start of democratic rule. As this coincided with Mexico's turn to host the Olympic Games, the government was desperately concerned to prevent Mexico's international image from tarnish. To this end, faced with mounting social unrest, on 2 October 1968, the president sent in the police and army to the Plaza de las Cuatro Culturas, Tlatelolco in the centre of Mexico City, to 'quell' the demonstration that was amassing there. In the process, these forces opened fire on the unarmed demonstrators. Although the full scale of the political violence has never been established with any degree of certainty, it is estimated that up to 500 demonstrators were killed, 2,500 wounded and 1,500 jailed.[29]

It is widely believed that one of the principal authors of the student massacre was the then minister for the interior, Luis Echeverría. Yet when Echeverría succeeded Gustavo Díaz Ordaz to the presidency in 1970, he sought to restore confidence in the party of state and to create, in appearance at least, a sense that it was less repressive and more open to democracy than during the preceding troubled years. To this end, as president, Echeverría loosened restrictions on the media, freed political prisoners, and courted leading intellectuals and cultural agents. Indeed, culture and the arts became pivotal in his populist project, at the centre of which stood the film industry. Despite the *Nuevo Cine* movement of the 1960s, which had opened space for filmmaking as a more experimental, independent practice, commercial cinema was firmly entrenched in a period of decline and decadence. Echeverría therefore set out to regenerate the ailing national industry, at the same time harnessing it to his nationalistic political project.

As part of this regeneration, the president's brother Rodolfo Echeverría, a professional actor, was appointed to the directorship of the Banco Cinematográfico and, through his leadership, yet another plan to restructure the national industry was designed and implemented. As David Maciel (1999: 201) notes: 'In no other presidential regime did the movie industry in general and certain filmmakers in particular receive more interest and financial support than during the years of [Echeverría's regime].' A series of reforms and improvements was set in motion. In terms of the industry's infrastructure, these included the establishment of three official production companies (Corporación Nacional Cinematográfica (CONACINE), Corporación Nacional Cinematográfica de Trabajadores de Estado I (CONACITE I) and Corporación Nacional Cinematográfica de Trabajadores de Estado II (CONACITE II)); the film school, the Centro de Capacitación Cinematográfica (CCC); and the foundation of the Cineteca Nacional. In the spheres of policy and politics of representation, President Echeverría himself intervened in debates on the state of the national industry and its products, decrying its tendency to place commercial concerns above questions of aesthetics and cultural value. Furthermore, distribution and screening policies were altered to ensure that more screen time was allocated to national productions.[30]

In short, the late 1960s and 1970s undoubtedly represent one of the most turbulent periods of political and social unrest in Mexico's history since the revolution. Nevertheless, in cultural terms, this period of turmoil coincided with one of the cinema's cyclical phases of renaissance. On the one hand, it is possible to view Echeverría's cultural policy more generally as a cynical attempt to co-opt artists, writers, intellectuals and directors, many of whom had been actively involved in the protest movements against political corruption and repression, and to contain their work within state-sanctioned structures. Indeed, Mora (1982: 113) notes that for some, it was impossible to forget Echeverría's role in the events of 1968, despite his pro-left and third-worldist foreign policy. On the other hand, the 1970s were without doubt a fertile period for the national cinematic industry and saw the consolidation of the careers of a number of important directors and the debut of others. Indeed, García Riera (1998: 278) is unequivocal on the vibrancy and uniqueness of this period. 'Con esa estatización – mayoritaria, no total, y forzada en buena medida – culminó en 1976 una época excepcional del cine mexicano.' / 'With this nationalisation – majority, not total, and to a good degree forced – in 1976 an exceptional period of the Mexican cinema culminated.' Noting the unusual level of state participation for a non-communist country, the Mexican critic goes on: 'Nunca antes habían accedido tantos y tan bien preparados directores a la industria cinematográfica ni se había disfrutado de mayor libertad en la realización de un cine de ideas avanzadas.' / 'Never before had so many well-prepared directors entered the film industry, nor had there ever been so much freedom in the production of a cinema of advanced ideas.'

For many critics, the succeeding period in Mexican film history is one of the country's darkest moments. It coincided with the presidential term of José López Portillo, who placed cinema, radio and television in the hands of his sister Margarita, whose name has become synonymous with the short-sighted and philistine policies she implemented. In effect, Margarita López Portillo reversed the policies brought in during the previous regime, dismantling key institutions including the Banco Cinematográfico and withdrawing support from CONACITE I and II. In this way, as David Maciel (1997: 98) notes, she eliminated 'almost all state-sponsored support from film production. These policies resulted in the near impossibility of securing production resources for Mexican filmmakers who were interested in making quality artistic movies.'

After the crisis years of López Portillo's *sexenio*, attempts were made to reinvigorate the national cinema and in 1983 the Instituto Mexicano de Cinematografía (IMCINE) was founded, under the directorship of director Alberto Isaac. Significantly, Mora (1989: 149) takes Isaac's statement, 'To rebuild a ruined cinema in a ruined country' on taking up his post, as the title for his final chapter on the 1981–89 period in national film history. As the brief history on IMCINE's website states, the institution was established to promote 'quality cinema' and to strengthen the three key areas of cinematic activity: production, exhibition and distribution, and the promotion of Mexican cinema of quality at both a national and international level.[31] As a government entity, subject not only to the vicissitudes of political appointments associated with the *sexenio* system and scarce resources, IMCINE has certainly not been exempt from problems and controversies. And yet, it is perhaps a sign of Mexican cinema's phoenix-like qualities that over recent years critics have started to detect signs of a return, if not to robust health, then certainly health.

In the early 1990s, a period that saw the emergence of what was termed the 'New Mexican Cinema', the title of an essay by Nissa Torrents (1993) declared 'Mexican Cinema Comes Alive'. Associated with a notion of 'quality' cinema, endowed with the power to win favour with the national audience and at the same time to gain critical acclaim on international film circuits, for Elissa J. Rashkin (2001) the New Mexican Cinema was, to some extent, spearheaded by significant numbers of women directors. Following in the footsteps of the early pioneers Adela Sequeyro and Matilde Landeta, the late 1980s and early 1990s witnessed the debut of the careers of Marisa Sistach, Busi Cortés, María Novaro and Dana Rotberg, to mention only some of the most prominent women directors.

Torrents's hopeful tone was echoed in 1997 by Maciel, who argued that there was much to be optimistic about:

> Above all else, though, the future of Mexican cinema will be determined by the creativity, tenacity and commitment of the various generations of filmmakers involved in this cinematic renaissance. Clearly, it is evident that there exists an abundance of exceptional talent in all phases and areas of filmmaking. There exists a new aggressive, self-reliant, and self-assured present and incoming generation of directors, actors, cinematographers, screenwriters and other members of the film community that have already demonstrated their artistic worth.
>
> (Maciel 1997: 117)

The upbeat tenor of Maciel's statement may be more symptomatic of a particular tendency towards wishful optimism in Mexican film scholarship, rather than a hard-headed critical evaluation of the actual state of national film culture. This tendency, which, in part, is the subject of Chapter 1, is couched in the language of renewal and regeneration, a critical striving for quality and improvement. Nevertheless, as we saw in the opening paragraphs of this introduction, the 1990s and the new century have indeed witnessed the premiere of a fairly steady, if not copious, stream of films that have captured both national and international audiences: from the controversial *La ley de Herodes* (Herod's Law, Luis Estrada, 2000), a hilarious parody of the PRI, to *Amores perros* which has now been consecrated as a modern classic in the British Film Institute's series of the same name by Paul Julian Smith (2003b).

A NOTE ON NATION, CINEMA AND MEDIUM SPECIFICITY

In the contemporary age of accelerated globalisation, the idea of the 'nation' and, by extension, the concept of 'national cinema', have been the subject of intense critical debate. To be sure, (audio)-visual products circulate today with unprecedented fluidity and are therefore consumed by a more diverse viewing public than ever before. Russian viewers, for example, have proved as avid consumers of Mexican soap operas as those in their original context of production. At the same time, the emergence of on-line trading organisations such as eBay makes it increasingly easy to obtain rare material on DVD, despite manufacturers' best efforts to codify the globe into viewing regions. It would be wrong to assume, however, that such fluid circulation is suddenly free from the power structures that have traditionally governed the flow of goods and knowledge since the advent of the colonial projects in the fifteenth century. Within globalised structures of power, Mexico, and Latin American more generally, are still more likely to be the receiver of cultural goods than the transmitter. In fact, as García Canclini (2000: 24) also notes, 9 per cent of the world's population lives in the European Union, which exports some 37.5 per cent of the cultural goods that are in circulation. By contrast, 7 per cent of the world's population lives in Latin America, and yet the subcontinent exports a mere 0.8 per cent of cultural goods. In short, whether today, or at the cinema's inception on the eve of the twentieth century, a Mexican film circulates in terms that are markedly different from a Hollywood production, or for that matter, a film of European origin.

This is not the place of offer a detailed overview of the way in which issues concerning the global flow of culture, goods and peoples have impacted on film scholarship specifically. It is helpful, however, to point the reader to Mette Hjort and Scott Mackenzie's edited collection of essays on the subject, *Cinema and Nation* (2000). Contributors to the volume take up a range of positions on the thorny question of the relationship between film and national culture. For example, in a reappraisal of an earlier classic essay on the question, British scholar Andrew Higson questions the usefulness of 'national cinema' as both a concept and approach, advocating instead an emphasis on cinema as a transnational enterprise: '[I]t is inappropriate to assume that cinema and film culture are bound by the limits of the nation-state. The complexities of the international film industry and the transnational movements of finance capital, filmmakers and films should put paid to that assumption' (Higson 2000: 73). Meanwhile, sociologist Philip Schlesinger sounds a note of caution:

> The new wave of concern with global interconnectedness should not make us now envisage the world as definitively 'postnational'. The continuing strong links between modes of social communication and national political spaces remain fundamental for conceptions of collective identity. And it is precisely that connectedness that informs, constructs, and reproduces the problematic of a national cinema.
>
> (Schlesinger 2000: 30)

Of these two positions, *Mexican National Cinema* is largely guided by the latter for reasons that have been implicit in the preceding sections. The nature of existing Mexican cinema scholarship with its strong national focus, combined with Knight's notion of the 'peculiarities' of Mexican history – especially in the twentieth century which saw the rise of a 'muscular' post-revolutionary state, attentive to the nation as a discursive formation – coalesce to suggest that the national is an appropriate paradigm through which to approach this regional cinema as an institution. This is not to deny this cinema's profound transnational status, however. Again, as should have become clear in the preceding sections of this introduction, the Mexican cinema *must* be understood in the context of wider developments, from the impact of Hollywood on national production, to the broader context of cinematic traditions at a subcontinental level, to events in international history.

Mexican National Cinema does not aim to be encyclopaedic. By necessity, it cannot offer detailed discussion of certain key figures and themes – the Mexican films of Luis Buñuel, or the career of Cantinflas, for example, are only mentioned in passing for they are admirably documented elsewhere.[32] *Mexican National Cinema* is structured around case studies of some fifteen films which exemplify the central themes and issues explored in the book, and which are discussed in the context of broader developments and in relation to similar films. At the same time, whilst this book is alert to the 'panorama' of Mexican cinema, the macro contexts of its development, it seeks to bring these into view via a focus on the micro – on the Mexican cinema's film texts, stars, spectators, on its major thematic preoccupations and generic formulae. In so doing, it aims at all times to foreground the question of medium specificity. For if, as Schlesinger (2000: 30) advocates, 'social communication and national political spaces remain fundamental for conceptions of collective identity', then the social communication at stake here is not just any form of communication. Rather, as a national institution, cinema is made up of audio-visual texts that appeal to a collective audience and have specific modes of address. In short, *Mexican National Cinema* places an emphasis on how the nation and its local and, inevitably, transnational concerns are figured and reconfigured *audio-visually.*

Chapter 1 explores the relationship between a film that has been consecrated as a classic of the Mexican cinema, Arcady Boytler's *La mujer del puerto* (1933) and Arturo Ripstein's iconoclastic remake of 1991. Focusing on the different treatments accorded to the theme of incest in the original and remake, and the historical moment in which each was made, the relationship between the two films becomes a vehicle via which to narrate a story of the development of the Mexican cinema. This story is bound up with the geo-politics of the Mexican nation and the quest for cultural modernity which, as a key theme, is woven throughout the pages of this book.

Chapter 2 turns to the cinematic representation of the Mexican revolution and moves between the modulations in the conflict's meanings as it became institutionalised as a key myth of origin in the nation's modern identity. Indeed, for many critics, the cinema is deemed to have played an important role in the dual processes of modernisation and 'Mexicanisation'. Chapter 3 offers an account of this role, exploring the origins and formation of the national audience, before analysing the relationship between screen and spectator in a case study of Emilio Fernández's *María Candelaria* (1943).

Chapters 4, 5 and 6 are concerned in different ways with questions of genre. Chapter 4 deals with melodrama as a mode with undoubted universal appeal, but key affinities with Mexican and Latin American culture more generally. The chapter focuses more specifically on the relationship between melodrama, masculinity and space at three important moments in national history: the 1940s, 1970s and 1990s. In Chapter 5, the road movie, as a quintessentially North American genre, is transported into the Mexican context and becomes a vehicle for understanding the ambiguous figure of the Indian in the national cultural imaginary. Finally, Chapter 6 casts an eye at the 3,000-kilometre border that separates Mexico from the United States, arguably one of the most conflictive dividing lines to separate two national entities, to explore the changing valences of this central cinematic trope in both the Hollywood and Mexican cinemas.

The 'Appendix: Filmography' provides an alphabetical listing of the films that have served as case studies throughout the book. Synopses and core information (e.g. producer, director, script, cinematographer, musical director, etc.) for each film provide a useful reference resource. At the end of the References section, a Web Resources section has also been included, which directs the reader to both Spanish and English language web sites where they may obtain more detailed information on the films discussed and links to other cinematographic forums.

1

REMAKING MEXICAN CINEMA

THE HAPPY ENDING

In the extraordinary epilogue of Arturo Ripstein's 1991 remake of Arcady Boytler's classic film *La mujer del puerto* (The Woman of the Port, 1933), an intertitle signals that the events that the viewer is about to witness take place five years after the last of the three versions of the same story that comprise the core narrative. Despite the time that has elapsed between this tripartite narrative and the epilogue, in the final moments of Ripstein's film the changes that have occurred in the closing scenes are also replete with repetitions. We are back in a brothel, a venue that has been one of the film's central dramatic spaces. Now, however, the brothel is called 'El Carmelo' rather than 'El Eneas' to indicate that the business has changed hands. El Marro (Damián Alcázar) is robed in the distinctive dressing gown of 'El Eneas's' erstwhile proprietor. The curtain lifts once more for the start of '*el acto internacional*'. As previously, the act involves Perla (Evangelina Sosa) performing fellatio on a member of the audience, in competition with Carmelo (Alejandro Parodi) at the piano, the latter attempting to hold a note for longer than it takes Perla to make her client reach his climax. Repetition, however, serves to underline one fundamental change that has taken place. In a narrative that has revolved around the violent intra-familial conflict triggered by the incestuous sibling relationship between El Marro and Perla, the enigmatic happy ending presents the viewer with a harmonious, if perverted, image of the family. The family unit consists of sibling lovers, El Marro and Perla, their mother Tomasa (Patricia Reyes Spíndola) and surrogate father-figure Carmelo. Perla is now pregnant with the couple's second child and the siblings' first-born is present in the wings of the stage on which her mother is about to perform.

The epilogue of the 1991 version of *La mujer del puerto* is rather hard to swallow on a number of counts. First, in its depiction of the harmonious family unit, Ripstein's remake transgresses the conventions of the happy ending, because as Murray Smith argues, 'for a happy ending to be recognized as such, we must have previously identified a morally desirable character and outcome' (Smith 1995: 215). The tripartite structure of *La mujer del puerto* with its alternative, grimly tragic outcomes to the incest, leaves us in no doubt that the epilogue represents the most optimistic, 'happy' outcome of those on offer.[1] And yet equally, it would be impossible to claim that the epilogue presents us with a 'morally' desirable resolution. Furthermore, if happy endings normally bring about narrative resolution, the epilogue poses more questions than answers: what are we to make of the way in which the film flaunts an exaggerated orality emblematised in the '*acto internacional*' and what is the significance of this perverse, incestuous family unit?

To say that this happy ending flagrantly flouts all taboos regarding incestuous desire hardly requires stating. Less immediately obvious, however, is the fact that *La mujer del puerto* is but one of a cluster of films made in the same period that explicitly revolves around the trauma of incest, taking Oedipal narratives to increasing extremes in ways that seem designed to shock the viewer. The guilty secret at the heart of both *El secreto de Romelia* (Romelia's Secret, Busi Cortés, 1988) and *Antiguo modelo* (Old-Fashioned Model, Raúl Araiza, 1991) revolves around brother–sister incest. There is something quietly unsettling about the relationship between the sibling couple Benjamín (Eduardo López Rojas) and Micaela (Malena Doria) in *La mujer de Benjamín* (Benjamin's Woman, Carlos Carrera, 1991). Incest is graphically explicit in *Angel de Fuego* (Angel of Fire, Dana Rotberg, 1991), a film about a father–daughter relationship and the daughter's attempts to receive atonement for the resulting pregnancy.[2] Finally, those films that do not touch on incest in some way are exceptions to a strong thematic thread that weaves throughout Ripstein's own filmography, from *El castillo de la pureza* (The Castle of Purity, 1972) through to *Principio y fin* (The Beginning and the End, 1993), *La reina de la noche* (Queen of the Night, 1994) and *Profundo carmesí* (Deep Crimson, 1996).[3] Indeed, I would go so far as to suggest that the prevalence of narratives that revolve around incestuous desire in the late 1980s and early 1990s is so striking as to betray a national obsession.

Finally, the ending of the remake is also difficult to assimilate because of its iconoclastic assault on the memory of Boytler's original *La mujer del puerto*. Endings, whether they provide narrative closure or remain ambiguously open, activate memory, cueing the spectator to review earlier events in the diegesis. In the case of the 1991 remake, however, the activation of memory is double. Conscious of the film's status as remake, the spectator is not only prompted to review earlier events in the diegesis, but also to recall the ending of the original on which it is based. Itself an adaptation of a literary text, namely a Guy de Maupassant short story 'Le Port', in Boytler's original, the sister Rosario, played to great critical acclaim by Andrea Palma, throws herself to an untimely death on discovering the incestuous act that she and her brother have unwittingly committed. The earlier film closes with a melodramatic shot of Alberto (Domingo Soler) at the scene of his sister's suicide, sobbing disconsolately – and melodramatically – into Rosario's shawl. Viewed in tandem, the radical differences between the endings of the original and remake – the tragic ending of incest punished by death versus the happy ending that revels in the perversity of incestuous desire – are, to say the least, striking.

In this chapter, the intergenerational relationship between original and remake and the connective theme of incest become a device to narrate a story about the development of the Mexican cinema in the context of historically contingent discourses of cultural modernity. Taking the happy ending of the remake of *La mujer del puerto* and the tragic ending of the original as a starting point, the chapter explores what is at stake in the radically different treatments accorded to incest in the two versions. Specifically, I aim to bring Ripstein's remake of *La mujer del puerto* into focus as an emblem of the incest narratives that propel a number of films released in the late 1980s and 1990s. The proliferation of increasingly explicit incest narratives suggests that as a theme, incest comes endowed with a surplus of cultural significance at this historical moment. Taking a backwards glance at the origins and development of the Mexican cinema, this chapter sets out to ask what is at stake.

THE GEO-POLITICS OF MEXICAN CINEMA

On 21 March 1895, the Lumière brothers projected their first feature, *Workers Leaving the Factory*. As any survey of the historical development of the cinema will testify, within a few years of this mythic point of cinematic origin, the medium was rapidly on its way to becoming a global phenomenon. Cinema's global status and the relationship between its metropolitan centres of origin and peripheral sites of reception can be loosely categorised in three stages. In the first, a network of venues was established in which audiences from around the world could view the first motion pictures that were produced in France, Germany, England and the United States. In the second, cameras were transported to locations outside their metropolitan centres of manufacture to capture local events. Finally, in the third, this new mode of communication established incipient, if unevenly developed industrial bases on a global scale.

Early cinema in Mexico was no exception to this model, a model that was, moreover, repeated across Latin America where 'the appearance and diffusion of the cinema [. . .] followed the patterns of neo-colonial dependency typical of the region's position in the global capitalist system at the turn of the century' (López 2000b: 48). In Mexico, the capital's 'residents lined up in [the] first movie queues to see such one-minute films as the *Card Players* [. . .] and other such brief performances that had premiered in Paris as recently as December 1895 and were already being shown around the world' (Mora 1989: 6). Such foreign footage was soon followed by material shot with imported equipment in Mexico itself, especially footage of President Porfirio Díaz, who was fond of mounting ceremonial displays of his power and quick to take advantage of the new visual technologies of film and photography to document that power. Finally, Mexico's first 'fiction film', *Don Juan Tenorio*, a one-reeler filmed by engineer Salvador Toscano Barragán, premiered in 1898. It was to be some thirty years, however, before the foundations of an industrial base were to be more firmly established.[4]

If cinema's near-simultaneous global impact is a constant in historical surveys of the medium, so too is the account of Hollywood's rise to dominance of world markets in the early decades of the twentieth century.[5] In this period, with Europe, its major competitor, involved in the First World War, Hollywood consolidated its industrial base with the development of star and studio systems, key film genres, and the establishment of directors and modes of film production. Hollywood's industrial consolidation made a profound impact on cinema as a medium with a globalised reach, as the world's film markets became saturated with its products. In an expanding global market for symbolic goods, Hollywood's rise to domi-nance prompted anxieties around the massification and standardisation of society that the large-scale dissemination of its cultural values was feared to engender.[6] Furthermore, despite the fact that Hollywood is clearly linked to a precise geo-graphical and cultural location, rarely are the values that a Hollywood film embodies considered to be linked to the national context of production. Rather, despite their national anchoring, these values pass as 'universal'.

Hollywood's rise to dominance coincided with Europe's involvement in the First World War; this period, of course, also coincided with a bellicose event in Mexican history, namely the 1910 revolution. The Mexican conflict was not only reported daily in the US newspapers and was a regular feature for newsreel companies, but also became a frequent backdrop in US feature films, which were populated with 'Mexican' characters.[7] These characters, however, often took the form of negative stereotypes, a phenomenon that became particularly accentuated in the aftermath of Pancho Villa's illegal incursion into US territory in 1916:

> Innate violence is the Mexican characteristic most often emphasised by North Americans; for them the Mexican is a villain capable of all kinds of criminal excess. From the beginning the North American cinema has portrayed the Mexican as irresponsible, treacherous, vengeful and prey to an uncontrolled sexuality. He is also represented physically in a specific way: his poncho and wide sombrero become a kind of uniform added to his dark skin portraying their southern neighbours, and this served the extra purpose of distinguishing the good from the evil people.
>
> (De Orellana 1993: 10)

Such images did not remain uncontested in Mexico, in which the state played an active, if not wholly successful, role in trying to ensure that films that featured denigrating stereotypes were not exhibited. Cinema audiences were encouraged to avoid films that contained offensive stereotypes and the Mexican government protested about them to its northern counterpart, as did Mexican consuls in other countries in which such films circulated. Furthermore, in solidarity with Mexico, a number of countries, particularly in the Spanish-speaking world, similarly attempted to limit the exhibition of denigrating images of Mexico and Mexicans. The activities of North American filmmakers within the Republic were restricted; and films that presented 'positive' images of Mexico were officially encouraged.

Indeed, as Emilio García Riera points out, between 1916 and 1920, the revolution is conspicuous in its absence from Mexican productions, for it was thought that to represent the conflict was to confirm Hollywood's worst stereotypical excesses (García Riera 1998: 33).[8] Ironically, Hollywood's negative attitude towards its southern neighbour was almost certainly toned down, not so much as a result of diplomatic and legislative action, than thanks to the fact that by the early 1920s Mexico was the most important Latin American consumer of its products. To put it bluntly, it simply did not make commercial sense to continue to produce images that ran the risk of offending the target audience.[9]

Commercial imperatives aside, this did not mean, however, that stereotypical representations of Mexicans simply disappeared. Rather, the narrative settings of the films in which they appeared were shifted to imaginary, non-specific Hispanic locations. The images themselves, with their powerful racist charge, persisted.[10] What is more, turning on an association between the Mexican and violent and sexual excess, Hollywood's early cinematic images of its southern neighbour were already well ensconced in both the North American popular imagination and the Mexican psyche. They hark back to Latin America's status within a world geo-political order in which, as Claudio Lomnitz states:

> [E]ven Latin America's status as 'Western' or 'non-Western' is ambiguous [. . .] [T]he continent has not usually been cast in the role that 'the Orient,' Africa, or Oceania have played in the Western imaginary – at least it has not often done so for the past couple of centuries. Mexico and Latin America have much more often been portrayed by Europeans and Americans as 'backward' than as radically different.
>
> (Lomnitz 2001: 127)

In short, Hollywood's images of Mexican greasers, bandits and sultry *señoritas* replicate an ingrained tradition of (visual) representation that is bound up with Mexico's colonial legacy. They exist on a continuum with the kinds of images that illustrated European accounts of the encounter with the 'new world' in the fifteenth and sixteenth centuries. Deploying key tropes of animalisation, sexualisation and infantilisation, as Ella Shohat and Robert Stam (1994: 137) argue, such colonialist discourse 'played a constitutive role in "figuring" European superiority'.[11]

Sexual and violent excess in the Hollywood cinema therefore simply took up where earlier visual regimes left off, playing a powerful audio-visual role in the on-going constitution of Mexico's inferiority, its backwardness. Part of a long-standing 'image problem', the hegemonic rise of Hollywood and the images that it produced assigned Mexico to an earlier, primitive position in relation to what Lomnitz terms a 'civilising horizon':

> The universal importance that all nation-states attribute to progress implies that there is always a [. . .] vanguard of progress on the

international level. This civilizing horizon is identified in terms of technological development, scientific advances, and the techniques used to
govern the population. The civilizing horizon serves to measure a
country's individual progress as well as different countries' relative progress. The parameters used tend to be produced in countries with robust
cultural and scientific infrastructures.

(Lomnitz 2001: 139)

Throughout the turbulent nineteenth century, projecting a national image
of stability, security and seriousness had never been an easy task. The stakes were,
however, high in countries like Mexico that 'have had to remind the world that
they have not been absent in the process of shaping the course of Western
civilization' (Lomnitz 2001: 235). Managing that image cinematographically –
whilst the cinema was potentially a powerful ideological force – was no less fraught
with problems. The economic, political and social instability of the immediate
aftermath of the revolution, coupled with a centuries-old 'image problem' compounded by recent events, meant that the country's relationship to an international
'vanguard of progress' was that of decidedly poor relation. Moreover, in cinematic
terms, by 1920 the technological, industrial and aesthetic vanguard was firmly
established in the US. If, following Lomnitz, the parameters used to determine
progress are set in countries with robust cultural and scientific infrastructures,
the vanguardist status of Hollywood posed a challenge to, and a paradox for, the
development of a Mexican cinema. Not only was Mexico dependent on the US
for technology, but, to access the 'civilising horizon', the Mexican cinema also
had to measure up to the aesthetic standards of production set by its northern
neighbour. That is, it had to emulate the standards of production set by a transnational cinema with an established repertoire of moving images that called into
question Mexico's very right to access the 'civilising horizon'.[12]

THE EARLY YEARS

It is unsurprising then that development of a basic infrastructure was both slow
and uneven, as is evinced in part by the dearth of enduring films produced in
Mexico prior to the 1930s. With the exception of *El automóvil gris* (The Grey
Automobile, Enrique Rosas, 1919) – a docu-drama based on a real-life series
of robberies of wealthy families in Mexico City that took place at the height of
the Revolution in 1915 – very few narrative films that made a lasting impact
were produced prior to the 1930s.[13] In fact, the 1920s witnessed a slump in film
production in general, due, in part, to a lack of official support for the medium.
Unlike the Soviet Union, whose post-revolutionary leadership was quick to
grasp the ideological potential of film and harness the medium for its ideological
project, the architects of cultural nationalism in Mexico were, to say the least, luke-
warm in their response to cinema.[14] Indeed, not without reason, the minister for

public education, José Vasconcelos, dismissed the cinema as a 'typically US cultural product impossible to develop as a national form' (López 2000a: 425).

Vasconcelos's dismissal was, to some extent at least, to prove excessively pessimistic as the advent in the 1930s of sound cinema and the ensuing Golden Age of Mexican cinema in the 1940s attest. To be sure, having already established its industrial base early on, Hollywood had certainly dominated global cinematic markets. By the 1930s, it had entered what has retrospectively become known as its 'classical' phase and had developed a cinematic idiom with global currency.[15] Nevertheless, the coming of sound gave rise to a temporary, if minor crisis, which provided an opportunity for Mexico (and the other Latin American countries with nascent industries at this point, Argentina and Brazil) to develop a national cinematic base. The need to reproduce dialogue demanded that Hollywood devise strategies for reaching audiences that did not speak English. Prior to the technological advances enabling dubbing, Hollywood's answer was to make foreign-language versions of its own English-language films. In Latin America these were known as the ill-fated 'Hispanic films'. Such films proved a disaster not only because they were expensive to make, but also on the grounds of unacceptable levels of hybridity which reveal a lack of cultural sensitivity on the part of their North American producers that verges on the comical. Or as director Alejandro Galindo (1985: 30) puts it: 'Los filmes "en español" que nos endilgaba Hollywood resultaban ser una ensalada. Los miembros de una misma familia hablaban con distintos acentos mezclados el asturiano, el argentino, el mexicano, el cubano y el andaluz.' / 'The films in Spanish that Hollywood landed us with ended up being a complete mix. Members of the same family spoke with different accents, mixing Asturian with Argentine, Mexican, Cuban and Andalusian accents.'

As technology advanced, Hollywood regained the ground it had briefly lost during the period of experimentation with its Hispanic movies from the late 1920s to the late 1930s. Nevertheless, the brief decline in Hollywood at this moment provided an important impetus for the development of a precarious industrial base in Mexico.[16] Scholars of the Mexican cinema are unanimous in their agreement that the 1930s represent a time of formal and generic experimentation that gave rise to key genres and a number of films that are now consecrated classics. The revolutionary state's promotion of *indigenismo* was reflected in films such as *Janitzio* (Carlos Navarro, 1934) and *Redes* (Nets, Fred Zinnemann, Emilio Gómez Muriel, Paul Strand and Agustín Chávez Velázquez, 1936). The decade also marked the end of the Revolution's absence from the nation's screens with the production of Fernando de Fuentes's trilogy *El compadre Mendoza* (Godfather Mendoza, 1933); *El prisionero trece* (Prisoner Number Thirteen, 1933); and *¡Vámonos con Pancho Villa!* (Let's Go with Pancho Villa!, 1935).

De Fuentes also directed the filmic phenomenon of the decade, the hugely popular and successful '*comedia ranchera*' (a musical comedy in a rural setting), *Allá en el Rancho Grande* (Over at the Big Ranch, 1936). Part of the trend known as '*añoranza porfiriana*' (films displaying nostalgia for the 'good old days' of the regime of Porfirio Díaz), *Allá en el Rancho Grande* looked back to a feudal pre-revolutionary, golden age with wistful longing. And finally, one of the Mexican cinema's most enduring figures, the prostitute, made her talking debut in the first Mexican sound film, *Santa* (Antonio Moreno, 1931). Based on the homonymous 1903 novel by Mexican writer Federico Gamboa, *Santa* was followed two years later by another literary adaptation, this time of a French short story: Arcady Boytler's *La mujer del puerto*.[17]

LA MUJER DEL PUERTO (1933): STORIES OF INCEST AND CULTURAL MODERNITY

Where the early films focused on specifically 'folkloric' or national historical themes and local forms – Mexico's indigenous heritage; the revolution; the popular music of *ranchera* songs and vaudeville comedy – the later brothel melodramas, particularly *La mujer del puerto*, looked beyond the national, in an effort to articulate internationally resonant themes and forms. Such an effort, however, does not make of *La mujer del puerto* an anti-nationalist narrative. Rather, Boytler's film is emblematic of a trend in cinematic cultural nationalism in the early years of sound cinema, a current which Aurelio de los Reyes (1987: 131) terms 'cosmopolitan' nationalism. That is, modernity and nationalism converge in Boytler's film which, as a cultural product, is involved in the manufacture of a national image that is intended for both internal and external consumption that bespeaks Mexico's status on the cutting edge of the 'civilising horizon'. It is in this context, I now argue, that we can start to unravel and make sense of the incest narrative and its tragic resolution in the denouement of *La mujer del puerto*.

It would be tempting to attribute the film's credentials as a form of 'cosmopolitan nationalism' to Boytler's Russian origins. The reality is, however, rather more complex than a simple matter of the director's country of birth. Unlike the more famous Soviet visitor to Mexico, Sergei Eisenstein, whose unfinished film *¡Que viva México!* has acquired mythic status in the mythologies of Mexican cinema, Boytler was an émigré who pointedly positioned his film within the parameters of a nascent national cinematic tradition. This is abundantly clear in the interviews and reviews that appeared at the time of the film's release. Asked, for example, by critic Esteban V. Escalante about how he viewed the development of cinema in Mexico, Boytler responded positively in the first person plural: 'Pues bien: veo un gran porvenir. Cada película buena que salga, será un gran empuje; y cada película regular también, porque es un paso adelante que nos hace reconocer los defectos en que involuntariamente hemos incurrido.' / 'Good: I can see a great future. Each good film that comes out will be a great push forward; and also each so-so film is also a step forward that makes us recognise the errors that we have made involuntarily' (De la Vega 1992b: 49). At the same time, Boytler strove to distinguish his film aesthetically from the cinematic idiom that was becoming dominant in his adopted national context, as the following comments demonstrate:

[S]e puede asegurar que en México se harán grandes películas. En este país hay un gran espíritu artístico, mucho elemento de soberbio valor, que hay que descubrir. Yo opino que no hay que hacer todas las películas demasiado vernáculas, para que las acepten y comprendan los demás países de habla española.

To be sure, great films will be made in Mexico. In this country, there is a great artistic spirit, many elements of magnificent value to be discovered. I think that not all films should be too vernacular so that they are accepted and understood in other Spanish-speaking countries.

(De la Vega 1992b: 47)

In order to grasp what is at stake in this rejection of the 'vernacular', we can profit by attending to the way in which *La mujer del puerto* dramatises the contradictions that pulsed through debates concerning identity and modernity in the post-revolutionary period. These debates divide along the metaphorical fault-line of the illusive 'civilising horizon'. On one side, we find the need to incorporate the *pueblo* – that amorphous entity engendered by the revolution – into the nation-space. On the other, we find the drive towards modernisation, expressed in the desire to measure up to the international standards of progress. Monsiváis (1994a: 1380) summarises the latter tendency, with its models located in the metropolitan centres of power, as a desire for recognition that 'en lo básico México pertenece incondicionalmente a la cultura occidental, a cuyo banquete se llega tarde pero con entusiasmo' / 'Mexico basically belongs unconditionally to Western culture, at whose feast it arrives belatedly but enthusiastically'.[18] Or as Ilan Stavans lucidly puts it:

Culture in Mexico is governed by two opposing sides, sharply divided by an open wound: on the one hand, a high-brow, Europeanized elite dream of inserting the nation's creative talent into a global stream of artistic consciousness; on the other, native art, a hybrid that results from ancient and borrowed elements, is produced by and for the masses.

(Stavans 1998: 31)[19]

In short, what makes of *La mujer del puerto* an exemplary text of 'cosmopolitan nationalism' is its disavowal of the vernacular, the local. Instead, the film seeks to place Mexico at the centre of an international cinematic vanguard of cultural modernity, where modernity is at once a theme – a story of the vicissitudes of modern life – and a technological category – as registered in its high production values, and embodied in its star, Andrea Palma.

As a number of recent studies have demonstrated, in the early twentieth century the cinema was a prime emblem and crucible of modernity and the processes of modernisation. Miriam Hansen is particularly eloquent on this matter, describing the cinema as:

a cultural formation that was [. . .] perceived as the incarnation of the modern, an aesthetic medium up-to-date with Fordist-Taylorist methods of industrial production and mass consumption, with drastic changes in social, sexual, and gender relations, in the material fabric of everyday life, in the organization of sensory perception and experience.

(Hansen 2000: 337)

Hollywood, moreover, 'figured as the very symbol of contemporaneity, the present, modern times'. If Hollywood represented the very symbol of contemporaneity, this was the present, and the future, to which modernising nations such as Mexico aspired to belong.[20]

If, following Hansen, modernisation brings about drastic changes in the social fabric, such changes are registered in Boytler's film in its narrative of familial disintegration. Inscribed at the heart of *La mujer del puerto*, the breakdown of the family unity harks back to the dislocations caused by the revolution and foreshadows those that were to be brought about by urbanisation and industrialisation, with incipient capitalist expansion in the 1930s, gathering pace in the 1940s. In this way, Boytler's film prefigures the popular *cabaretera* films of the 1940s, such as *La mujer sin alma* (Woman Without a Soul, Fernando de Fuentes, 1943), *Las abandonadas* (Abandoned Women, Emilio Fernández, 1944), *Salón México* (Emilio Fernández, 1948), *Aventurera* (The Adventuress, Alberto Gout, 1949), and *Víctimas del pecado* (Victims of Sin, Emilio Fernández, 1950). *La mujer del puerto* starkly chronicles the dissolution of the family unit that is its central focus, in which the transition to a more modern mode of social organisation is experienced as dispossession and dislocation. The mother-figure is conspicuous by her absence; the brother, Alberto, has left for sea prior to the story's initiation; and, on the death of her father, at the mercy of such unscrupulous men as Basilio (Antonio Polo), Rosario's fall into prostitution is as inevitable as it is irrevocable. In short, Boytler's film palpably registers the 'drastic changes in social, sexual and gender relations' (Hansen 2000: 337), depicting the modern age experienced as disorder.[21]

Alongside and as a corollary of its narrative of modernity experienced as disorder, *La mujer del puerto* offers its viewers a frank and, for its time, explicit exploration of liberalised sexual mores. Indeed, Paulo Antonio Paranaguá's brief synopsis of Boytler's film (1995: 226) notes how 'The film's depiction of inadvertent incest shocked contemporary audiences. Escaping official censorship, it enjoyed great popularity largely due to the controversy.'[22] The film's risqué edge is not confined, however, to the incest motif alone. Its sexual daring is also evident in the scenes set in the brothel, Salón Nicanor in Veracruz, in which we witness close-up, point-of-view shots of couples locked in amorous embrace. And, in a striking sequence, a shot of Andrea Palma is traversed by superimposed images of a multitude of men who cross the star's body, giving visual expression to the words that Rosario will later utter to her brother Alberto: 'veo a tantos hombres, todos tienen la misma cara para mí' / 'I see so many men, they all have the same face for me'.[23]

Figure 1.1 La mujer del puerto (Arcady Boytler, 1933)

Source: Filmoteca de la UNAM

If *La mujer del puerto* tells a quintessential story about modern life, it does so in a suitably sophisticated filmic idiom. The film's high production values were singled out for comment in the critical reception of Boytler's film at the time of its first release. Indeed, critical acclaim for *La mujer del puerto* places the film consistently on a par with the best of international productions, noting its high production values that made of it an instant landmark within its national cinematic context. In December 1933, for instance, *Mundo cinematográfico* declared: 'Creemos sinceramente que *La mujer del puerto* será la obra que venga a marcar un adelanto definitivo dentro de nuestra cinematografía. [. . .] Puede compararse ventajosamente con cualquier producción extranjera de calidad.' / 'We sincerely believe that *La mujer del puerto* will be the work that comes to mark a definitive advance in our cinematography [. . .] It compares favourably to any foreign production of quality' (De la Vega 1992b: 54). Similarly, in February 1934, *Filmográfico* made the following comparison: 'Las más grandiosas realizaciones del cine extranjero palidecen junto a esta historia intensamente dramática y real.' / 'The greatest productions in foreign cinema pale besides this intensely dramatic and real story.' And the same source was to claim: '*La mujer del puerto* es una cinta internacional, que, como se desarrolla en el puerto de Veracruz, bien podría haberse registrado en Shanghai o en Conchinchina.' / '*The Woman of the Port* is an international film and, played out in the port of Veracruz, could equally have taken place in Shanghai or on the other side of the world' (De la Vega 1992b: 55).

The film's claim to international status was not limited to its high production values, considered comparable with those to be found in Hollywood or European cinema, or to its cosmopolitan location alone. In the film's female star, Andrea Palma, Boytler had found a leading lady of international, indeed, 'universal' standing. In an interview, Palma herself was under no illusion as to why she had been selected for the female leading role: '[É]l [Boytler] no desea esa belleza de la campesina mexicana, sino algo un poco más universal.' / '[H]e [Boytler] doesn't want the kind of beauty embodied in the Mexican peasant, rather something a little more universal' (De la Vega 1992b: 65). Palma's comment alludes to an archetypal construction of female beauty in the Mexican cinema, associated with a glamorised and whitened version of the country's indigenous heritage. The actors who were to embody this feminine ideal most perfectly were Dolores del Río and María Félix, stars whose film careers by far eclipsed that of Palma.[24] In fact, it was Del Río and María Félix, and not Palma, who were to become the cinema's enduring female stars. Unlike Palma, their star persona was pointedly shaped by and shaping of what were presented as quintessentially Mexican cultural traits.

Palma's performance as Rosario in *La mujer del puerto*, by contrast, emphatically eschewed such local traits. Rather, the Mexican actor became associated with two major North American stars: '[E]n la publicidad que se ha hecho a la película, se compara a Andrea Palma con las grandes estrellas y aun se ha dicho que supera a Greta Garbo.' / 'In the film's publicity, Andrea Palma has been compared with the great stars and it has even been said that she is better than Greta Garbo' (De la Vega 1992b: 56). It was, however, Marlene Dietrich with whom Palma became most firmly linked. This association is nowhere more apparent than in the ubiquitous production still that haunts the history of the Mexican cinema, featuring a desultory Palma in her long evening gown, arms crossed and cigarette in mouth. Palma's performance in her role as Rosario was then, to some considerable degree, indebted to her celebrated Hollywood-based counterpart, a fact that the actor was not shy to publicise. Like many of her compatriots, she had recently returned from California:

En Hollywood, yo llegaba a las nueve, me sentaba en el set y miraba todo para que no se me fuera detalle. Eso sí. Cuando regresé sabía más que nadie: de pestañas postizas, de caminar, de los ángulos correctos. A Marlene le ponían un espejo enfrente de la escena para poderse observar y lo mismo hice yo cuando llegué a México [. . .] Aquello fue más que una escuela para mí.

In Hollywood, I arrived at nine, sat down on set and watched everything so as not to miss a detail. And yes. When I returned I knew more than anybody: about false eyelashes, how to walk, and all the correct angles. They used to put a mirror in front of Marlene on set so that she could watch herself and I did the same when I got back to Mexico [. . .] That was more than a school for me.

(De los Reyes 1987: 128)

Palma's mimicry of Dietrich as invoked in this quotation, in particular the detail of the mirror, serves as an apt metaphor for Mexico–Hollywood relations in this period and underlines the fundamental irony that subtends Mexico's aspiration to cinematic modernity. That is, despite the distorted, stereotypical images of Mexicans emanating from Hollywood in the early years, for many scholars of this national cinema, Mexico's reflection and refraction of Hollywood are central to an understanding of its development. Indeed, in an essay devoted to the relationship between Hollywood and Latin American cinema more generally, in a clear reference to *La mujer del puerto*, Monsiváis has argued:

Para que las fórmulas del cine norteamericano puedan asimilarse y 'nacionalizarse', el requisito previo es el avasallamiento. En América Latina el público se deslumbra con los Monstruos Sagrados, las escenografías, la técnica de Hollywood. [. . .] Las actrices de los años treintas ubican sin dificultades a sus role-models, y verbigracia, Andrea Palma, que en Hollywood hacía sombreros, en México se propone emular a Marlene Dietrich, y rediseña su rostro para volverlo misterioso y distante.

Subjugation is the prerequisite for the formulas of the North-American cinema to be assimilated and 'nationalised'. In Latin America, audiences are dazzled by the sacred cows, set design, Hollywood's technology. [. . .] Actresses in the thirties find their role models without difficulty, and for example, Andrea Palma, who made hats in Hollywood, in Mexico sets out to emulate Marlene Dietrich and redesigns her face to make it mysterious and distant.

(Monsiváis 2000: 56)

How though finally, might a nexus of modernity as technological/aesthetic category and sexual liberalisation impact upon our understanding of the tragic ending of the original *La mujer del puerto*? Is there, moreover, a link between colonial mimicry – the Hollywood hat-maker who 'redesigns' her face on return to Mexico – and incestuous desire punished by death? The answer, I suggest, lies with another cultural import that had made its way to Mexico during this period, via the United States from Europe: psychoanalysis.[25]

In *American Encounters* (1998), José Limón explores what he terms the 'Americanisation' of psychoanalysis and its impact on the first of a series of influential studies of the Mexican character, namely Samuel Ramos's *El perfil del hombre y la cultura en México* (Profile of Man and Culture in Mexico). Published in 1934, Ramos's text clearly bears the imprint of the 'Americanisation' of psychoanalysis and in particular the ideas of Alfred Adler, whose work the Mexican intellectual had read 'with great approbation' (Limón 1998: 85) some time between Adler's 1911 break with Freud and the 1930s. As Limón notes, Ramos's landmark study of the Mexican character marks a significant change in the intellectual climate of the day, and particularly in attitudes towards the Mexican masses. Where intellectuals and cultural ideologues such as the anthropologist Manuel Gamio had previously looked to the masses, to forge 'an indigenous-based cultural nationalism' (Limón 1998: 76), Ramos's text took a dim view of the common man (the masculine, as Limón (1998: 77) observes 'is not entirely accidental in Ramos'). More specifically, the hostility revealed in Ramos's study was targeted at what he perceived as the common man's inferiority complex – manifest in the violence and sexual innuendo at play in his use of language – an inferiority complex that was not confined to the lower classes. Rather, although accentuated in the 'common man', his inferiority was symptomatic of a more widespread Mexican condition.

For Ramos, the Mexican's inferiority complex was rooted in the Conquest, whereby Mexico 'at first found itself in the same relationship to the civilized world as that of a child to his parents. It [i.e. pre-Conquest indigenous civilisation] entered Western history at a time when a mature civilization already prevailed, something which an infantile spirit can only half understand' (Limón 1998: 76). As this reference to a historically located infantile trauma exemplifies, Ramos's study was essentially a psycho-cultural analysis of the deep-seated complexes afflicting the contemporary Mexican: complexes that were erected on the 'theoretical scaffolding' (Limón 1998: 86) of psychoanalytic theory, particularly the work of Adler. What is more, this psycho-cultural analysis was, ultimately, a normative discourse, particularly where the lower-class male libido was concerned: 'The clear implication is that they [lower-class males] must be reeducated and if not, subjected to effective social controls to ensure their compliance with the social order' (Limón 1998: 86).

As Limón (1998: 83) maintains: 'We cannot fully understand these negations of the erotic in Mexican lower-class male life unless we link them to a larger negating discourse flowing from the transformation of Freudian psychoanalysis as it was transplanted to the United States.' Filmed in 1933 and released in February 1934, the Americanisation of psychoanalysis would also seem a compelling interpretative matrix though which to read *La mujer del puerto* and particularly the puzzle of the film's tragic resolution of the involuntary incest. That is, to the degree that Boytler's film – with its sexually explicit brothel scenes – arguably leaves less to the viewer's imagination than most films of the period, the extreme conservatism of the ending becomes rather difficult to reconcile. The difficulty of the ending comes into even sharper focus when we consider it in relation to the Maupassant short story on which the film is based, in which the French writer leaves the fate that befalls the incestuous siblings ambivalently open: the drunk brother Célestin is guided by his equally inebriated companions back up to the

Figure 1.2 La mujer del puerto (Arcady Boytler, 1933)

Source: Filmoteca de la UNAM

room in which his sister Françoise is weeping disconsolately at the foot of the 'couche criminelle'. In the translation from European literary text to Mexican filmic text – that is to say, from metropolitan centre to post-colonial periphery – why should the ambiguity of the source text undergo such an unambiguous transformation? This is a difficult question to answer with any certainty. However, the solution to the enigma of the resolution may lie in the fissure or 'open wound', to return to Stavans's formulation, that divides Mexican culture between the local, the popular and the specific on the one hand, and the universal and the elite, on the other.

In cinematic terms, as we have seen, in its pursuit of access to the civilising horizon, the Mexican cinema looked to Hollywood as the vanguard of progress and modernity. That is to say, it sought to emulate the technological and aesthetic standards established by a cinema whose moving images, with their emphasis on Mexico as a site of violence and sexual excess, served precisely to call into question Mexico's access to the civilising horizon, to reaffirm its backward condition. The United States, as we have seen, was also the port of entry for another myth of progress; a myth that proceeded through psychoanalysis understood as a narrative of civilised advance and a way of leaving the distasteful, the primitive, behind.

39

If the quest for (cinematic) modernity is played out at an extra-diegetic level in the discursive structures of production and reception that surround *La mujer del puerto*, in Palma's performance and in the film's high production values, this pursuit of modernity is also replicated generically in its narrative workings, particularly in the resolution to the incest motif. The ultimate taboo, incest is a motif that endures across time and culture as an emblem of the negative pole of the civilised/non-civilised and the modern/pre-modern power dynamic. At the level of narrative content, to raise the spectre of incest is to offer a warning about what will befall the subject that is not modern. That is to say, by rehearsing a narrative of incestuous desire, and punishing the consummation of that desire, *La mujer del puerto* denounces a category from which it wishes to distance itself – the savage, pre-modern. By meting out punishment on that which stands outside the order of civilisation, the film reinforces and supports a cinematic quest for access to the civilising horizon. What is more, viewed through a psychoanalytically informed reading of the 'civilising horizon', the tragic ending of Boytler's original is, in fact, by one reckoning, a 'happy ending'. By meting out punishment to those that would transgress the norms of civilised order, *La mujer del puerto* signals Mexico's belated, but enthusiastic arrival at the privileged feast of Western civilisation.

So, as I have argued, the resolution to the incest in Boytler's film can be understood in the context of a range of factors concerning Mexico's status within a geo-political arena in which the nation has historically been assigned to an earlier, primitive position in relation to the 'civilising horizon'. How though are we to approach Ripstein's 1991 remake? How, moreover, are we to understand what the director, in interview with Sergio de la Mora (1999: 11), calls the 'most atrocious happy family ever depicted on film'? Having established critical reception of the original *La mujer del puerto* at the time of its production, we can start to sketch out answers to these questions, and particularly to the enigma of the ending of the remake, by exploring the film's enduring status as a classic text in Mexican film-lore. It will then become possible to locate the remake within its contextual setting, namely the debates around civilisation and modernity which forcefully reasserted themselves on the national agenda in the 1980s and 1990s.

LA MUJER DEL PUERTO: THE 1991 REMAKE

In an illuminating essay on the questions posed by the filmic adaptation of literary texts, Catherine Grant offers an overview of recent debate in the field. Drawing on the work of John Ellis (1982), Grant argues for an understanding of the literary adaptation in terms of a trade in which 'the most important act that films and their surrounding discourses need to perform in order to communicate unequivocally their status as adaptations is to [make their audiences] *recall* the adapted work, or the cultural memory of it' (Grant 2002: 57). Although Grant's comments are set to launch a discussion of a literary adaptation, her emphasis on recall and cultural memory are suggestive when attempting to analyse the relationship between the two versions of *La mujer del puerto*, and particularly the different inflections that each gives to the thematisation of incest. This is because the notion of cultural memory invokes more than simple recall of, for example, plot, character or even star persona. It also signals the symbolic and affective power that a particular film text exerts on collective memory.[26] Significantly, the excessive ending of Ripstein's remake not only invites the viewer to recall the tragic ending of the original; it also conjures a memory of a film text to which considerable cultural prestige has accrued. Not only did *La mujer del puerto* receive praise from its contemporary reviewers; it has since passed into Mexican film-lore as a classic within the national canon, a film whose promise of an auspicious, commercially viable, international future for the nascent industry is, moreover, remembered with a high degree of nostalgia. A flavour of this nostalgia can be detected in the views of two contemporary protagonists of Mexican cinema scholarship.

The acerbic and often hostile Jorge Ayala Blanco (1993: 110) attests to *La mujer del puerto*'s classic status in *La aventura del cine mexicano*. Singling out Andrea Palma's performance as Rosario, in characteristically dense, descriptive prose, Ayala Blanco notes:

> Como se ha escrito en múltiples ocasiones, Andrea Palma es una especie de Marlene Dietrich veracruzana. Con voz grave, ademanes despectivos, gesto siempre adusto, ojos adormilados, cigarrillo colgando de los labios, irresistible mirada pérfida, mejillas hundidas y cubierta de encajes negros, Andrea Palma es una vampiresa magnífica, la mujer fatal e indomeñable para quien Arcady Boytler ha retenido la preferencia baudeleriana por el sabor del veneno y la distancia ante el espectáculo de la carroña viviente.

> As has been written on multiple occasions, Andrea Palma is a kind of Marlene Dietrich from Veracruz. With her deep voice, contemptuous gestures, look of constant severity, sleepy eyes, cigarette hanging from her lips, irresistible treacherous gaze, sunken cheeks and swathed in black lace, Andrea Palma is a magnificent vampiress, the indomitable femme fatale for whom Boytler has retained the Baudelairean preference for the taste of poison and distance before the spectacle of live carrion.
>
> (Ayala Blanco 1993: 111)

Similarly, whilst acknowledging the uneven quality of Boytler's film, Emilio García Riera offers a superlative evaluation of Palma's performance:

> En medio de un batiburrillo que se quiere a la vez trágico y frívolo, algo mantiene el interés a lo largo de la película: la presencia privilegiada de Andrea Palma, elegante y lejana. *En el debut más llamativo que actriz alguna haya tenido en el cine nacional, la señora Palma logró trascender su clara imitación de Marlene Dietrich*, comunicar a su interpretación una

delicadeza conmovedora y proponer una de las escasas imágenes míticas del cine mexicano de la época: su lánguida silueta, apoyada en el quicio de una puerta [. . .] sobresale como una expresión de la belleza desolada, de la 'flor en el fango'.

Amidst a hodgepodge that tries to be tragic and frivolous at the same time, something maintains interest throughout the film: the privileged presence of the elegant and distant Andrea Palma. *In the most striking debut that an actress has ever had in the national cinema, Palma managed to transcend her clear imitation of Marlene Dietrich*, and in her interpretation get across a moving delicacy and present one of the scarce mythical scenes of the Mexican cinema of the period; her languid silhouette leaning against a doorjamb [. . .] stands out as an expression of desolate beauty, of the 'flower in the mire'.

(García Riera 1992: 108, emphasis added)

In short, both Ayala Blanco and García Riera concur that, despite Palma's clear mimicry of her Hollywood counterpart, the Mexican actor manages to produce a stellar performance. At the same time, this performance has come to emblematise a crucial moment in which the national cinema almost, but not quite, measured up to the 'international' standards – or the 'civilising horizon' – set by Hollywood. The evaluations of Ayala Blanco and García Riera do not simply reveal nostalgia for a classic film, however. They also exemplify a current running through Mexican cinema scholarship that is permeated with a critical discourse which expresses a desire for renewal and regeneration, a constant striving for improvement. Within this discourse, Boytler's *La mujer del puerto* is a totemic text, an early example of what the national industry aspired to, but never quite achieved.

It should perhaps not surprise us then that there appears to be something compelling about Boytler's 1933 film as a site of return. Indeed, Ripstein's remake is but one of four versions of *La mujer del puerto*. Other reworkings include *La mujer del puerto* (Emilio Gómez Muriel, 1949), *En carne viva* (In the Flesh, Alberto Gout, 1950) and *La diosa del puerto* (Goddess of the Port, Luis Quintanilla Rico, 1990). What is more, the fact that Quintanilla Rico and Ripstein's versions were made almost simultaneously, combined with the proliferation of films that focus in one form or another on incestuous desire – from *La mujer de Benjamín* to *Angel de Fuego* – surely requires further comment. As I indicated in the introduction, the prevalence of narratives that revolve around incestuous desire in the late 1980s and early 1990s suggests that as a theme, incest has resonances that are in some way symptomatic of this particular cultural moment.

If Boytler's original was made at a time when debates around Mexico's status within the international geo-political order were coursing through national cultural politics, then so too was Ripstein's remake. As Susan Dever (2003: 49) has argued in *Celluloid Nationalism and Other Melodramas*, a constellation of factors meant that in the 1990s, 'high-stakes nation-building reopened the debate on the meaning of civilisation'. To gloss and expand slightly on Dever's fascinating analysis, these factors can be summed up as follows. With changes to the 1917 Constitution, this period saw the re-emergence of previously disenfranchised groups into the national arena. On the one hand, the clergy, who had been locked out of the political sphere since the nineteenth-century separation of church and state, were reincorporated into political life. On the other, in the run-up to the quincentenary commemoration of the 'discovery' of the New World in 1992, indigenous rights surfaced with renewed vigour. (Although, as Dever (2003: 49) cautions, the fact that disenfranchised groups emerged at this point, is not synonymous with their empowerment.) Meanwhile, a new breed of politician made his (the pronoun is intentional) entry into national politics. To borrow a phrase from Roderic Ai Camp (2000), this was 'the time of the technocrats': the age of a political elite, educated in US Ivy League institutions of higher education, who sought to insert Mexico into the global economy via the Free Trade Agreement, a trilateral trade pact between Mexico, Canada and the United States that was eventually ratified in 1994.

Developments in the socio-political sphere, in turn, were registered in the field of culture. For Dever (2003: 51) and other commentators (Bartra 2002), the influential art exhibition 'Mexico Splendors of Thirty Centuries' crystallises this phenomenon clearly with its 'carefully framed national portrait' which serves as a barometer to gauge the negotiations for power involved in the 'high-stakes nation building'. This exhibition became a form of ambassadorial showcase for Mexican official culture. Having opened in the north, in the Metropolitan Museum of Art, New York in 1990, where it acquired the cosmopolitan seal of legitimacy, it then travelled south to Mexico, where it was designed 'to appeal to middle-class Mexicans who were wavering between the possibilities for new civilization (free trade and big business) and old barbarism (protected production and small collectives)' (Dever 2003: 51). Here, then, we can see the re-emergence of the topoi of the debates being held in the 1930s.

It is in the context of a 'reanimated rhetoric on salvation-through-civilization [bearing] an uncanny resemblance to Golden Age cinema's proselytizing of fifty years ago' (Dever 2003: 51), that we can start to unravel the meaning of the 'atrocious' family unit in the epilogue of Ripstein's remake of *La mujer del puerto*. As we have seen, at a thematic level, Boytler's original signals the modern condition in the form of the drastic changes that took place in the social fabric in the early twentieth century. Yet, as a cultural product made in the post-colonial periphery – a periphery that harboured the 'Europeanized dream of inserting the nation's creative talent into a global stream of artistic consciousness' (Stavans 1998: 31) – the film symbolically deals with sexual desire associated with these changes. It is a desire which at once stands as a transgression of the order of civilisation, but which simultaneously is recuperated through punishment by death. In this way, the film adheres to, and endorses, the myth of progress understood through psychoanalytic theory as a normative narrative of civilised advance.

By contrast, Ripstein's remake, made at a moment in which parallel debates held currency in the sphere of national cultural politics, nevertheless adopts a different approach to the incest theme. Although the narrative structure of the remake departs significantly from the original, it nevertheless remains faithful to the 'salacious' tone of Boytler's film. In so doing, it reflects the liberal sexual mores and relaxed codes of censorship of the late twentieth century. Where, however, the original recuperates the risqué eroticism by punishing the heroine with suicide in the closing sequence, the remake offers no such recuperation, of course closing with the 'atrocious' sequence of the incestuous family unit. In fact, it would not be an exaggeration to state that Ripstein's *La mujer del puerto* seems to exult in showing the squalor, depravity and baseness of human life in Veracruz, which is, in the words of Paranaguá (1997: 204) '[un] puerto tropical y cosmopolita venido a menos, decadente como todas las mitologías clásicas del cine mexicano y como el mismo México contemporáneo' / '[a] tropical and cosmopolitan port gone to seed, decadent like all the classic mythologies of Mexican cinema and like contemporary Mexico itself'.

As Paranaguá's statement obliquely signals, with its conflation of cinema and nation, it is possible to read the remake as a comment on the state of both the cinema and the nation. This comment, moreover, with its intensely self-conscious assault on the original – nowhere more evident than in the ending – would be tempting to characterise as 'postmodern'. In fact, in many ways, *La mujer del puerto* might be seen to bear all the hallmarks of postmodernism understood as an intensely self-reflexive mode of representation in which simulacra, irony and pastiche have become watchwords. That this is the case is clear from the opening titles of Ripstein's film, which roll to the musical accompaniment of '*Wenn die Soldaten*', sung by none other than Andrea Palma's alter ego, Marlene Dietrich. The credits then fade to an opening sequence in black and white, featuring steamships entering the port of Veracruz, incorporated directly from Boytler's original. The tripartite structure of the film then progresses from Marro's story – the most faithful of the three to the original – through those of Perla and Tomasa to the epilogue. Progression is, however, a misleading term to describe the relationship between the different stories for they defy both temporal and narrative logic. As the narrative circles back upon itself – for example, in one version Perla commits suicide; in another she does not – the viewer is denied the security that linearity would confer.

The dense web of references to the original, combined with the circularity and profound narrative ambivalence of Ripstein's remake, would seem to invite its categorisation as postmodern artefact *par excellence*. By the same token, it is also perhaps tempting to read the ending of Ripstein's remake as a form of parodic, self-reflexive meditation on the resonances of the original film's denouement. The original punishes incest; the remake exults in incestuous sexuality. In this way, on a symbolic level, the remake sets the scene to assail the myth of progress that the first film articulates. Such an interpretation works, to some extent, particularly when we take into account the discourses in circulation concerning civilisation that form the backdrop to the remake. There is nevertheless a problem associated with such a reading; in particular we must scrutinise the teleological narrative which drives the question of postmodernity in the Latin American context.

The status and significance of the postmodern as aesthetic practice and temporal marker have become a hotly debated issue in Latin American studies. For some, the advent of postmodernity, and particularly the emphasis that postmodern discourses would place on a notion of the decentred West, was hailed as a cause for celebration. As George Yúdice notes, the late Nobel Laureate, Octavio Paz was amongst the first to embrace the implications of postmodernity in 1950, when he declared:

> We have lived on the periphery of history. Today the center, the nucleus of world society has come apart and we have all become peripheral beings, even the Europeans and the North Americans. We are all on the margin because there is no longer any center.
>
> (Yúdice 1992: 5)

Other Latin American cultural critics are, however, rather less sanguine about the implications of metropolitan debates on postmodernity for an understanding of the region's geo-political status, for the term is bound up in precisely the kind of teleological narrative of progress, whereby modernity, once achieved, gives way to 'postmodernity'. Or as Claudio Lomnitz puts it, referring to the cultural and social transformations that, like Dever, he perceives to take place in a specifically Mexican context:

> At that time many a social diagnostician thought that Mexico had contracted 'postmodernity' [. . .] Nevertheless, this notion was soon corrected by Roger Bartra (1987) who, having carefully analyzed Mexico's symptoms, came to the sobering conclusion that, although indeed strange things were happening regarding modernity in Mexico, these might more aptly be described as a particular form of dismodernity or, more playfully, as 'dis-motherism': a mixture of a quite postmodern *desmadre* (chaos) and continuing aspirations to an unachieved modernity.
>
> (Lomnitz 2001: 110)

In short, the ending of Ripstein's remake, whilst it mimics to perfection a brand of postmodern irony – not least in the final shot, in which Patricia Reyes Spíndola as Tomasa stares directly into the camera, smoking a cigarette in a desultory manner in an intensely knowing nod to Andrea Palma's imitation of Dietrich – can be more appropriately understood as a form of 'dismodern' irony. As one of a series of remakes, and made within one year of Quintanilla Rico's version, Ripstein's *La mujer del puerto*, almost despite itself, attests to the 'continuing aspirations to an unachieved modernity', which is here figured cinematographically. At the same time, the ending, with its iconoclastic assault on that of the original, calls into question the very same narrative of progress that animated cultural, social and political debate at the time of the first film's making.

45

THE ULTIMATE 'DISMODERN' IRONY

There is one final irony about the remake, however, which requires comment for it not only illuminates the interplay between Boytler and Ripstein's films, but also sheds light on the role of the filmmaker in Mexico – and Latin America more generally – in the contemporary cultural moment. Once again, at the heart of this irony is the conflation of cinema and nationhood. The emphasis on an excessive, oral sexuality in Ripstein's remake, concluding with the happy ending of consummated incestuous sexuality, can be read as recognition that the dream of cosmopolitan nationalism which found expression in a cinematic idiom of the 1930s is a failed project. This is not to deny that the Mexican cinema, to requote Boytler, did indeed 'come to be understood and accepted in other Spanish-speaking countries'; for it did. In 1937, Boytler himself directed *¡Así es mi tierra!* (That's my Country!) and *Aguila o sol* (Heads or Tails), both featuring the comic actor Cantinflas, who was to go on to become a national star with precisely the kind of transnational appeal to which Boytler would seem to have aspired with his earlier film. In other words, Mexican cinema was understood and accepted in other Spanish-speaking countries: it simply did not do so in the universalising terms invoked by Boytler and the contemporary critics of his earlier, more aesthetically ambitious film. Rather, as Ana López has convincingly established, the critical and commercial success of the Mexican cinema during its heyday of the 1940s was precisely founded upon its circulation of images of the local, the folkloric, and the popular that held widespread appeal for audiences across Latin America so that by 1943:

> [T]he best and most popular films of that year [. . .] for the most part abandoned foreign exoticism and left behind 'universalizing' or Pan-Latin Americanist tendencies to focus on markedly 'Mexican' themes and problems. These themes – *indigenismo*, the Revolution, the melodramatic angst of urban life, and, of course, *rancheras* – would constitute the backbone of the Mexican cinema's popularity in Latin America.
>
> (López 1994: 9)

If, in part, Ripstein's self-reflexive, overtly cinematic dialogue with the original signals the return of the repressed in its emphasis on the base, the bodily and the low, this dialogue is, nevertheless, underpinned by a paradox. In the 1990s, an age of ever-diminishing cinema budgets and heightened competition with both television and Hollywood, Ripstein's films, and Ripstein himself as auteur, are to be found primarily on an international 'art house' circuit. Or in the words of López:

> In an international context, this 'new' Mexican cinema speaks with a different voice to a radically different audience. The international market it seeks is no longer defined by language or geography, but by a network

of financers and distributors that direct it north (to the U.S.) rather than south, and to elite rather than mass audiences.

(López 1994: 12)

Emblematic of what Marvin D'Lugo (2003: 110) terms an 'authorial icon', Ripstein – alongside other seminal Latin American directors, amongst them Cuban Tomás Gutiérrez Alea and Argentine Fernando Solanas – now represents Mexican national culture within the global market. As a prestigious aesthetic product, Ripstein's remake of *La mujer del puerto* and its presentation of modernity as a failed project, comes to stand for a cosmopolitan, internationally recognised cinema. In other words, the success of Mexican cinema – and this observation could be extended to much contemporary Latin American cinema more generally – is predicated on the failure of modernity in this geo-political location. In Ripstein as an auteur, Boytler's dream of cosmopolitan nationalism is, to some extent, imperfectly achieved.

2

THE MEXICAN REVOLUTION AS
MOVING MEMORY

WATCHING THE REVOLUTION

In a classic vignette from the literature of the Mexican revolution, in *El águila y la serpiente* (The Eagle and the Serpent, 1928) Martín Luis Guzmán recalls an early audience of the moving image. The scene involves a group of revolutionary soldiers at the Convention of Aguascalientes in 1914, who have gathered to view a newsreel projected onto a makeshift screen. Chronicling the historical events that were unfolding around the assembled revolutionaries and focusing particularly on the leading figures of those events, in the newsreel one revolutionary *caudillo* in particular, namely Constitutionalist leader Venustiano Carranza, elicits a memorable reaction:[1]

> Don Venustiano, por supuesto, era el personaje que más a menudo volvía a la pantalla. Sus apariciones, más y más frecuentes, habían venido haciéndose, como debía esperarse, más y más ingratas para el público convencionista. De los siseos mezclados con aplauso en las primeras veces en que se le vio, se fue pasando a los siseos francos; luego, al escándalo.

> Don Venustiano, of course, was the figure who appeared most often on the screen. His ever more frequent appearances had, as was only to be expected, become increasingly disagreeable for the Convention audience. The hisses mixed with applause that greeted his first appearances, soon became pure hisses; then uproar.

> (Guzmán [1928] 1991: 353)

Having arrived late to the packed venue, for lack of space, Guzmán and his two companions are forced to watch the newsreel from behind the curtain that serves as a screen. The newsreel is, however, cut short abruptly, for the makeshift auditorium degenerates into pandemonium:

> Y de ese modo, de etapa en etapa, se alcanzó al fin, al proyectarse la escena en que se veía a Carranza entrando a caballo en la ciudad de México, una especie de batahola de infierno que culminó en dos disparos.

48

Ambos proyectiles atravesaron el telón, exactamente en el lugar donde se dibujaba el pecho del Primer Jefe, y vinieron a incrustarse en la pared, una a medio metro por encima de Lucio Blanco, y el otro, más cerca aún entre la cabeza de Domínguez y la mía.

And in this way, bit by bit, the uproar reached its climax in the scene in which Carranza was seen entering Mexico City on horseback, in a hellish din, culminating in two gunshots.

Both projectiles hit the screen at the exact spot where the chest of the Supreme Commander was outlined and ended up embedded in the wall, one, half a metre above Lucio Blanco and the other, closer still, between Domínguez's head and mine.

(Guzmán [1928] 1991: 353)

For Guzmán and his companions, the appearance of Venustiano Carranza on the makeshift screen in 1914 had comic, if nearly tragic consequences. It is unlikely that this *caudillo*, or indeed any of the other key revolutionary figures – Emiliano Zapata, Pancho Villa and Alvaro Obregón – had the same effect when they appeared on screen before the audiences of Carmen Toscano's *Memorias de un mexicano* (Memories of a Mexican). Released in 1950, and comprised of footage selected and edited from her father, Salvador Toscano's archive of material filmed just prior to, during and in the immediate aftermath of the armed conflict some thirty years previously, *Memorias de un mexicano* offered its audience a fascinating historical panorama of the still relatively recent bellicose events – from the final moments of Porfirio Díaz's dictatorship; through the years of violent factional struggle from 1910–17; up to the electoral campaign of 1923 that propelled Plutarco Elías Calles to the presidency.

As fascinating as this historical material was (and still is), what for the 1914 revolutionary audience of Guzmán's account caused such uproar would, by 1950, certainly have lost its explosive charge. With nearly three decades separating this audience from the events depicted on screen, in the ensuing years the revolution had undergone a process of institutionalisation and passed into the domains of collective memory. In this way, the 1950s audience came to *Memorias de un mexicano* as viewers embedded in socio-cultural structures in which the revolution's meanings were constructed and promoted in an on-going process that involved the selective appropriation of elements of the past that corresponded to the needs of the present. Even if this were not the case, to put it with comic book starkness, with more than half a century's experience of film viewing behind it, the 1950s audience, unlike its earlier counterpart, would clearly be able to distinguish between screen and real life.

Not spurred on to action maybe, in the same way as the 1914 revolutionaries caught up in the violence and emotion of the armed struggle, audiences in the 1950s would undoubtedly still have been moved by *Memorias de un mexicano*. Audiences who saw the Toscanos' film in 1950 were made up both of those for

49

whom the revolution was a living memory and, increasingly, of those for whom it was, following Marianne Hirsch, a postmemory; whilst the armed struggle preceded their birth, it nevertheless represented a potent memory text.[2] Both categories of spectator would arguably have been better acquainted with the conflict in representational forms other than the spectacle of the moving image of early actualities film.

On the one hand, this audience in 1950 might have been familiar with still photographs of the conflict, such as those that make up the Casasola Archive.[3] Numbering some 600,000 negatives, images from this rich source achieved widespread dissemination with the publication of the *Historia gráfica de la revolución* circa 1940. By the 1940s, as Carlos Monsiváis (1981a) notes, photographs that depicted the violent phase of the revolution started to receive renewed attention, particularly by viewers who had not experienced events first-hand, in a process whereby a suspiciously small number of images were singled out for repeated exposure. In this way, a select handful of photographs – images such as *Zapatistas en Sanborns* (1914) or *Villa en la silla presidencial* (1914) – acquired iconic status, coming to emblematise the revolution in the popular imagination.

On the other hand, metropolitan audiences in 1950 would also have had experience of the revolution's iconography that had gradually insinuated itself into their everyday lived environment in a variety of state-sponsored guises. Such iconic representations of the revolution took the form of the muralists' painted representations of the struggle, and the rituals and statues of *caudillos* and other symbols related to the struggle that were erected throughout the Republic.[4] And finally, many members of the audience of *Memorias de un mexicano* in 1950 would, of course, have been familiar with the growing body of feature films produced in the aftermath: films such as *Flor silvestre* (Wild Flower, Emilio Fernández, 1943) and *Enamorada* (A Woman in Love, Emilio Fernández, 1946), in which the revolution figured either as a backdrop or as the main theme.

By contrast, where early film footage survived the neglect and destruction that have been the fate of much early cinema the world over, the politics and logistics of screening what had in effect become outdated material, would have led to the confinement of any such extant footage to the archive.[5] In other words, *Memorias de un mexicano* would, we can imagine, initially have caused quite a stir with its 1950s audiences, on one level, precisely because after three decades dominated by fiction films and other modes of representation of the event of most importance in the nation's recent history, the Toscanos' film (re)acquainted them with the revolution as moving image. That is, as an edited compilation of early actualities footage, *Memorias de un mexicano* afforded privileged access to what Ivone Margulies (2003: 1) terms 'the epistemological promise of referential images: that what we see refers to an existing reality'.

In this preamble, I have placed an emphasis on the gap that separates, on the one hand, those revolutionary viewers who saw the newsreels at the height of the conflict in the permanent and makeshift auditoriums such as that described by Guzmán, which had sprung up across the Republic, and, on the other, those who experienced the conflict as moving, (post) memory in 1950. This is because in this chapter I wish to explore the function of the revolution in the nation's audio-visual imaginary in these key post-revolutionary years, weaving in and out of a detailed case study of *Memorias de un mexicano* and debates in cultural history and memory.

FROM FACTION TO FICTION:
FILM AND MEMORY

The revolution acted as magnet for photographers and filmmakers from both home and abroad, who hooked up with the different armed factions to record their feats for a domestic audience, in the first instance at least, hungry for news and views of the unfolding events. In fact, the outbreak of the revolution in 1910 provided an opportunity for the city-based cameramen to extend their itineraries and broaden their visual repertoires. And, in due course, as Julianne Burton notes, the revolution transformed the way in which the medium of film was deployed:

> High angles, immobile cameras, and long shots of indigenous peoples performing and workers parading before a Europeanized oligarchy, gave way to shots of swirling masses in motion on their own behalf. From their position of privileged superiority, often literally as well as figuratively on the dais of the dictator, cameramen descended into the street; from the sheltered urban spaces of the bourgeoisie, they fanned out into the contested countryside.
>
> (Burton 1990: 13)

Although Díaz's overthrow and the revolutionary years coincided with innovations in cinematic language, from the static camera of the Lumière films, to the mobility and editing associated especially with D. W. Griffiths, the changes described by Burton go beyond the technical and have clear ideological hues. Hitherto yoked to the constraints imposed by the self-aggrandising tendencies of the *Porfiriato*, the outbreak of the revolution in 1910 entailed the freedom to film differently. In short, the revolution not only generated new kinds of images – locomotives packed with combatants, multitudes gathering to greet the arrival of a revolutionary *caudillo* – it also provided unprecedented points of view, breaking with the circumscribed modes of seeing associated with the *Porfiriato*.

The soon to-be-deposed dictator Porfirio Díaz had quickly grasped the efficacy of the new audio-visual medium in his project of self-aggrandisement when, in 1895 cinema arrived in Mexico. The revolutionary *caudillos* were no less canny in their appropriation of the ideological and commemorative potential of film. Notably, of the four most politically (and visually) prominent *caudillos* (Zapata, Villa, Carranza and Obregón), Villa's relationship with the moving image is the stuff of legend. On signing an exclusive contract with the North American Mutual

Film Co., Villa stage-managed elements of his role in the conflict, arranging for battles to be fought and hangings performed by the light of day to ensure that they could be filmed.[6] Despite such manipulative and openly propagandistic manoeuvres on the part of their subjects, filmmakers cleaved to a belief in the scientific impartiality of medium:

> [F]rom the moment cinema arrived in Mexico, intellectuals linked it to the illustrated press and, following the positivist spirit of the era, to science. In that context, fiction cinema was rejected because of its potential to dupe the public: the cinema was a science and as such should show truths.
>
> (De los Reyes 1995a: 65)

Early audiences of the moving image similarly appeared to harbour illusions as to the truth-value of what they saw on screen, as illustrated by the classic vignette from the literature of the revolution with which I opened this chapter. As the example of the revolutionary crowd evoked by Guzmán at the Convention of Aguascalientes demonstrates, such was the power of photographic realism to convince, that this unruly bunch became, momentarily at least, unable to distinguish between reality and representation. Both stances – that of the filmmakers who cleaved to the scientific basis of film and that of the audience who were moved to shoot at the screen – are, however, vectors of the same phenomenon; both turn on the power of photographic realism to register the visible world. Furthermore, the ideological status of this powerful visual medium at this historical juncture also serves to explain, in part, why from 1916 on, film that focused on the revolution ceased to appear with such frequency on the nation's screens.

In his important work on early cinema and society in Mexico, Aurelio de los Reyes argues that a constellation of factors led to the revolution's disappearance from the Republic's screens. First, and as we saw in Chapter 1, it was felt that the revolution played a significant role in the deterioration of Mexico's image abroad (particularly in the US), an image that the state was keen to 'sanitise'. Such images of conflict were considered to confirm Hollywood's images of Mexicans as prone to excesses of violence. Second, some five years into the upheaval, a general 'battle fatigue' started to prevail, which was felt particularly strongly by metropolitan Mexicans who, once eager for views of the conflict, were rapidly becoming wearied by the problems that the armed struggle was causing in their daily life. Third, when Carranza acceded to power in 1917, in the interests of promoting greater stability and social quiescence, the newly established ruling elite actively took steps to prevent the presentation of film footage that might stir the masses to take up arms once again. Hence, De los Reyes (1987: 66) concludes there was a tacit consensus to ignore the revolution. In its early phase, the revolution had transformed the way in which the medium was used, allowing filmmakers to take to the streets and countryside to capture the uprising of the masses in motion. Ironically, it was precisely film's 'provocative mimesis' (Margulies 2003: 2), its ability to convince and influence, that brought this activity to an abrupt halt. From 1916 on, film-making instead took on increasingly nationalistic and narrative hues and started to focus its lens on less bellicose subjects such as landscapes, '*tipos mexicanos*' or the safely distant pre-Columbian past.

Although actuality films that focused on the conflict disappeared prematurely, this did not, and indeed, within the terms of reference that governed the post-revolutionary state's legitimacy, *could* not, spell the disappearance of the revolution from the nation's (audio)visual imaginary altogether. This legitimacy was predicated on the state's status as heir to the revolutionary project, whose values it promoted and would carry forward. As noted, in the aftermath of the violent phase, it fell to feature film and to photography – along with muralism, rituals, official commemorations, monuments etc. – to install the memory of the revo-lution at the centre of the processes of national 'imagining'. Indeed, discourses of memory came to play an important role in the post-revolutionary drive to institutionalise the armed struggle as a foundational narrative of identity, where identity was to be forged on a notion of national unity. In fact, unity was a political exigency at this time because, as Alan Knight declares at the opening of his monumental two-volume study of the revolution:

> Mexico of 1910 was, borrowing Lesley Simpson's phrase, 'many Mexicos', less a nation than a geographical expression, a mosaic of regions and communities, introverted and jealous, ethnically and physically fragmented, and lacking common national sentiments; these sentiments came after the revolution and were [. . .] its offspring rather than its parents.
>
> (Knight 1986: 2)

If, as Knight's comments suggest, Mexico was more a collection of fragments than coherent whole in 1910, so too was the revolution, which was ultimately a highly factionalised and bitter civil war. For the revolution to function within the post-revolutionary political and cultural imaginary as the desired unifying, foundational narrative of identity, it therefore had to be remembered and thereby *reinvented* as what it was not: a unified struggle propelled by a set of coherent aims and ideals. Furthermore, given that it was the middle-class, conservative Constitutionalists embodied by (the hissed at) Carranza and Obregón who emerged as victorious (and not the *campesinos* or radicals, represented by Villa and Zapata), the revolution had to be retrospectively re-presented not only as coherent, but also (in appearance at least) as propelled by a social and political *revolutionary* agenda.

The dynamics of post-revolutionary audio-visual discourses of memory can therefore usefully be understood in the light of theories of collective memory, which, as influential scholars such as Benedict Anderson (1983) have established, is crucial to the formation of national identities. Nancy Wood provides a help-ful definition of this particular inflection of memory which she establishes in opposition to individual memory as 'that which testifies to a will or desire on the part of some social group or disposition of power to select and organize representations of the past so that these will be embraced by individuals as their own'. And she continues, 'If particular representations of the past have permeated the public domain, it is because they embody an intentionality – social, political, institutional and so on – that promotes or authorizes their entry' (Wood 1999: 2). Such conceptions of memory have clearly influenced approaches to the cultural politics of representation of the revolution in Mexican studies, as evidenced for example by Thomas Benjamin's excellent book *La Revolución: Mexico's Great Revolution as Memory and Myth, History* (2000). Nevertheless it would be wrong to overplay the notion of memory as a wholly 'top-down', uniform construct in post-revolutionary cultural politics. Rather, Mary Kay Vaughan recommends that 'the post-revolutionary state's cultural politics are better understood as an improvised, multivalent, accumulative process that grew through interaction between state and society' (Vaughan 2001: 472).

Indeed, something of the rugged, uneven contours of the conflict's post-revolutionary commemoration that bespeaks the relationship between state and society can be discerned by tracing the thematic development of some of the feature films in which the revolution figures as a central theme. In so doing, it is possible to grasp how, in the period 1930–50, the cinematic representation of the revolution gradually fell within the parameters set for it by official rhetoric. At the same time, in following through the development of the revolution's representation, the ambivalence of the relationship that obtains between memory and the moving image becomes apparent. This ambivalence is predicated on two key factors. On the one hand, the narrative and editing strategies of feature film – the flashback, the fade-in etc. – echo many of memory's key tropes; similarly the non-fiction film functions as a form of repository of memory.[7] On the other, however, as Tom Gunning has pointed out, 'images in their mass-produced form recall less those "honey-combs" of memory [. . .] than recycled discards of the all too familiar.' In short, 'the proliferation of moving images threatens, as in Plato, to destroy rather than to preserve memory' (Gunning 2000: 318). In what follows, it is these tensions and ambiguities between film as material base akin to memory and as an entity that paradoxically can also serve to occlude memory that I wish to explore in the context of the filmic representation of the revolution.

REVIEWING THE REVOLUTION

The revolution's exit from the nation's screens in 1916 – although, as outlined above, for tangible reasons – was both abrupt and premature. It was not until the 1930s and the advent of sound cinema that the revolution erupted back onto the nation's screens with Fernando de Fuentes's revolutionary trilogy – *El compadre Mendoza* (Godfather Mendoza, 1933); *El prisionero trece* (Prisoner Number Thirteen, 1933); and *¡Vámonos con Pancho Villa!* (Let's Go with Pancho Villa!,

1935). The gap of some ten years between the end of the violence and the revolution's reappearance on screen can be understood, on one level and in part, in the light of the post-revolutionary state's neglect of the still relatively new technology of film. Seemingly blind to cinema's capacity to reach out to and communicate with a mass audience, the state opted instead to promote muralism as a national art form. As we saw in Chapter 1, the cinema was initially treated with a degree of distrust as an essentially foreign import and therefore inimical to the project of cultural nationalism. On another level, the absence of the revolution from the nation's screens speaks volumes about the precariousness post-revolutionary political stability in the 1920s. The decade witnessed the *Delahuerta* uprising in 1924 and the more serious *Cristero* rebellion that spanned the years 1926–29, both putting the uneasy peace to the test.[8] The absence of the revolution also conveys the force of a denial: a wilful amnesia on the part of filmmakers working within the institutional structures of the nascent national industry to block out traumatic memories of the recent past.

The reappearance of the revolution in the form of the De Fuentes trilogy signals for many critics a watershed both in the history of the national cinema and representations of the civil war.[9] For example, Burton-Carvajal (1997: 211) describes De Fuentes as 'widely regarded as Mexico's most important director of the initial sound period, [who] made two of the most clear-eyed and powerful films ever produced on the theme of the revolution (*El compadre Mendoza* [. . .] and *¡Vámonos con Pancho Villa!*).' And for John Mraz, these two films are:

> the best films made on [the] struggle [. . .]. Contrary to the great majority of movies about this event, these works by de Fuentes do not in any way glorify the civil war and the people – usually male leaders, rarely women – who made it. [. . .] [T]hey exude a disenchantment with the revolution's shortcomings, instead of celebrating its achievements.
>
> (Mraz 1999: 148)

To be sure, it is significant that all three films represent the recent conflict in a specific idiom. Each focuses on some form of human relationship that culminates in a betrayal. Moreover, the relationships in question clearly function as metaphors for the revolution itself, and particularly the ultimate betrayal of its more radical, utopian ideals.

El compadre Mendoza centres on the bonds of allegiance between two symbolically charged figures: wealthy landowner Rosalío Mendoza (Alfredo del Diestro) and the man who, in the course of the film, becomes his best friend, *Zapatista* general Felipe Nieto (Antonio R. Frausto). Despite the fact Mendoza owes his life to Nieto, who also becomes godfather to the landowner's son, at the end Mendoza literally sells his friend out. Accepting money offered by the Carrancistas that will facilitate his family's escape from their hacienda, Mendoza betrays Nieto: an act that ultimately leads to his *compadre*'s death.

Likewise, in *El prisionero trece*, drunken colonel Carrasco (Alfredo del Diestro) is bribed by a friend to release some jailed revolutionaries, substituting them with another prisoner who turns out to be the son that Carrasco has not seen since he was a child. Unable to save his son from the firing squad, the film is prevented from degenerating into utter bathos when Carrasco awakens to discover that the traumatic events have all been nothing more than a nightmare. This dream device was in fact a narrative strategy imposed by the censors to temper the harsh infanticidal ending of the original version. Nevertheless, this imposition hardly detracts from the bitter criticism that *El prisionero trece* directs at the corruption and betrayal that constitute the revolution in De Fuentes's film.

Finally, *¡Vámonos con Pancho Villa!* follows the fate of six *rancheros*, 'los Leones', who join up with the forces of Pancho Villa and who, one by one, meet their deaths, their loyalty to the legendary *caudillo* rewarded with his utter indifference to their plight.

As this brief overview demonstrates, all three films emphatically highlight not the triumphs and achievements of the revolution, but its shortcomings.[10] By focusing on interpersonal relationships that turn on the bonds of allegiance and trust and which ultimately end in tragedy, all three films provide a bold critique of the revolution's fratricidal factionalism.[11]

The cultural and political climate of the 1930s that had provided De Fuentes with the creative space to explore the internecine conflicts of the revolution and the light-touch censorship that we observed in Chapter 1, had largely vanished by the 1940s. For example, Emilio García Riera (1998: 131) cites the official censor of the period, Felipe Gregorio Castillo, who was of the opinion that: '[Y]a no debían hacerse películas como *El compadre Mendoza* por presentar "aspectos vergonzosos de la revolución" y que, si de él hubiera dependido diez años atrás, la cinta de De Fuentes nunca hubiera sido filmada.' / '[F]ilms like *El compadre Mendoza* should no longer be made, for they showed "shameful aspects of the revolution" and if it had been up to him ten years ago, De Fuentes's film would never have been made.' García Riera concludes therefore that 'Se veía pues como obligatorio que el cine mexicano fuera un espejo embellecedor del país.' / 'It was seen as obligatory that the Mexican cinema was a mirror that beautified the country.' How, though, are we to understand the censor's comments? What had changed in the intervening ten years that would prompt such a gesture of retrospective censorship?

In the excellent introduction to *Fragments of a Golden Age* (2001), Gil Joseph, Anne Rubenstein and Eric Zolov argue that 1940 represents a pivotal, if contradictory, moment in Mexican historiography. For these critics, 1940 marks the beginning of the end of revolutionary promise. This was the moment when the (relatively) radical potential of Lázaro Cárdenas's 1934–40 regime (with its expropriation of the national oil reserves and land redistribution programmes) had evaporated and politics took a sharp turn to the right under Manuel Avila Camacho (1940–46) – a turn that became even more accentuated under Miguel Alemán (1946–52). With the onset of the 'economic miracle' triggered by the global dislocations of the Second World War, the country became increasingly urban and consumer oriented.

In the 1940s, therefore, the revolution parted company with the residues of radicalism which the term conventionally might connote. Ironically, however, this parting of ways coincided with the moment at which the revolution as epic and its pantheon of heroes started to acquire increased symbolic power as a legitimising, foundational myth that became ever more harnessed to the official unifying rhetoric of '*lo mexicano*':

> Embodied politically in the new, one-party state orchestrated by the Partido Nacional Revolucionario (which was founded in 1929 and rebaptized as the Partido Revolucionario Mexicano in 1938 and the Partido Revolucionario Institucional in 1946), Mexicans across class, regional, ethnic, race, gender and generational lines were exhorted by their rulers to feel part of the new 'Revolutionary Family' to which they belonged by birth and which spoke in their name.
>
> (Joseph *et al.* 2001: 8)

In a nutshell, this is what had changed between the making of De Fuentes's trilogy and the 1940s context of Gregorio Castillo's condemnatory comments. Given that the dissolution of bonds of social and familial kinship functions as a central metaphor for the revolution across the films that comprise De Fuentes's trilogy, it is hardly surprising that the official censor should articulate his retrospective condemnation in the 1940s. *El compadre Mendoza* (and for that matter, *El prisionero trece* and *¡Vámonos con Pancho Villa!*) cut to the quick of the filial and familial union that underpinned the myth of 'Revolutionary Family' and its attendant ideologies. From this point on, the revolution was to be represented and remembered differently:

> [C]oncerned to legitimate the ruling party as sole heir of the founding cataclysm, the official account conflates the Revolutionaries into the same camp, eliding the fact that [. . .] this struggle was defined more by the warfare between the Revolutionaries than by the battle of Old and New Orders.
>
> (Mraz 1999: 149)

Post 1940, in the interests of national unity, the divisions and internal struggles of the revolution were to all intents and purposes to be erased from collective memory.

Having traced some of the vicissitudes of the filmic representation – albeit fictional – of the revolution and the links to official discourses of national identity, I want now to return to *Memorias de un mexicano*. We last saw the Toscanos' film in the introductory remarks to this chapter, where we attempted to imagine the kind of viewing experience it might have represented for its audience in 1950.

Unlikely to have elicited the kind of audience reaction as that of the unruly and gun-toting revolutionaries described by Guzmán, viewers in 1950 of Toscano's actuality footage, now rendered documentary, nonetheless cannot fail to have been moved by this monumental memory image.

REVISING THE REVOLUTION:
FROM DOCUMENT TO DOCUMENTARY

Memorias de un mexicano comprises a panoramic overview of early twentieth-century Mexican history in the form of a chronologically organised series of actualities presented explicitly as filtered through, and therefore a visualisation of, the memory of the Mexican of the film's title. On the death of her father in 1947, and as a commemoration of his life's work, Carmen Toscano set about selecting and editing the material of which *Memorias de un mexicano* is constituted. In this sense, the film stands as a daughter's homage to her father, while the film as the act of memory signalled by the title is (by one reading) that of Salvador Toscano as eye-witness to the dramatic events that were to shape his country's political and cultural history throughout the course of the twentieth century.

The issue of memory – or, more to the point, the issue of *whose* memories are presented – is, however, more complicated than the film's title will allow. The daughter's presence in *Memorias de un mexicano* is not only evident in the processes of selection and edition: processes that are, of course, redolent of the structure of condensation that is one of memory's key tropes. In her re-presentation of archival material, Carmen Toscano also opted to impose a sound track on what was, of course, originally silent footage.[12] It is the multiple levels on which we can understand this auditory narrative and its relationship to the moving visual image of memory that will be of central significance in this discussion of *Memorias de un mexicano*.

The audio dimension consists of sound effects, a musical score and a narrative voice-over. So, for example, a range of sound effects are synchronised with the action on screen. Cries of '*¡Viva!*', implicitly issued by the crowds captured on film, greet the appearance first of Díaz, and then, without marking any form of ideological distinction between them, the *caudillos* Madero, Zapata, Villa and Carranza are similarly hailed by such cries. Battle scenes are accompanied by gunshots and steam locomotives emit puffing noises. Arranged by Jorge Pérez H., the musical score marks the changing emotional tenor of the on-screen action. It runs the gamut from the lively *corridos* of Madero, Zapata, Villa, Carranza and Obregón to the sombre music that signals the murder of Madero and Pino Suárez at the hands of Huerta in the scenes filmed in the capital during the *Decena trágica* (tragic ten days) of 1914.

Superimposed on this ambient soundtrack is the voice of an unnamed and unseen male narrator, the other Mexican of the title who provides historical orientation to the footage. This fictional creation's story, spoken by Manuel Bernal, and penned by Carmen Toscano, begins after an initial intertitle that informs the audience about the provenance of the footage it is to witness:

> En 1897 el ingeniero Salvador Toscano abrió el primer cine en México y comenzó a fotografiar escenas de la vida mexicana que fueron el principio de la valiosa colección que ha sido utilizada en esta película.

> In 1897 the engineer Salvador Toscano opened the first cinema in Mexico and started to photograph scenes from Mexican life that were the beginnings of the valuable collection that has been used in this film.

As the fictional narrator informs us, 1897 is also the year of his birth. Without doubt, this is no simple coincidence. By establishing an explicit link between, on the one hand, the birth of the narrator, whose memories the audience will witness, and on the other, the birth of cinema in Mexico, *Memorias de un mexicano* sets up an a priori relationship between film and memory. Celluloid, it seems to suggest, is the very stuff on which memory is imprinted: film and memory are in this way established as somehow analogous. If celluloid is the material base of memory and the scenes projected onto the screen implicitly offer direct access onto the past, it is significant to note that from the vantage point of 1950, this (unnamed) Mexican's memories focus tightly upon a key historical event: the revolution. Memory as presented here exists then as a configuration of film and revolution which, in turn, is also a (curiously) family affair.

The narrator not only provides a commentary on the imagistic history as it unfolds on screen; he also recounts a family narrative, a personal story that is intertwined with the events of public history. Thus the audience discovers that the narrator's father is a supporter of Porfirio Díaz, whom he accompanies on official tours of the Republic. The narrator also has an uncle, Tío Luis, who is a supporter of Villa, much to the disgust of his *Porfirista* brother. Nevertheless, when the narrator's father leaves Mexico in 1911 on the same ship that transports the deposed dictator into exile in Europe, he entrusts his son's care into the hands of Luis. Nephew and uncle, however, enjoy a stormy relationship in their travels with the revolutionaries. The two become enemies when, in 1914, the narrator sides with Carranza against Villa. Finally, though, with the surrender of Villa, the narrator and Luis are reconciled. What, then, are we to make of the soundtrack generally and in particular its familial dimension? Why this kind of personal narrative and not, say, a more conventionally 'objective' voice-over?

On the one hand, the actuality film to which *Memorias de un mexicano* reintroduced its audience in 1950, is, particularly during its early sequences, characteristic of what Tom Gunning (1990) has termed early 'cinema of attractions', which he argues is 'presentational' rather than 'representational'. Early actuality films provoked astonishment in their audiences, who thrilled at the sight of moving images, at first, precisely because they moved. Unlike later, narrative-driven cinema, their appeal lay in their ability to display and show, rather than tell. Although the revolution marked a break with the circumscribed modes of seeing associated with the *Porfiriato*, *Memorias de un mexicano* nevertheless largely conforms to the tenets of theatrical display of early cinema. However, as Angel Miquel argues, as early as 1928, such archaic film language bored critics and the general public in equal measure, to the extent that Toscano's films

> a duras penas se mantuvieron tres días en cartelera. Hacía tiempo que el lenguaje del cine había cambiado y ver esas tomas fijas de desfiles y cañonazos resultaba insoportablemente aburrido para los espectadores comunes acostumbrados a la dinámica del cine Hollywoodense, y también para los conocedores que habían podido disfrutar en México, por ejemplo, *El crucero Potemkin* de Eisenstein.

> barely managed to run for three days. Cinematic language had changed some time ago and to see these fixed shots of processions and canon fire proved unbearably boring for ordinary spectators who were used to the dynamics of the Hollywood cinema, and also for those connoisseurs who had, for example, enjoyed Eisenstein's *Battleship Potemkin*.
>
> (Miquel 1997: 88)

Already tedious for audiences in 1928, such material would have been doubly so for later generations of spectators. In 1950, the soundtrack with its voice-over, musical score and sound effects represented a strategy to provide the footage with a more contemporaneous narrative structure – one that served to ensure the fuller engagement of a 1950s audience with the spectacle of an outmoded early cinematic form. There is, however, more at stake in the audience's engagement with the moving images on screen than a simple experiential gap in viewing horizons. To grasp something of this, we can profit by attending to two overlapping issues – namely the historicity of documentary as a mode of representation, and the change that the revolution's status underwent in collective memory circa 1940 and its link to official nationalist rhetoric.

Until recently, it has been commonplace in film studies to posit the simultaneous origins of early cinema and documentary form in the period 1895–1905. Thus, for example, Charles Ramírez Berg (1999: 365) suggests: 'A key distinguishing feature of Mexican cinema is the fact that for its first 20 years, from 1896 until 1916, Mexican film production was almost exclusively a documentary practice.' Bill Nichols has, however, questioned the legitimacy of this twin birth. Instead, he notes that documentary film is a historically contingent form whose emergence must be located instead to the 1920s and early 1930s. Indeed, the emergence of documentary 'involves the combination of three pre-existing elements – photographic realism, narrative structure, and modernist fragmentation – along with a new emphasis on the rhetoric of social persuasion'. What is more, Nichols continues:

[A] wave of documentary activity takes shape at the point when cinema comes into the direct service of various, already active efforts to build national identity during the 1920s and 1930s. Documentary film affirms, or contests, the power of the state. It addresses issues of public importance and affirms or contests the role of the state in confronting these issues.

(Nichols 2001: 562)

In other words, prior to this confluence of factors, imbued with the power of indexicality, film was certainly underpinned by an impulse to document. Without the existence of narrative codes and conventions and modernist practices of fragmentation and a concomitant reflexive foregrounding of questions of perception, film could not, however, be classified as documentary.

The imposition of the audio narrative structure onto the selected and edited footage that is *Memorias de un mexicano*, is, on one level, a prime illustration of the historically contingent status of documentary form. The imposition of the soundtrack serves to underline the fact that, whilst early cinema certainly displayed a latent impulse to document, devoid of narrative and editing, it lacked the rhetorical power to argue and persuade. With the addition of the narrative voice-over and sound effects, the moving spectacle of the revolution became endowed with the significance of historical time and meaning: it acquired the potential precisely to argue and persuade. At the same time, however, *Memorias de un mexicano* is not only an illustration of gap between early cinema and documentary form; it is also revealing of how, in the 1940s, the relative pluralism that had permitted De Fuentes to make his critical revolutionary trilogy effectively evaporated. Rather, *Memorias de un mexicano* constitutes a prime example of the attempts to install the memory of the revolution at the centre of the processes of national 'imagining'.

Cinematic spectatorship of actualities rendered documentary form, therefore, constitutes an act of collective memory with clear ideological ramifications that are linked to the historical circumstances of the film's production and consumption. What is more if, on one level, *Memorias de un mexicano* deployed a voice-over narrative in order to engage its audience with the potentially tedious spectacle of early cinematic form, on another, its favoured narrative trope – the patriarchal family – was wholly consonant and coalesced with two key idioms of national belonging. On the one hand, it did not simply draw on just any narrative convention; rather it drew on conventions associated with an existent cinematic genre, the revolutionary melodrama. On the other hand, this genre was in turn co-extensive with the official rhetoric and ideology of the new 'Revolutionary Family'. It is, therefore, instructive to take a brief detour through this key genre of the Mexican cinema – namely, revolutionary melodrama – for *Memorias de un mexicano* converges with its conventions in significant ways.

In a suggestive discussion, Deborah E. Mistron (1984) notes that this genre, which arose in the late 1930s with films such as *La adelita* (Guillermo Hernández Gómez, 1937) and was common during the 1940s, enshrines a paradox. Whereas melodrama tends to place an emphasis on the individual and the preservation of the status quo, revolution suggests precisely the inverse – namely, an expression of the collective will and the possibility of radical change to the traditional order that melodrama would preserve. Centring her essay primarily on Emilio Fernández's *Flor silvestre* (Wild Flower, 1943) and *Enamorada* (Woman in Love, 1946), Mistron homes in on the status and significance of the family in these films. As the sacrosanct institution at the heart of the life of the nation, the family functions as a unit on which the destructive force and violence of the revolution is played out and from whose fragments the post-revolutionary future is born. Unlike other deeply conservative examples of the genre, such as *Vino el remolino y nos alevantó* (The Whirlwind Came and Awakened Us, Juan Bustillo Oro, 1949) – a film that views the dynamism of the revolution as a serious threat to the family and social stability more generally – Mistron notes that Fernández's films offer a more nuanced vision of the changes wrought by the revolution, even if they are not lacking in conservative elements. Neither *Flor silvestre* nor *Enamorada* fights shy of showing the cataclysmic violence of the revolution as a force that irrevocably tears the unity of the family apart. Nor, however, do these films erase thorny issues concerning the deeply embedded class conflicts of pre-revolutionary society.

Flor silvestre focuses on a cross-class relationship between the wealthy son of a landowner, José Luis (Pedro Armendáriz) and a poor peasant Esperanza (Dolores del Río). As his choice of partner demonstrates, José Luis identifies with the nobler revolutionary aims of social equality and as a result is disowned by his family. In the course of film, the viewer witnesses the violence that the abrupt transition from one social system to another entails. When a pair of renegade revolutionaries murders his estranged father, José Luis is forced to seek vengeance, killing one of the revolutionaries; the surviving revolutionary then kidnaps Esperanza and their baby son, and José Luis is killed in the rescue attempt. On one level then, the revolution brings nothing but anguish and sorrow. However, the film is narrated in the form of a flashback, from a present-day perspective from which an older Esperanza recounts to her son the turbulent story of origins that surrounds his birth. For Mistron, this device serves a vital narrative and ideological purpose, for the story that Esperanza relates is one of personal and also national origins:

> [T]he revolution is seen as the painful birth of a new generation of families who are able to live in the more just and equitable society envisioned and created by those who came before. As a result, *Flor silvestre* is able to affirm the traditional values of the melodrama – the family and fatherland – at the same time that it affirms radical social changes, for the painful transitional phase is set in the past and is shown to contain the seeds of a new and better present.
>
> (Mistron 1984: 52)

If for Mistron, melodramas such as *Flor silvestre* and *Enamorada* constitute a (strange) hybrid genre, in generic terms, so too does *Memorias de un mexicano.*

Ostensibly a documentary, at the same time the film draws on codes and conventions proper to the revolutionary melodrama. Indeed significantly, the family of the unnamed narrator in *Memorias de un mexicano* is beset by similar disputes and fallings out that replicate those that were played out at a national level in the internecine conflicts with which the revolution was riven and also in revolutionary melodramas of the 1940s. That the narrator's family serves as a metaphor with clearly national and indeed nationalist implications is made explicit at a number of points. For example, when uncle and nephew part company, the latter declares: 'como nosotros se había dividido todo el país' / 'just like us, the whole country had divided'. But more importantly, this fictional, anonymous family, like the nation, is reconciled in what is ultimately a narrative of cohesion and identification that embraces all factions involved in the struggle – Porfirians, Zapatistas, Maderistas, Villistas, Carrancistas.[13] In a short essay on the film, Margarita de Orellana argues that in this all-embracing ideological eclecticism,

> [t]here is a simulation of 'collective memory' that manifests itself in this cross between the voice of the 'Mexican' and the documentary images. All to whom this (hi)story is shown are positioned in this intermediate space, which presumes a memory beyond that of the speaker and his family. Between the voice and the document, a simulation of a common past is evoked, assumed, described as unquestionable – even more unquestionable when the film tries to commemorate it.
>
> (De Orellana 1990: 214)

The memories signalled by the film's title therefore are not exclusively those of the unnamed narrator, mediated by the lens of Salvador Toscano. Rather, in the act of cinematic spectatorship, they become those of the national audience situated in 1950, an audience that looks back with the narrator at scenes of the nation's collective past.

In fact, *Memorias de un mexicano* is not only indebted to the revolutionary melodrama via its rendering of the revolution as a family affair. It also employs a narrative device similar to the flashback deployed in *Flor silvestre*, which Ayala Blanco (1985: 34) has noted as being common to feature films of the era. *Flor silvestre* closes with an image of Esperanza and her son, the symbolic embodiment of the new society engendered by the revolution, as they gaze out across the rural landscape that used to belong to José Luis's father, but now belongs to the people. So too, the final sequences of *Memorias de un mexicano* afford the audience with a panoramic vista of the nation's modern capital, which it surveys with the unnamed and unseen narrator. It is to this urban landscape that I now wish to turn, to explore the way in which the new and implicitly improved present is manifest in visual terms as explicitly linked to a project of modernisation of sensory perception.

MEMORY AND THE MOBILE GAZE

That the memories of the film's narrator have, through the act of spectatorship, become those of its 1950 audience is made explicit in these final scenes which culminate in the supreme symbol of the reified armed struggle in the form of the Monument to the Revolution that stands in the Plaza de la República in Mexico City. The year is 1950 and, after twenty-six years in exile, the narrator surveys this scene of bustling modernity over which images from the past are superimposed. At this sight, he comments:

> Y ahora regreso después de 26 años. México ya no es la vieja ciudad en que nací. Un ritmo más acelerado parece mover la nación pero en el fondo del nuevo México viven las ideales del pasado: el derecho, la libertad, la justicia. Lo mismo en la independencia que en la reforma que en la revolución: hay un pueblo invariable en sus esperanzas, en sus luchas que no han sido en vano. Me parece mirar escurrir las imágenes del pasado en las arterias de la ciudad y siento que algo de mi mismo habrá de perdurar mientras el recuerdo de lo que he vivido palpite en la memoria de cualquier mexicano.

> And now I return after 26 years. Mexico is no longer the old city in which I was born. A more accelerated rhythm appears to move the nation but the ideals of the past live at the heart of this new Mexico: the law, liberty and justice. The same as during Independence, and the Reform, as in the revolution: a people who are constant in their hopes and struggles, which have not been in vain. I seem to see images from the past flow through the arteries of the city and I feel that something of me will have to endure as long as the memory of what I have lived palpitates in the memory of all Mexicans.

The status and significance of memory could not be more explicit: memory functions as a conduit to modernity. Memory (or more to the point, an official version of it) exists not in the succession of images that fills the screen – as the film itself would seem to urge us to believe – but rather in the relationship between the screen and spectator, whose memories these become. In this account, memory is effectively constituted in the act of cinematic spectatorship, making of it, not an audio-visual object as such, but rather an audio-visually mediated *relationship* to the past. What is more, as the final scenes make clear, memory (as audio-visual relationship to the past) is articulated as a trope within an overarching nationalist narrative of modernisation.

If memory is conjured into existence in the screen–spectator relationship, modernity is similarly presented not as an object, but rather in terms of a relationship with specific audio-visual qualities. That is to say, despite the suggestion in the final scenes that modernity exists as an object of vision in the form of the spectacle of accelerated pace of life in the modern metropolis; modernity is posited in important ways as bound up with memory and presented as what we might term a genealogy of (audio)visuality. This becomes clear if we 'rewind', so to speak, first to the opening moments of *Memorias de un mexicano* and then 'fast forward' to the closing scenes in order to view them in tandem.

The opening credits of *Memorias de un mexicano* are presented in the form of a photograph album, the pages of which turn to reveal the names of those involved in the film's production, which are superimposed on still images of buildings. On the one hand, the photograph album, with its associations with the commemoration of the family as socio-cultural institution, obviously chimes with the familial story at the centre of the narrator's commentary discussed earlier. On the other, it has further connotations that emerge in the interplay of audio and visual narratives. After the still photographic images of the credit sequence, the narrator commences his narrative, accompanied by a succession of still architectural images:

> 1897: el año en que yo nací. Cuántas cosas han pasado desde entonces. El perfil de las cúpulas no había sido ocultado por los rascacielos y aún parecía cercano el espíritu de la colonia.

> 1897: the year in which I was born. So many things have happened since then. Skyscrapers had not hidden the view of the domes and the spirit of the colony still seemed to be close by.

The narrative transition from domes to skyscrapers, or tradition to anticipated (but, as yet, 'invisible') modernity, is then followed by a sequence of moving images made in 1897 that visually privilege scenes of mobility. Indeed, many of the early sections of the film are devoted to notions of travel and movement: from bicycles to mechanised modes of transport including trains, planes and ships, parades and the arrival of international visitors to Mexico. This transition is echoed in the narrator's words:

> Ciudad tranquila, apenas se conmovió con la llegada del nuevo invento que con su magia podía transportar al espectador a lugares tan remotos como Mérida en Yucatán o al Paseo de los Cocos en Veracruz sin moverse de su asiento.

> Tranquil city, it was hardly disturbed by the arrival of the new invention which with its magic could transport spectators to places as remote as Mérida in the Yucatan Peninsula, or the Paseo de los Cocos in Veracruz without having to move from their seats.

If these opening filmic images foreground what Ana López (2000b: 56) calls an 'extraordinary catalogue of mobility', the viewer in 1950 has to be reminded that this was once extraordinary, for the latter is perfectly accustomed to the spectacle of motion. In so doing, *Memorias de un mexicano* signals an important shift in visual experience that took place in 1897 with the opening of Salvador Toscano's first cinema: from the stasis of the photographic image to the mobility of film. Visually speaking, the film reminds its audience, the world changed at this moment. Strikingly, this gesture of making the familiar – the mobile gaze – strange, is echoed again in the closing sequence.

The final sequence, as we have noted, chronicles the spectacle of the modern metropolis that the narrator (and with him, the viewer) encounters on his return to Mexico from exile in 1950. On one level, the question of the narrator's exile is a pragmatic narrative device. Once the violent phase of the revolution had come to an end, what we might term actualities fatigue set in, which led to the curtailment of Salvador Toscano's filmmaking activities.[14] On another level, however, this return to Mexico after twenty-six years allows the narrator to come to the spectacle of the modern Mexican metropolis with fresh eyes, to marvel at the wonders of development that, thanks to the revolution, have transformed the Republic in the ensuing years. Via this narrative technique, the viewer is also made to step back from what for him/her constitutes a scene that is rapidly becoming part of everyday urban reality. The viewer is invited to appreciate the progress that, according to the filmic logic of *Memorias*, Mexico was enjoying in 1950 thanks to the cohesive force of the revolution.

This vision of urban-based modernity, with its emphasis on movement, also reverberated in the narrative voice-over in which a series of terms denoting motion become audible:

> Un *ritmo* más *acelerado* parece *mover* la nación [. . .] Me parece mirar *escurrir* las imágenes del pasado en las arterias de la ciudad y siento que algo de mi mismo habrá de perdurar mientras el recuerdo de lo que he vivido *palpite* en la memoria de cualquier mexicano.

> A more *accelerated rhythm* appears to *move* the nation [. . .] I seem to see images from the past *flow* through the arteries of the city and I feel that something of me will endure as long as the memory of what I have lived *palpitates* in the memory of all Mexicans.

> (Emphasis added)

And there on screen are twin emblems of the technological advances of modern life that move before the viewer's eyes: the circulating automobiles, and the multiple exposures whereby images from the past are superimposed on scenes from the present. Present and past, modernity and memory, are bound together in these multiple exposures in delicate equilibrium. The backwards motion that is a defining trope of memory is counter-arrested by the relentlessly forward thrust of film, which culminates here in a celebration of the modernity that the revolution as historical process has brought to the nation. At the same time, the forward thrust of progressive modernity is balanced by the backward gaze of memory to

Figure 2.1 Memorias de un mexicano (Carmen Toscano, 1950)

Source: Fundación Carmen Toscano

Figure 2.2 Memorias de un mexicano (Carmen Toscano, 1950)

Source: Fundación Carmen Toscano

underscore the notion that the revolution as tradition and historical process has brought stability: stability that is also echoed in the audio narrative.

Modernity, however, is not simply conjured as an object of vision in the conjunction of image and sound of the final sequence. It is also signalled at the level of the cinematic signifier itself, insofar as the multiple exposures of these closing moments, whilst certainly not the ultimate in cinematic technology, nevertheless register a distinct break with the early cinematic form of the preceding sequences.[15]

As we saw in Chapter 1, Miriam Hansen (2000: 342) has explored the relationship between cinema and modernity, noting that (Hollywood) cinema played a key role in mediating and negotiating the effects of modernity. Following Kracauer, Hansen goes on to argue that these effects were most palpable and irreversible at the level of the senses. Cinema mediated modernity, she suggests, not simply by providing its viewers with models of modern mores and values with which to identify. In addition to what films showed, a key facet of cinema's mediation of modernity resided in the way it 'opened up hitherto unperceived modes of sensory perception and experience' (Hansen 2000: 344).

Taking my cue from Hansen, I want to suggest that *Memorias de un mexicano*, in its journey through memory to modernity, responds to and registers modernity as a shift in visual experience. Or to put this slightly differently, historical memory is deployed to mediate and foreground visual memory. That is, the edited footage transports the viewer back to a visual 'origin' located in the pre-filmic stasis of the photographic image, which it animates in the re-presentation of early actuality film, culminating in the technological 'progress' figured in the final double exposures of images of past and present. In this way, modernity is registered in terms of the shifts that have occurred in modes of experiencing the world visually. Modernity, as it is visually memorialised in Toscano's film, is not so much about *what* one sees as *how* one sees.

FROM SHOOTING TO APPLAUDING

I opened this chapter with the literary scene of the revolutionaries at the Convention of Aguascalientes, who flocked to view a newsreel of the historic events through which they were living and who, at the sight of Carranza, issued hisses followed by gunshots. I want to close with an account of another audience, this time dating from the 1950s, that is to say, roughly contemporaneous with the audience of *Memorias de un mexicano*. Anne Rubenstein describes this audience and its practices in the context of a wonderful essay on the death of Pedro Infante, in which she argues:

> Movie-going was a relatively new form of behavior, and a highly contested one, though it was extremely popular. Mexicans in the 1950s had not completely settled on proper movie house etiquette: one

fan magazine reported on a 1956 controversy over whether or not to applaud.

(Rubenstein 2001: 217)

Although I have alluded to these two audiences throughout, this chapter has focused predominantly on screens and more particularly the screen as a site of visual memory. Rubenstein's observation about audience etiquette in the 1950s, nevertheless, prefigures the subject of the next chapter. That audiences in the 1950s debated whether to applaud at the screen rather than shoot at it as their revolutionary predecessors in Guzmán's account, is, I suggest, a measure of the shifts in sensory perception that had taken place between 1914 and mid century. This, in turn, is an index of modernity understood not in terms of changes in attitudes and behaviours, nor in terms of visible signs of progress such as the bustling metropolitan centres. Rather, as Hansen has demonstrated, modernity is equally a shift that takes place in the visual experience of the world. Viewing early film footage such as that of which *Memorias de un mexicano* is comprised, not only affords us a glimpse of what people saw, but also *how* they saw. Having focused on the revolution as moving image of memory, in the next chapter, taking my inspiration from the work of Rubenstein amongst others, I wish to focus more fully on questions of the audience and spectatorship in the history and development of the Mexican cinema.

3

THE FORMATION OF A
NATIONAL CINEMA AUDIENCE

IN THE BEGINNING . . .

En el principio creó Dios la sala y las butacas. Y advirtió que las butacas
estaban vacías y decidió formar al hombre y la mujer para poblar la sala
de sonidos aprobatorios.

In the beginning, God created the movie theatre and seats. And He
noticed that the seats were empty and decided to create man and woman
to fill the movie theatre with approving sounds.

(Monsiváis 1994a: 176)

For all that it is lighthearted, Carlos Monsiváis's irreverent take on the Creation
myth that posits God as the ultimate maker of an audience that came into existence
just after the movie theatre, alerts us to a number of more serious questions
concerning the origins and formation of this neglected figure in accounts of
Mexican cinema. What kinds of people have traditionally made up the audience
in Mexico and how have audiences changed over time? What factors have defined
and determined the characteristics of the movie-going experience? How do we
understand the historical formation of the spectator, and what is the nature of the
latter's relationship to the screen? Is there moreover anything culturally specific
about Mexican spectatorship?

Monsiváis's witty take on the Creation myth is by no means his only contribution to our understanding of the cinema audience in Mexico. In the frequently
cited essay, playfully titled 'Vino todo el pueblo pero no cupo en la pantalla: notas
sobre el público del cine en México' ('All the People Came and Did Not Fit onto
the Screen: Notes on the Cinema Audience in Mexico'), the cultural critic places
an emphasis on the impact that the cinema made on this 'divine' creation and
specifically, the cinema's role in the modernising and nationalising processes at
work in the first half of the twentieth century. As Mexico made the precipitous
transition from a predominantly rural to urban, Catholic to secular and pre-
modern to modern cultural/political entity, the results were invariably chaotic and
incomplete. In the face of the breaks and discontinuities, the gaps and aporias
inherent in these modernising processes, the role of the mass media, and especially
the cinema and radio, was of prime significance.[1] Or as Monsiváis puts it:

With hindsight, we can see the basic function of the electronic media at their first important moment of power: they mediate between the shock of industrialisation and the rural and urban experience which has not been prepared in any way for this giant change, a process that from the 40s modifies the idea of the nation.

(Monsiváis 1995: 151)

The suggestive title of Monsiváis's essay – 'All the People Came and Did Not Fit onto the Screen' – neatly signals the importance of the cinema's function as cultural mediator that was predicated on a dynamic screen/spectator relationship. The cinematic experience promoted spectatorial identifications with a repertoire of new and traditional images associated with *lo mexicano* that were played out on screen. Indeed, the national inflections of spectatorship are further underlined in the original title, in which the Spanish word '*pueblo*' could equally have been translated as 'nation'. Finally, the ludic hyperbole of the title also signals the phenomenal popularity of the cinema during the Golden Age: not just some, rather *all* the people came. The act of viewing as a social practice is therefore clearly a key and crucial issue for an understanding of how 'all the people', or the 'whole nation' of Monsiváis's title, might have experienced *mexicanidad* and modernity and, importantly, incorporated these configurations into their daily lives as part of the complex landscape of constantly shifting identities.[2]

In their groundbreaking book *Unthinking Eurocentrism* (1994), Ella Shohat and Robert Stam similarly make explicit the link between spectatorship and nationhood. Building on and extending Benedict Anderson's notion of the nineteenth-century nation as an imagined community forged by print capitalism, they argue that in the twentieth century:

[T]he cinema's institutional ritual of gathering a community – spectators who share a region, language, and culture – homologizes, in a sense, the symbolic gathering of the nation. Anderson's sense of the nation as 'horizontal comradeship' evokes the movie audience as a provisional 'nation' forged by spectatorship.

(Shohat and Stam 1994: 103)

Elsewhere in the same volume, Shohat and Stam offer a cogent summary of the issues with which those interested in spectatorship – and more to the point, what they term an 'ethnography of spectatorship' – must grapple:

Any comprehensive ethnography of spectatorship, we would argue, must distinguish between multiple registers:

1. the spectator as fashioned by the text itself (through focalization, point-of-view conventions, narrative structuring, *mise-en-scène*);
2. the spectator as fashioned by the (diverse and evolving) technical apparatuses (movie theater, domestic VCR interactive technologies);

3. the spectator as fashioned by the institutional contexts of spectator-ship (social ritual of movie-going, classroom analysis, cinémateque);
4. the spectator as fashioned by ambient discourses and ideologies; and
5. the actual spectator as embodied, raced, gendered, and historically situated.

(Shohat and Stam 1994: 350)

In this chapter, I am concerned with the consumption of film images in Mexico and the idea of national belonging forged through the act of spectatorship. Focusing primarily, but not exclusively, on early cinema through to the Golden Age of the 1940s, I weave in and out of these five registers of spectatorship.[3] In so doing, I aim to highlight what Judith Mayne (1993) has termed the 'paradoxes of spectatorship' which, in a nutshell, turn on the opposition between the spectator as historical subject versus the spectator as theoretical or textual construct. This opposition stands at the centre of my own discussion of spectatorship which counterbalances an understanding, on the one hand, of the Mexican spectator as a material presence who frequented the movie theatres of the Republic; and on the other, the spectator as an ideological and historical construct, conjured into existence via an engagement with the film text.

ALL THE PEOPLE STARTED TO COME

It has often been commented that Porfirio Díaz is considered the first star of the Mexican cinema (López 2000b: 62). The *Porfiriato* not only saw a proliferation of commemorative monuments dedicated to the president, but, as briefly noted in Chapter 2, the dictator took advantage of the new visual technologies of film and photography to document and augment his presidential power. If Díaz was the first star attraction of the new technology, the dictator, his family and key government officials were also amongst the first Mexican spectators of the moving image in Mexico. Prior to the first public screening in the Plateros Pharmacy in 1896, the Lumières' representatives in Mexico arranged a private screening at Chapultepec Castle exclusively for the dictator and his entourage. According to Gustavo García (1999: 5), 'for his part, [Díaz] "appeared pleased." It was said that he jumped for joy in the presence of this new toy.' Quick to deploy the new visual technology of the moving image in his project of self-aggrandisement, the dictator and his entourage were also unequivocal as to the essentially passive role designated to the popular masses in this spectacle of power: 'el pueblo es la masa pintoresca cuya función única es aplaudir el paso del cortejo'/ 'the people are the picturesque mass whose only function is to applaud the passing cortège' (Bonfil 1994: 14).

Notwithstanding the elitist assumptions underpinning Porfirian politics of vision, accounts of the practice of early consumption of the moving image suggest that Mexicans of all classes and regional affiliations, like their counterparts across the world, embraced the new technology with bedazzled excitement. Moreover, this form of entertainment displayed certain democratising tendencies that were unprecedented in the sphere of Mexican cultural consumption which, prior to the advent of the moving image, was organised along starkly classist lines. In this rigid equation, the subaltern classes were aficionados of bullfighting, cockfighting and popular theatre; the social elite enjoyed the European-modelled delights of the opera, fine art and classical theatre. Where the church had previously been one of the few public spaces in which different sectors of society would have encountered one another in their leisure time, the cinema represented a new point of contact in this hierarchical society. Indeed, Aurelio de los Reyes invokes an audience scenario that reveals not only that the new invention cut across class divisions, but also that it was a pleasure in which women could legitimately indulge:

El sueño invadía a todas las clases sociales y no era extraño ver en los cinematógrafos a señoras de vaporosa 'toilette', elevado sombrero de plumas, guantes y abanico, sentadas al lado de una señora con trenza suelta o de columpio, rebozo de bolita y criatura en los brazos. En los cinematógrafos la sociedad se mezclaba democráticamente.

The dream invaded all social classes and in the movie theatre it was not uncommon to see ladies of extravagant 'toilette', high, feathered hat, gloves and fan, seated beside a woman with a loose or looped plait, shawl and babe in arms. In the movie theatres society mixed democratically.

(De los Reyes 1996a: 91)[4]

Carlos Bonfil also conjures up this phenomenon with an eloquence that evokes the frisson of danger that characterises the elite's incursion onto uncharted social terrain:

Frecuentar el cinematógrafo es para la buena sociedad criolla el equivalente a una incursión temeraria en una zona de tolerancia; es alternar con la plebe, compartir sus goces y padecer sus entusiasmos; es abdicar, por un instante, de la urbanidad y el decoro en el roce con la chusma.

To frequent the movie theatre for Creole high society is the equivalent of a bold incursion into a zone of tolerance; it is to mix with the masses, share their pleasures and endure their enthusiasms; it is to abdicate, for a moment, urbanity and decorum in the brush with the rabble.

(Bonfil 1997: 130)

This is not to suggest, however, that the upper echelons of Mexican society uniformly endorsed the new medium or that it was completely free from the social hierarchies that were deeply ingrained in the mindset of the late *Porfiriato*. The intellectual elite in particular lamented the fact that their wealthy peers seemed to favour the cinema over other forms of entertainment more 'appropriate' to their status, such as the opera. The temporary sites of exhibition (*carpas* and other forms of makeshift construction) and, by 1906, the permanent movie theatres that were starting to replace these early venues were not in the first instance hierarchically divided. Nevertheless, divisions were established on an ad hoc basis, insofar as some cinemas charged a higher admission fee than others.

The consumption of early moving images may have revealed certain democratising tendencies. These were not without attendant conflicts and tensions. One thing is for certain, however. From its earliest days, the consumption of the moving image became associated with new social behaviour and practices. De los Reyes ([1981] 1993b: 279) offers a concrete example when he notes that the moment at which courting couples started to kiss in public can be pinpointed with some degree of accuracy to the period 1920–24. Influenced by the divas of early Italian cinema, the coy kiss on the hand or the cheek started to be replaced in the Hollywood cinema by the kiss on the mouth, which in turn had ramifications for codes of erotic conduct in both the Mexican cinema and cinema audience.[5] Furthermore, in keeping with what appears to be standard behaviour displayed in movie theatres elsewhere across the globe, Mexican audiences took advantage of the darkened auditorium to indulge in amorous activities of their own. Such activities did not pass without note by the authorities, and in 1921 a law was passed to ensure that movie theatres were equipped with sufficient lighting of a green hue so as not to hamper viewing, but also to prevent 'immoral' behaviour (De los Reyes [1981] 1993b: 279). For all that the authorities had to contend with 'anti-social' activities related to the new form of entertainment – and at the more serious end of the 'anti-social' scale, certain movie theatres were frequented by prostitutes, or were targeted by petty thieves – cinema-going also brought about improvements in other areas of life. In particular, the incidence in the suicide rate and alcoholism was noted to decline in the early decades of the twentieth century, as this pastime became an increasingly popular form of family entertainment (De los Reyes [1981] 1993b: 76).

On the whole, early audiences comprised of a broad spectrum of Mexican society; by the 1930s and especially the 1940s the national industry became more established and cinema-going soon became an everyday social practice. This period, of course, coincided with the mass migration from countryside to the cities: it is estimated, for example, that the population of Mexico City increased by nearly 500 per cent between 1920 and 1950 (Levi 2001: 334). With mass migration, particularly in the period of accelerated industrialisation and the aggressive capitalist economic policies pursued during the regime of Miguel Alemán in the 1940s, the number of cinemas grew exponentially. In 1938 there were fewer than 500 permanent cinemas in the whole country (Rubenstein 2000: 647). By 1945 this number had risen to 1,400 and, according to Julia Tuñón (1998: 57), movie-going had displaced other forms of activity (including bull and cock-fighting, sport and the *carpas*) as the most popular form of entertainment amongst the subaltern classes.

It was this audience, newly arrived and more than likely bewildered by the size, accelerated pace and anonymity of life in the major urban centres, that emerged as the principal consumers of the national film product. Although it is dangerous to generalise, the social elite was not overall as enthused by the increasing supply of films produced on national soil, films that in differing degrees purported to reflect local concerns. The social elite had a greater predilection for the 'superior' foreign imports (particularly those from Hollywood, of course) with their higher production values. As one commentator, the actor, songwriter and director José Bohr put it:

> Recuerdo que la élite no era muy afecta a nuestro cine. Nuestro éxito estaba en la clase media y cuando llevábamos las películas a los barrios, entonces hacíamos un gran negocio. Pero en los estrenos siempre salíamos perdiendo, eran más bien para la crítica, para los diarios. Desgraciadamente la clase alta tiene un acendrado esnobismo: todo lo importado huele mejor.

> I remember that the elite was not very fond of our cinema. Our success lay in the middle class when we took the movies to the *barrios*, and then we did great business. But at the premières we always ended up losing money, they were more for the critics and the newspapers. Unfortunately, the upper class has an ingrained snobbism: to it, all imported products smell better.
>
> (Bohr, cited in Tuñón 1998: 62)

Bohr's comments are revealing on a number of levels. First, they clearly signal the emergence of the discursive structures of a critical apparatus dedicated to the dissemination and promotion of film consumption in this period. Indeed, excluding the regular film columns that appeared in daily newspapers such as *El universal*, Paranaguá (1999: 81) lists some twenty-seven specialised publications that appeared between the 1930s and 1950s. Primarily based in the capital, these include the relatively long-running *Mundo cinematográfico* (1930–38), *Cinema Reporter* (1938–65) and *México Cinema* (1942–59), and more short-lived publications such as *Diario fílmico mexicano* (1943–44) and *Estrellita* (1947). Second, the elite was (and arguably still is) remarkably easy to define. Given the pronounced social immobility that has tended to characterise Mexican society, as a class it has remained fairly static since the colonial period. As Tuñón observes, however, defining the middle class, or more accurately, the middle classes in the 1940s is a different matter altogether:

> La categoría de clase media es compleja y polémica [. . .] Las clases medias en México a menudo se confunden con el proletariado y otras veces incluyen a pequeños o muy pequeños burgueses. Bajo la denominación de clase media caben diferentes grupos, desde los sectores medio

que nombró Marx, refiriéndose a pequeños artesanos, comerciantes y profesionistas independientes, hasta los empleados de sueldo fijo, surgidos del desarrollo económico.

The category of middle class is complex and polemical [. . .] The middle classes in Mexico are often confused with the proletariat and at other times include the petit or 'very' petit bourgeoisie. Different groups fit into the category of middle class, from the middle sectors that Marx named, referring to artisans, shopkeepers and independent professionals to fixed wage employees who emerged with economic development.

(Tuñón 1998: 60)[6]

In the 1940s, the national cinema found its audience in this vast and amorphous middle class, for whom the regular (generally, once or twice) weekly outing to the movies became part of the rhythm of family life, and an integral component in the rituals of courtship. For those metropolitan spectators who had recently abandoned the close-knit security of rural village life, the cinema offered a form of collective public experience that provided a refuge from the alienating effects of urban life. For others, Monsiváis suggests (1995: 149), the regular outing to the cinema had quasi didactic connotations, initiating the illiterate masses into the rituals of modern life. The 'lessons' to be learned in the movie theatre were multivalent: how to adjust to an increasingly secular outlook; how to adapt to one's place in a more socially complex environment; how to cope in a community in which traditional gender roles were rapidly being eroded; how to become a consumer in a society increasingly driven by capitalist accumulation; how to identify with cultural practices and symbols divested of their erstwhile regional associations and now harnessed to the concept of the centralised nation.[7]

For all that 'the middle class' was an amorphous label in the 1940s; this did not mean that there were no distinctions in practices of film consumption across this broad spectrum. As Bohr's comments also evince, there were different categories of movie theatre that attracted different kinds of audiences. At the upper end of the scale were the first-run cinemas. Of the ninety-six cinemas in Mexico City in 1946, nine were first-run (Tuñón 1998: 57), which in practice not only meant that they premiered films, but also were more luxurious and charged higher admission fees. In his nostalgic chronicle of life in Mexico City in *Los años de oro* (Golden Years), Manuel Magaña Contreras describes the look of such premium movie theatres and tellingly suggests how they made spectators of a particular social class – namely his own, as the use of the first person plural signals – feel:

Cines de lujo, verdaderos palacios en que *los espectadores nos sentíamos gente digna*, lo fueron las salas cinematográficas Alameda, Palacio Chino, Magerit (hoy cine Variedades), Regis, Chapultepec, Roble, Olimpia, Rex, Colonial, Teresa, Palacio y muchos más.

El precio en las salas de primera categoría, dotados [*sic*] de alfombras, escalinatas, pinturas, candiles, lujosas cortinas, y hasta de muebles estilo Luis XVI en los recibidores, fue de $4.00.

Luxury cinemas, real palaces in which *we spectators felt like dignified people*, those were the Alameda, Palacio Chino, Magerit (today Variedades cinema), Regis, Chapultepec, Roble, Olimpia, Rex, Colonial, Teresa, Palacio and many more.

The cost of the first class movie theatres, fitted with carpets, flights of stairs, paintings, chandeliers, luxury curtains and even Louis XVI-style furniture in the entrance, was $4.00.

> (Contreras Magaña 1996: 166; emphasis added)

Those who frequented such cinemas dressed in accordance with their luxurious surroundings. Both sexes went attired in their Sunday best for the occasion: for men this included suit, overcoat, hat and gloves; women wore a 'well-cut' dress, gloves, hat and fur stole (Contreras Magaña 1996: 167).

During the so-called 'Golden Years' that Contreras Magaña evokes, however, the minimum weekly wage stood between $3.00 and $1.65 (Tuñón 1998: 58). The 'palaces' frequented by Contreras Magaña and his ilk were therefore clearly beyond the economic reach of the vast majority of regular cinema-goers. At the other end of the scale, catering for the masses, were the so-called *cines de piojitos* (flea pits), which charged an admission fee of just $0.80 for up to three films. Such cinemas were located in the working class *barrios* that already had a tradition of popular entertainment as the site of the *carpas*. These venues, which date back to the 1870s, had come into their own in the 1920s (flourishing especially in the 1930s), and took the form of itinerant shows that featured acrobatics, slapstick comedy, clowns, skits and other forms of 'low-brow' entertainment, similar to vaudeville.[8] Many performers rose up through the *carpas* to achieve national fame on the celluloid screen. The comedians Cantinflas (Mario Moreno) and Tin Tan (Germán Valdés) were, of course, the most famous and successful of such stars, their cheeky, roguish characters embodying elements modelled on the popular audiences – their modes of speech, dress and social conduct – who were naturally their most devoted fans.[9]

Contreras Magaña's account of the *cines de piojo* is noteworthy not only in its romanticised vision of such venues: 'Cines de *piojito* se le denominó afectuosamente, y se constituyeron en un lugar que todo mundo consideraba como si fuera propio, debido a la cordialidad entre el personal de dichos centros de espectáculos y las familias del rumbo.' / 'They were affectionately called flea pits, and became a place that everyone considered their own, owing to the cordiality between the staff of such venues and the families of the neighbourhood' (1996: 168). (One suspects that this particular chronicler of Mexico City's 'Golden Years' did not count himself amongst the 'todo mundo' who considered such movie theatres their own).

Despite himself, Contreras Magaña also betrays an attitude that is verging on the contemptuous towards national cinematic production and its popular audience. This hint of contempt becomes clear if we read between the lines of this chronicler's nostalgic account. Amongst those movies that he highlights as on exhibition in the years in question, he is careful to include only Mexican films 'porque si nos gustó el cine de casa es porque reflejaba nuestra identidad' / 'because if we liked our home-produced cinema it was because it reflected our identity' (1996: 167). The use of the inclusive first person plural is noteworthy here. For, when he turns to list the kinds of films that were exhibited in the poorer neighbourhoods, he rather undercuts this position:

> Naturalmente, en los cines de piojito no únicamente eran exhibidas películas mexicanas del Charro Negro, las de gangsters de Juan Orol, las de Joaquín Padarvé, de Gloria Marín y Jorge Negrete, de la familia Soler o de Cantinflas, de Mapy Cortés o Arturo de Córdoba [*sic*] o de La Devoradora María Félix, sino también los filmes norteamericanos en glorioso technicolor [. . .] [E]n los barrios, el público era conocedor exigente.

> Naturally, in the flea pits Mexican films were not the only films exhibited – Charro Negro films, Juan Orol's gangster films, Joaquín Padarvé, Gloria Marín and Jorge Negrete, those of the Soler family or Cantinflas, Mapy Cortés or Arturo de Córdova or the 'Devouress' María Félix films – but also North American films in all their glorious technicolor [. . .] [I]n the *barrios* the audience was a demanding connoisseur.
>
> (Contreras Magaña 1996: 168)

Ironically, this statement and particularly the disclaimer 'Mexican films were not the only films exhibited', contains a clear assumption. That is, the audiences that frequented the *cines de piojito* may have occupied a lower rung on the social scale; nevertheless (like their chronicler) they were 'discerning' enough to appreciate the implicitly superior ('in all their glorious Technicolor') foreign product.

Via the foregoing snapshot, my aim has been to delineate a socio-cultural sketch of how the audience was formed from the early days of the movie image through to the establishment of the national industry in the 1940s. In this period its consumers were drawn primarily from amongst the expanding and amorphous middle classes, for whom movie-going became an integral part of family ritual. This was the Golden Age of the Mexican film consumption, 'there was one public. No matter how different the spectators might be from one another in social or economic terms, from the days of the Nickleodeon, film exhibition and production addressed themselves to a mythical, unique, and homogenous mass audience' (Paranaguá 1998: 33).

Having, so to speak, focused the limelight on this popular audience, the relationship between the screen and national spectator nevertheless remains obscure and requires further elucidation. Largely inspired, it would seem, by the analysis of Monsiváis in 'All the People Came but Did not Fit on the Screen', it has become commonplace to claim that the cinema indeed played a key role in the dual cultural processes of modernisation and 'Mexicanisation'. And here it is worth citing Monsiváis once more, who in another essay on the audience states:

> It was in front of the screen that the public acquired, to the best of its ability, the new language of modern life. This modernization was only skin-deep, a varnish that nevertheless helped audiences to understand some of the changes affecting their lives [. . .] For the audience, the 'myths' of Mexican cinema were bridges of understanding, privileged faces that stood for a collective biography, the embodiment of past and present experience.
>
> (Monsiváis 1990: 86)

If the analogy between cinema and modernisation seems obvious on some levels, what is less clear is exactly how the spectator is fashioned as modern by 'the text itself (through focalization, point-of-view conventions [etc.]' (Shohat and Stam 1994: 350). In what follows, I build on the analysis of the 'real' audience laid out in this section, by offering a close reading of a film that has been consecrated as a classic within the national canon and, I suggest, offers fertile terrain on which to explore the dynamics of the screen–spectator relationship.

ALL THE PEOPLE WENT, OR REMEMBERED GOING TO SEE . . . *MARÍA CANDELARIA*

Based on an analysis of the exhibition 'Revisión del Cine Mexicano' (December 1990 to February 1991), the first section of Nestor García Canclini's study *Los nuevos espectadores* focuses on an analysis of the results of questionnaires given to visitors to the commemorative show, which are compared with the opinions of a range of specialist commentators, participants in the national industry. By counterbalancing specialist commentaries with those opinions expressed by the general public to the exhibition, the anthropologist and his team of collaborators set out to address specific questions pertaining to the Mexican cinema and its audience. Mindful that the views expressed offered an insight into the Mexican cinema from the historical perspective of the end of the twentieth century, these included questions that attempted to elicit responses to modes and memories of spectatorship in the 1940s and 1950s. To this end, respondents were asked to list the three national films that they considered most important. Of these, a significant number (47 per cent) singled out the same trio: *María Candelaria* (20 per cent); *Nosotros los pobres* (14.6 per cent); *Allá en el Rancho Grande* (12 per cent).

That *María Candelaria* occupies prime position in this group's predilections, however, arguably tells us more about the nostalgia that underpins the Golden

Age of Mexican cinema and its mythologies than it does about the reception of Emilio Fernández's film. Furthermore, despite the fact that *María Candelaria* was the first Mexican film to garner international recognition – it won prizes at Cannes in 1946 and Locarno in 1947 – it has fared less well in the estimation of Mexican film critics. For instance, García Riera argues that the social and political conflicts that traversed the film's context of production are sacrificed to its melodramatic proclivities:

> Las calamidades abatidas sobre la impoluta heroína son más resultado de la casualidad o la mala suerte que de las causas sociales, políticas y económicas que desfavorecen a un importante sector de la población del país. El melodrama hace privar sus razones sobre cualquier otra, pese a que la trama se ubica en vísperas de la revolución.

> The calamities that befall the innocent heroine are more a result of chance or bad luck than social, political or economic causes that go against the interests of an important sector of the country. The logic of melodrama overwhelms all others, despite the fact that the plot takes place on the eve of the Revolution.
>
> (García Riera 1992, vol. 3: 67)

To some extent, García Riera has a valid point. Locked into the melodramatic tragedy that is the fate of what Monsiváis has termed the 'mythic couple of the Mexican cinema' comprising Dolores del Río and Pedro Armendáriz, *María Candelaria* offers little in the way of direct social criticism.[10] I wish to suggest, however, that as a film text that is invoked with the nostalgic fondness for a lost past by its popular audience, *María Candelaria* nevertheless does offer us a window onto politics. These politics are not conventional 'politics' grounded in social reality. Rather *María Candelaria* offers an intriguing insight into the politics of spectatorship in Mexico that is at once historical and contemporaneous with the film's context of production. As the case study that follows seeks to demonstrate, it is a film text that allows us to explore the modernising and 'Mexicanising' processes at work in the viewing experience alluded to by Monsiváis and in this way, start to sketch out the cultural specificity of spectatorship in the context of this national cinema.[11]

If, as García Riera contends, *María Candelaria* does not engage with conflict at a socio-historical level, at the centre of Fernández's film lies a contest between two clearly delineated gazes with their origins in the colonial period. The loci of these gazes are embodied in the unnamed painter (Alberto Galán) and Lorenzo Rafael (Pedro Armendáriz) who represent white *criollo* versus indigenous Mexico respectively. Through an exploration of the cultural ramifications of this contest, I wish to map out a historical context in which to insert looking relations in the Mexican cinema. More to the point, I want to imagine how the film appealed on a textual level to the kind of 'real' urban audience outlined in the preceding section. This imaginary spectator was newly arrived in the city and 'constituted by the ambient discourses and ideologies [that traverse the text]' (Shohat and Stam 1994: 350) in that he/she is caught between allegiances to traditional bonds of community and the emerging social structures of metropolitan life. This spectator is, moreover, in Shohat and Stam's terms, an embodied subject, and more precisely a racially inscribed subject. And here we would do well to recall the two *señoras*, who sat side by side at an early screening evoked by De los Reyes (1996b: 91): the *señora* of 'extravagant "toilette"', and the *señora* with a loose or ringed plait shawl [*rebozo*] and babe in arms'. The difference to which De los Reyes alludes here is not only social; it is racial, for the second *señora*'s plaited hair and shawl mark her as an indigenous woman. The two *señoras* remind us that in the cinema's symbolic gathering of the nation, Mexico is essentially a *mestizo* entity, the product of the colonial encounter between Indians, Spaniards (and Africans). The politics of *mestizaje* are, I suggest, furthermore a key to an understanding of the politics of spectatorship that are played out in *María Candelaria*.[12]

The two characters in Fernández's film, the painter and Lorenzo Rafael, engage in a struggle over the right to possess María Candelaria (Dolores del Río) which is presented in both visual and economic terms. The spectator witnesses this conflict in the scene set, significantly, in a marketplace in which the painter first encounters María Candelaria. He offers to purchase all María Candelaria's flowers, a transaction that would resolve the couple's economic problems, in return for permission to paint her. Lorenzo Rafael angrily denies him consent and, muttering some unsubtitled words in Nahua, hastily sends María Candelaria away. Later in the film, after Lorenzo Rafael's imprisonment, he stubbornly refuses the painter the right to represent María Candelaria, accepting the painter's 'sweetener' also to paint him, but is emphatic that 'en lo tocante a María Candelaria, yo prefiero que no'/ 'as far as painting María Candelaria is concerned, I prefer you not to'. Such a substitution (him for her), however, is not a viable option. Within the painter (and the film's) visual economy, María Candelaria's commodity value resides in what she represents, namely 'el rostro mismo de México'/ 'the very face of Mexico'. Or, as an object belonging to an enduring Western painterly tradition, namely the female nude, María Candelaria might more aptly be described as 'the very body of Mexico'.[13] In other words, the contest that lies at the heart of the film revolves around the right to gaze not just upon a woman, but upon the (feminine) embodiment of the nation.

That the film semiotises María Candelaria as 'Mexico' is made abundantly clear throughout it. Moreover 'Mexico', as embodied (and en*visag*ed?) by María Candelaria is an essentially hybrid entity. In her detailed discussion of the film, Joanne Hershfield points out that the opening sequence establishes an association between the female indigenous subject, the pre-Columbian past and the post-Columbian present:

A montage of pre-Columbian images illustrating this indigenous past ends with a shot of a young Indian woman standing next to the stone figure of an Aztec woman that has the same high cheekbones and proud facial expression as the live woman. [. . .] Fernández's shot specifically links that past to the present through his representation of Mexico's 'eternal' Indianness.

(Hershfield 1996: 55)

This metonymic chain of associations, in which woman-as-cultural-artefact links past to present, is further extended to María Candelaria, whose parallel status in the frame narrative as artefact is manifest in the presence of the fateful painting and the curiosity that it arouses. She too is linked to the imagistic dialogue between pre-Columbian past and post-Columbian present established within the film's diegesis and made explicit in the painter's explanation as to what the famous painting depicts: '. . . una india de pura raza mexicana. Como puede usted ver, esta indígena tenía la belleza de las antiguas princesas que vinieron a sojuzgar los conquistadores.'/ '. . . an Indian of pure Mexican race. As you can see, this Indian possessed the beauty of the ancient princesses whom the *conquistadores* came to subjugate.'[14]

But even as María Candelaria is associated with pure indigenous 'essence', she is also an embodiment of the post-Columbian Mexican Virgin of Guadalupe, the patron saint of Mexico.[15] There are two key moments in the film in which this association is dramatically crystallised. The most obvious occurs after Lorenzo Rafael is imprisoned, when María Candelaria visits the church to remonstrate with a statue of the Virgin: '[Y] tú ¿por qué no me oyes? [. . .] con nosotros eres dura.'/ '[W]hy don't you listen to me? [. . .] you are hard on us.' At this point, the camera cuts from María Candelaria, with her hands in a gesture of prayer and uplifted face framed by her shawl, to the statue of the Virgin in order to draw a clear visual analogy between the two figures. Less obviously, but no less significantly, earlier on in the film Lupe (Margarita Cortés), María Candelaria's jealous rival for Lorenzo Rafael's affections, casts a stone shattering an image of the Virgin of Guadalupe in María Candelaria's humble home. This act of violent iconoclasm prefigures the circumstances of the latter's tragic demise, stoned to death by members of her own community. Given the Virgin of Guadalupe's status as a unifying national symbol in Mexico, the pure and virginal María Candelaria's own symbolic burden as 'the very face/body of Mexico' is further reinforced.

By foregrounding the conflict in the main body of the narrative between the white *criollo* painter and the indigenous Lorenzo Rafael over the right to possess María Candelaria as quintessential 'Mexican' artefact, the film invokes an originary moment in the history of looking relations in Mexico. Such a history has been plotted by ethno-historian Serge Gruzinski in his fascinating book *Images at War* (2001) which, as the title signals, narrates the conquest of Mexico and the colonial society to which it gave rise in terms of a visual conflict. That is to say, Gruzinski reads the conquest and colonisation of Mexico as a struggle by one culture to impose a system of visual representation upon another in an analysis in which concepts of the gaze and power occupy charged and contested positions. A number

Figure 3.1 María Candelaria (Emilio Fernández, 1943)

Source: Televisa

of points emerge from the study which are extremely productive for the present discussion of spectatorship in the Mexican cinema. The first is Gruzinski's notion of the Conquest as a clash between two competing and radically different visual traditions in which he notes 'a quite different abyss separated the two worlds: the Indians did not share the Spanish conception of the image' (Gruzinski 2001: 49). The abyss separating the two revolves around the fact that where Christian iconography is predicated upon the notion of representation, such a concept cannot readily be transferred to comparable indigenous iconographic traditions. That is to say, the Spaniards' relationship to their religious icons was founded upon an essential understanding of the distinction between the signifier and the signified: an icon of the Virgin Mary is *not* the Virgin Mary but an anthropomorphically fashioned object that stands in for a transcendentally located entity that is other to the icon itself. By contrast, the indigenous eye recognised no such radical split between signifier and signified in a belief system in which the 'divine' is not transcendental, but instead effective presence and immanence. Gruzinski elaborates upon the indigenous system of 'representation' by recourse to the Nahua term *ixiptla*:

> The Nahua notion [*ixiptla*] did not take a similarity in shape for granted [. . .] The *ixiptla* was the container for a power, the localizable, epiphanic presence, the actualization of the power infused into an object, a 'being

here', native thought did not take the time to distinguish between divine essence and material support. It was neither an appearance nor a visual illusion harkening back to an elsewhere, or a beyond. In this sense the *ixiptla* emphasized the immanence of the forces surrounding us; whereas the Christian image, in a reverse, upward motion, is meant to raise us toward a personal god, the copy moving toward its prototype, guided by the resemblance uniting them.

(Gruzinski 2001: 51)

Given the radically different indigenous and Spanish visual systems, the colonisation of Mexico not only involved the imposition of Catholic icons, but also the re-education of the indigenous gaze through a politics of the image which consisted of saturating the visual sphere with a new social and cultural imaginary. In this way, the image came to play a constitutive role in the construction of colonial society, whereby:

The image unveiled its new body, whose visible flesh covered its invisible soul to the Indian. Through the use of perspective, the image gave the Indian a spectator's external point of view but a privileged one; his gaze and body fully participated in the contemplation the image had established. He became a spectator ideally endowed with a 'moral eye'; free and faith would enable him to gain mastery over the true image in order to escape the trickery of the demon and the traps of idolatry.

(Gruzinski 2001: 95)

It does not require too much imagination to see that the immensity and complexity of the task of visual colonisation in hand was to produce uneven, contested effects and that the carefully orchestrated politics of the image was to run out of the church's control. The resulting war of images, according to Gruzinski, gave rise to an essentially hybrid cultural imaginary. Hybrid, it must be stressed, not only in the sense of physical objects that partook of both indigenous and Spanish systems of representation; but hybrid also precisely at the level of the gaze, in that two very different systems for visualising the world converged in the colonised viewing subject.

As William Rowe and Vivian Shelling (1991: 45) point out, Gruzinski's analysis of colonial relations is extremely valuable for 'the comprehensiveness with which it distinguishes between different levels and modes of interaction without reducing them to the binary of dominant versus subordinated'. Having taken a brief detour via Gruzinski's exploration of colonial looking relations, I want now to consider how such a refusal of reduction might inflect an understanding of the visual struggle between the painter and Lorenzo Rafael over the right to possess María Candelaria. Reading Fernández's film through the prism of Gruzinski's analysis, I would suggest that the narrative syncretically encodes María Candelaria simultaneously as indigenous 'idol' and Catholic 'icon' precisely through her association

84

with, and status as, a visual image. As such, she becomes the locus of a visual conflict which echoes the encounter between the colonising gaze of the *criollo* painter and the resistant gaze of the indigenous male subject, who hurries to hide away his 'effigy' (idol or icon?). In this way, Lorenzo Rafael's action can be seen to replicate that of the post-conquest Indians, who according to Gruzinski (2001: 52) '[f]aced with Spanish idolocastry, the natives organized their riposte. It was mainly a defensive one, where they tried to shield their gods from the invaders by all means possible.'

This visual conflict, nevertheless, raises not only colonial, but also gender issues. To the critical eye steeped in the traditions of feminist film and visual theory, the resonances of María Candelaria's positioning hardly require spelling out. As the film invokes an originary colonial scenario, it also reproduces a time-honoured trope whereby Woman (in this case Indigenous Woman) functions as object-of-the-gaze thereby providing the grounds for an exchange of looks.

As a mediating object with symbolic resonances, María Candelaria (both woman and painted image) bespeaks the different histories that fuse to make modern Mexico. But, more than this, her 'Mexican embodiment' points to the co-existence within the film of different loci of the gaze. Furthermore, if María Candelaria, visually codified as cultural artefact, represents the conceptual space for an exchange of competing looks with vestiges of colonial looking relations, then there is a third party in this visual conflict whose gaze has yet to come into focus within this section of the discussion – namely, the spectator of the film, who is implicitly positioned within the overlapping and contradictory discourses of 1940s modernisation and these older, colonial-looking relations. This viewing subject of *María Candelaria* is structured into the film text in quite specific ways that require further elucidation and which revolve around the presence of the painting in which a series of meanings is condensed. Moreover, this painting is linked to the modernisation of the spectator's gaze. In what follows, I shall explore how the spectator's gaze is structured into the film before considering what is at stake in such a structuring of the gaze.

LOOKING OUTSIDE *MARÍA CANDELARIA*

A particularly striking feature of the frame-narrative in which the unnamed painter starts to reveal María Candelaria's story to a woman journalist, is the way in which it sets the spectator up in the expectation that he is to see the image depicted upon the canvas.[16] This expectation is, however, thoroughly thwarted. Anticipation is built up gradually across a number of shots and is intensified by the painter's hyperbolic language when referring to the image: 'Hay cosas que nada más con tocarlas sangran – ¿me entiende usted? – ésta es una de ellas. Hace ya muchos años que pinté ese cuadro pero no puedo pensar en él con más que horror porque fue causa de una tragedia.'/ 'There are things that simply by being touched bleed – do you understand me? – this is one of them. I painted this painting many years

Figure 3.2 María Candelaria (Emilio Fernández, 1943)

Source: Televisa

ago but I cannot think of it without horror because it was the cause of a tragedy.' Finally, the painter reluctantly agrees to show the notorious painting to the woman journalist, whose surprise is registered in a medium close-up of her face whereby the camera occupies the place of the easel. At this point, filmic convention dictates a reverse shot from the journalist's point of view, which of course would afford the spectator a glimpse of the image. But no such shot occurs and the spectator is left as the only participant in the scene not to have caught sight of the image on the canvas. Although the painting does not make another appearance until towards the end of the film – when the spectator, unlike the villagers, is privy to its making and thereby witnesses María Candelaria's refusal to model naked – nevertheless, the image on the canvas is never manifest visually except via others' reaction to it.

Given that the spectator's heightened expectation of seeing the canvas is structured into the film through elements of *mise-en-scène*, dialogue and point-of-view conventions, why does the spectator never get to see the fatal image? To understand the spectator's frustrated gaze, I suggest that it is essential now to extend our understanding of the audience set out in the first section of this chapter. We need to modify this viewing subject, and to read him or her in broad cultural terms as constituted by what Ella Shohat and Robert Stam term 'ambient discourses and ideologies', which in the case of 1940s Mexico, revolve around cultural nationalism.

86

As should be abundantly clear by this point in my study, the cinema's peak in the 1940s in Mexico coincided with the heightened cultural nationalism of the post-revolutionary period, a project in which, as throughout the colonial period as detailed by Gruzinski, the visual was to occupy a privileged position. Graphic historian John Mraz argues that 1940s cultural nationalism must be seen as a product of an 'authentic' search for identity and an ideological imposition. The first was a consequence of having lived through a revolution (1910–20) that redefined Mexico, and the processes of urbanisation and industrialisation that were transforming the country. The second was an imposition of the political ideology of *Alemanismo* (a political ideology named after President Miguel Alemán, 1940–46), which utilised nationalism to cover up US domination and to obfuscate class struggle. As Mraz states:

El periodo [. . .] estaba marcado por el desarrollo de la ideología de una mexicanidad sin contradicciones. Las divergencias y diferencias que habían caracterizado al cardenismo fueron reemplazadas por una insistencia en la 'unidad nacional'. Carlos Monsiváis definió el espíritu de la época así: 'Nada de "país plural" o de "diversidad de culturas", *México es uno.*'

The period was marked by the development of the ideology of a form of 'Mexicanness' without contradictions. The divergences and differences that had characterised *Cardenismo* were replaced by an insistence on 'national unity'. Carlos Monsiváis defined the spirit of the epoch as 'Nothing to do with "plural country" or "diversity of cultures", *Mexico is one.*'

(Mraz 1996: 86)

The challenge that confronted cultural nationalism, then, was how to create a coherent notion of Mexican identity in the face of the fissures and discontinuities that were the product of a multi-ethnic body politic. As an integral dimension of cultural nationalism, *indigenista* discourses sought to retrieve a pristine notion of the myriad and diverse Indian communities and to incorporate it within the boundaries of the modern nation-state. This retrieval took place across a range of cultural spheres, including the visual arts and film and, to put it crudely, involved a celebratory and yet deeply ambivalent representation of the 'Indian' as a national figure. The 'Indian' was at once revered as the receptacle of authentically Mexican values, yet whose resistance to the processes of modernisation threatened to call them into question.[17]

At the forefront of cinematic cultural nationalism, Emilio 'el Indio' Fernández has passed into Mexican film-lore as the originator of a specifically Mexican national cinema. Julia Tuñón (1995: 184) states that his 'basic concern was to produce a Mexican cinema: "I dreamt and am still dreaming of a different cinema, of course, but Mexican, pure. Now I have this great desire to mexicanise the

Mexicans, for we are becoming Americanised."' To 'Mexicanise the Mexicans' involved, on the one hand, a new repertoire of stories and images; it also entailed, on the other, mobilising the spectator, by drawing upon historically contingent looking relations. In other words, to pick up on Gruzinski's tantalisingly open subtitle – *Images at War: Mexico from Columbus to Blade Runner (1492–2019)* – in the twentieth century, the moving image takes up where the still, sacred image of previous epochs left off. Only, if previously the church had striven to Christianise the gaze, it fell to cinema in the twentieth century to modernise and 'Mexicanise' that same gaze.[18] Indeed, in his study, Gruzinski picks up on the modernising role of the cinema in the 1940s, remarking:

> The images of Mexican cinema, during its Golden Age in particular, prepared the farmer and town masses for the trauma of the industrialization of the 40s; they carried an *imaginaire* that, in league with the radio, either undermined or actualized traditions by initiating the crowds to the modern world through its mythic figures, such as Pedro Armendáriz, Dolores del Río, María Félix and many others. From the late 30s on, the flood of cinematographic images wove a new consensus centered on the new values of city, technology, illusions of consumerism, and even at times the assimilation of the most denigrating stereotypes.
>
> (Gruzinski 2001: 222)

Furthermore, in a brief but suggestive footnote that focuses specifically on *María Candelaria*, Gruzinski suggests that this 'fresco-film [. . .] also told the story of an image: a painting, symbol of modern Mexico' (2001: 266). If, as Gruzinski argues, cinema was involved in the process of modernisation, why then was the very subject of this process (i.e. the spectator) prevented from seeing this symbol of modern Mexico? How, moreover, can an absent painting symbolise a nation? I would like to suggest that these basic paradoxes lend themselves to a particular reading of the relationship between the 1940s viewing subject and the on-screen painting. Namely, the modernity of this symbol can only be apprehended by the modernised gaze, a gaze structured into the film text, and one that was being actively produced by and through the cinematic experience.

In *María Candelaria*, if the spectator constitutes a frustrated participant in the struggle to see the painting, his gaze is, nevertheless, confronted with a range of looking relations: these alternately promote identification with the characters on the screen and prevent such identification from taking place. Such identification and distanciation – particularly with the painter and with the indigenous denizens of Xochimilco – at once reverberate with the power dynamics of the colonial visual sphere, and, at the same time, are constitutive of the modernising process. The painter himself may, as Gruzinski's footnote suggests, be the creator of a 'symbol of modern Mexico', but this does not imply that the film presents him as necessarily the locus of the modern gaze. Insofar as the painter's gaze is associated with elite cultural values, with ties to colonial social relations, his character invites little or no spectatorial identification.[19] As Hershfield (1996: 57) argues, the painter's intervention in the frame narrative can be read as an attempt to absolve himself of his guilt in the murder of María Candelaria. No matter how much he may deny his agency in the frame narrative – ('hay veces cuando la vida le convierte a uno en instrumento de la desgracia ajena'/ 'there are times when life converts one into an instrument of other people's misfortunes') – as María Candelaria's story unfolds, the painter's fundamental misunderstanding of the culture into which he has intruded becomes clear to the spectator.[20] Drawing the indigenous Other into his own iconographic scheme, in a gesture that echoes an older colonising gaze, leads to her death. Or to put it another way, within the visual logic of *María Candelaria*, looks can, and indeed do, kill.

Significantly, however, the painter is not the sole locus of the deadly look; his gaze is conjoined with that of the Indian villagers who perform the actual murder, stoning María Candelaria to death. Moreover, just as the spectator (recognises and) rejects participation in the painter's colonising gaze, the film prevents identification with the Indian denizens of Xochimilco. On the one hand, the film sets up a clear distinction between María Candelaria and Lorenzo Rafael and what Emilio García Riera terms as the *populacho*.[21] On the whole, the *populacho* is presented as a collective, as at the beginning of the film when the villagers prevent María Candelaria from selling her flowers; or again in the final scenes when she is stoned to death. Collective cinematic identity by definition functions here to prevent close spectatorial identification. Furthermore, those members of the *populacho* who are individuated are presented as violently jealous (Lupe), as shrill (La chismosa; Lupe Inclán), or as downright primitive (La huesera; Lupe del Castillo).

Identification and distanciation are promoted not only in terms of characterisation, however, but also at the level of the gaze. For the gaze associated with the *populacho* is suffused with dissonant vestiges of both pre- and post-Conquest looking relations and is presented, moreover, as decidedly pre-modern. The palimpsestic complexity of this gaze is manifest in two key iconoclastic moments of the film. First, there is the scene already mentioned, in which Lupe jealously casts the stone, shattering María Candelaria's icon of the Virgin of Guadalupe. As suggested earlier, this scene at once establishes a link between the Virgin and María Candelaria and also prefigures her violent murder at the end of film. Where in the earlier scene Lupe's iconoclastic impulse is directed towards an image – that is to say, towards the signifier – in the later scene the target of the *populacho*'s scandalised violence is instead the signified (María Candelaria) and not the signifier (the painting). Viewed in tandem, these two iconoclastic moments bespeak a profoundly ambivalent attitude towards the concept of visual representation. To the extent that there is a slippage between signifier and signified, I would suggest that these acts of iconoclasm reveal vestiges of a pre-conquest visual schemata that find echo in Gruzinski's explanation of *ixiptla*. This slippage between signifier and signified within the terms of the film has disastrous consequences for the object of this gaze, María Candelaria.

Nevertheless, if these iconoclastic acts resonate with pre-Conquest looking relations the same pre-Conquest gaze is overwritten with what Gruzinski terms the post-Conquest 'moral eye'. According to Gruzinski, during the colonial war of images, the Spaniards imposed their Christian concept of morality on the indigenous masses. It is this imposed colonial 'moral eye' that is so scandalised by María Candelaria's 'immoral' act of posing nude. However, the film associates the scandalised eye not with insight, but with metaphorical blindness. In this context, it is interesting to note that Alexander S. Dawson, in his discussion of *indigenista* discourses in the period 1920–40, argues that influential *indigenistas* such as Carlos Basauri

> applauded the absence of Catholic domination in [some indigenous] communities by commenting that 'among some tribes the virginity of women is not held in the same high esteem as can be seen among Western cultures'. This fact showed that indigenous peoples were in some sense far more liberated than most Mexicans, and offered a future course for change.
>
> (Dawson 1998: 290)

Clearly, the Xochimilcans depicted in Fernández's film do not belong to the 'enlightened' Indians celebrated by Basauri. However, the film does espouse the latter's view extra-diegetically in the way in which it promotes spectatorial distanciation from the 'primitive' gaze of these Indian subjects.

This distanciation takes place on a number of levels. First, the opening intertitles describe the events about to be witnessed as 'una tragedia de amor arrancada de un rincón indígena de México, Xochimilco en el año 1909'/ 'a tragedy of love snatched from an indigenous corner of Mexico, Xochimilco in the year 1909'. In this way, the urban spectator viewing the film in the 1940s is distanced both temporally and geographically from the events on the screen. Second, in general terms and as suggested, given that the convention of cinematic identification is predicated upon individualisation, the *populacho* as collective protagonist prevents identification. Third, the spectator is apprised of information – María Candelaria does not in fact pose naked – that the violent *populacho* does not possess. The spectator's superior knowledge ultimately confirms the *populacho*'s scandalised morality as hollow. And fourth, the spectator, whilst he does not get to see the final painting itself, nevertheless does witness the scene of its making and therefore catches sight of the naked model (Nieves) on whose body the final, composite image is based.

This last point is crucially important to an understanding of the modernising process at work in the viewing experience. Even though the spectator knows that María Candelaria does not pose naked for the image, the distance and fundamental difference between the pre-modern gaze of the *populacho* and the spectator's 'gaze-being-modernised' is ultimately reinforced by the act of witnessing the scene of painting. What for the *populacho* is so scandalous as to lead it to commit murder, for the spectator of the film in the 1940s is perfectly acceptable. The naked model

Nieves is introduced so unobtrusively as to pass as 'normal' and as such serves as an index of the modernity of the 'liberated' gaze.

All this is to say that the spectator of *María Candelaria* is presented with the spectacle of looking relations in which certain, historically resonant gazes are intimately associated with violence and death. What, though, are the ideological implications of such an association for an understanding of the positioning of the spectator within the on-going war of images in 1940s Mexican cinema? I want to suggest that the clue to understanding spectatorial positioning lies in the painting, whose presence, *Meninas*-like, haunts both the film and this discussion. In fact, Velázquez's seminal painting arguably holds the key to the final significance that I wish to attach to the painted image and attendant issues of spectatorship in *María Candelaria*. Post-Foucault, *Las Meninas* has become synonymous with self-reflexivity, where the painting-within-the-painting signals the work of (painterly) representation. Furthermore, *Las Meninas* is widely considered the first painting within the canon of Western art history to foreground the position of the spectator.

To return to Fernández's film, the painting-within-the-film can be seen to share an analogous status to that of its art-historical counterpart.[22] In *María Candelaria*, however, if the painting foregrounds the work of representation, then this self-reflexive gesture points to the cinematic apparatus itself. And in Fernández's film, the combination of the invisible painting and the painting as signifier of the work of cinematic representation is consistent with the fact that the spectator is not privileged with so much as a glimpse of the symbol of 'México moderno'. Why might this be so? I would like to suggest that this is because '*México moderno*' does not exist as an object, but instead as a relationship: '*México moderno*' cannot be represented on the canvas, but instead resides in the relay of looks between the screen and the spectator. Moreover, as I have shown, this relay of looks is older than cinema itself, imbued as it is with the charged and contested remnants of nearly 500 years of looking relations.

NOTES ON THE CINEMA AUDIENCE AFTER THE GOLDEN AGE

As this chapter has set out to establish, the period known as the Golden Age of Mexican cinema was not simply, with caveats, a Golden Age of production.[23] Rather, it was also a mythical moment of cinema consumption: a moment at which 'all the people' – or, at least, more than before and since – went to the movies and in so doing, participated in the everyday rituals of belonging to the modern nation. This was an undeniably novel phenomenon. For the first time in the history of the cinema, spectators were able to enjoy a reasonably sustained, regular repertoire of films in their own language, featuring local songs and music, dealing with issues specific to national cultural identity, which were embodied by range of stars that were fast becoming established as household names.

91

If the Golden Age can be measured in terms of an increase in production and a relatively socially diverse, yet homogeneous, audience profile, the same neat equation does not work for the long period of aesthetic and economic crisis and decline into which the Mexican cinema fell, post-1950. In fact, production continued at a relatively stable rate, certainly until the late 1960s. And, for example, a record of 136 features was produced in 1958. In the 1950s, however, the mythical audience of the Golden Age started to fragment. 'All the people' dropped off to 'some of the people', or different people for different kinds of films. Paranaguá puts this in the following terms:

> [A]fter World War II, [the Golden Age] model of film consumption begins to collapse. Producers [. . .] had the intuition that the growing middle class introduced differenciation [*sic*] among the film public. In Argentina as well as Mexico, they tried to respond to this new situation by producing more ambitious and expensive films in order to attract that new middle class, whose tastes and aspirations were different from those of the popular, almost completely illiterate spectators who supported the local industry. This attempt was a failure because the middle class preferred foreign films to their poor local imitations.
>
> (Paranaguá 1998: 33)

As Paranaguá admits, the question of periodisation is a complex matter and fraught with problems. Nevertheless, at some point in the 1950s it seems clear that the national cinema lost what we might term its 'comfortably' middle-class segment. Post-1950s developments in the Mexican cinema, and particularly the greater fragmentation and polarisation of the audience, are attributable to a number of factors. On the one hand, as always, whatever happened to the Mexican industry must be understood in the light of parallel developments in Hollywood cinema. After the years 1939–45, when the attentions of the northern industry had been channelled into ideological support of the war effort, Hollywood set out to regain its Latin American markets once more. To this end, as Eduardo de la Vega (1999: 165) observes, the financial and technological support that the US had extended to the Mexican industry dried up.[24] This, coupled with a decline in investment rates, resulting in less investment per film, lead to a stream of low-budget, formula-based films designed to appeal to a specific audience – namely, the urban popular classes – rather than the more all-embracing tendencies of films produced in the Golden Age. Low production values were further compounded by the closed-shop policies pursued by the unions associated with the cinematic industry, which prevented the entry of new blood, particularly the debut of directors. And finally, of course, in July 1950 the television arrived in Mexico. It was to be some time before this new audio-visual medium was to achieve the saturation that it enjoys today, when it is common to find a television in the humblest of homes in the most impoverished of shanty towns. Nevertheless, the arrival of the television is a useful barometer for the cinema audience in the

1950s. For this new technology was in the first instance beyond the financial grasp of the urban popular classes, who increasingly made up the primary audience for national cinematic production.[25]

If the audience for the national film product was increasingly composed of the vast urban popular classes, this was unsurprisingly reflected in the kinds of genres that prospered in the post-1950 period. These included: urban melodramas, set in working-class *barrios* which built on the success of a cluster of 1948 films *Nosotros los pobres* (We the Poor, Ismael Rodríguez) and *Hay lugar para dos* (There's Room for Two, Alejandro Galindo); and an upsurge in *cabareteras*, or brothel melodramas that reflected the emergent, erotically risqué nightlife and featured exotic female stars who became associated with the genre: the Cubans María Antonia Pons and Ninón Sevilla, Marga López and Yolanda Montes 'Tongolele' amongst others; comedies featuring Tin Tan, Cantinflas and Resortes. Finally, 1952 saw the emergence of a peculiarly Mexican genre, *el cine de luchadores* (or wrestling films), which featured masked wrestlers who engaged in battles against a range of stock evil characters, from mummies, to vampires and Martians. Trading on the phenomenal popularity of wrestling as a sport in the 1930s and 1940s, and its translation into the extremely successful *fotonovelas*, the genre produced a mythic star of the screen – El Santo, who became a quintessentially Mexican superhero. With some 150 *cine de luchador* films produced between 1952 and the demise of the genre in 1983, quantity triumphed over quality. For all that they were formulaic and the last word in kitsch, these films and their hero-stars proved a huge box-office success. According to Nelson Carro (1984: 47), they found their principal audiences amongst the provincial popular classes and became the idol *par excellence* of Mexican boys who would wrestle in the cinema aisles at the end of the show.[26]

Just as that key myth, the Golden Age of national production is almost certainly doomed to remain a point of no return, so too has the Golden Age of consumption been equally elusive. This phenomenon is without doubt part of a wider trend in Latin American cinema, in which, as Marvin D'Lugo has noted (2003: 103), in the 1980s this regional cinema suffered the long-term loss of more than half of the movie-going audience. Indeed, in an essay originally published in Spanish in 1993, García Canclini ominously asked 'Will there be Latin American cinema in the year 2000?', to which the logical corollary is: 'Will there be a Latin American audience for regionally produced films?' The national and international success of films such as *Amores perros* (Alejandro González Iñárritu, 2000), *Y tu mamá también* (And Your Mother Too, Alfonso Cuarón, 2001), suggest that the answer is a qualified yes. Indeed, despite the pessimistic title of his essay, García Canclini nevertheless offers a more up-beat conclusion:

> Nations and ethnicities continue to exist. The key problem seems not to be the risk that globalization will erase them but rather to understand how ethnic, regional, and national identities reconstitute themselves through processes of intercultural hybridization. If we conceive of nations

as multidetermined scenarios, where diverse symbolic systems intersect and interpenetrate, the question is what kind of cinema and television narrates heterogeneity and the coexistence of various codes in a single group, and even in a single subject.

(García Canclini 1997: 257)

As my case study of the looking relations in one particular text, *María Candelaria*, during the Golden Age of consumption demonstrates, nations – and more to point, the Mexican nation – has always been a 'multidetermined' scenario in which 'diverse symbolic systems intersect and interpenetrate'. Furthermore, any attempt to account for the gathering of community that is the act of spectatorship must take the long view and explore the resonances of looking relations understood as a historically inflected category. Nevertheless, whereas the Golden Age audience of *María Candelaria* can be located with a degree of ease in the nation's movie theatres, today's audience and the dynamics of spectatorship must be sought across the 'diverse and evolving technical apparatuses' (Shohat and Stam 1994: 350) and also in relationship to increasingly complex transnational productions.

4

MELODRAMA, MASCULINITY AND THE POLITICS OF SPACE

THE UBIQUITY OF MELODRAMA

Ningún otro género, ni el de terror – y no es que falten motivos – ni el de aventuras – y no es que no haya grandes selvas y ríos – ha logrado cuajar en la región como el melodrama. Cómo si en él se hallara el modo de expresión más abierto de vivir y sentir de nuestras gentes.

No other genre, neither horror – and motives [for horror] are certainly not lacking – nor adventure films – and it is not that there are no great jungles and rivers – has managed to take off in Latin America like melodrama. It is as if the way our people live and feel finds its most open expression in melodrama.

(Martín-Barbero 1987: 243)

In a global market that is governed by the asymmetrical circulation of goods, melodrama, with its universal appeal, is undoubtedly one of Latin America's most successful cultural exports in the form of the *telenovela*, or soap opera. Perhaps unsurprisingly, the success of melodrama is not limited to the small screen. Films that contain elements that facilitate their consideration under the rubric of melodrama – briefly, an emphasis on human relationships and emotions, dramatic *mise-en-scène* and excess – abound across the cinemas of the region. The Mexican cinema is no exception in this sub-continental phenomenon.[1] Examples of melodrama traverse the decades and include: *Santa* (Antonio Moreno, 1931); *La mujer del puerto* (The Woman of the Port, Arcady Boytler, 1933); *Allá en el Rancho Grande* (Over at the Big Ranch, Fernando de Fuentes,1936); *Flor silvestre* (Wild Flower, Emilio Fernández, 1943); *Nosotros los pobres* (We the Poor, Ismael Rodríguez, 1947); *Sensualidad* (Sensuality, Alberto Gout, 1950); *Dos tipos de cuidado* (Two Careful Fellows, Ismael Rodríguez, 1952); *La soldadera* (The Female Soldier, José Bolaños, 1966); *La pasión según Berenice* (The Passion of Berenice, Jaime Humberto Hermosillo, 1975); *El secreto de Romelia* (Romelia's Secret, Busi Cortés, 1988); *La mujer de Benjamín* (Benjamin's Woman, Carlos Carrera, 1991). In no sense exhaustive, this list nonetheless raises two salient issues. On the one hand, melodrama is undoubtedly a ubiquitous film mode in Mexico with transhistorical significance. On the other, its very ubiquity, embracing rural comedy (*Allá en el Rancho Grande*, etc.), revolutionary drama (*La soldadera*, etc.) and urban 'weepies' (*Nosotros los pobres*, etc.) suggests that genre analysis is beset by a number of problems.

Robert Stam offers a concise summary of some of these problems, placing an emphasis on the question of cultural specificity:

> First, there is the question of *extension*. Some generic labels [. . .] are too broad to be useful, whereas others [. . .] are too narrow. Second there is the danger of *normativism*, of having a preconceived *a priori* idea of what a genre film should do, rather than seeing genre merely as a trampoline for creativity and innovation. Third, genre is sometimes imagined to be *monolithic*, as if films belonged only to one genre. [. . .] Fourth genre criticism is often plagued by *biologism*. The etymological roots of the word 'genre' in tropes of biology and birth [. . .] promote a kind of essentialism. Much genre criticism suffers from *Hollywoodcentrism*, a provinciality which leads analysts to restrict their attention to the Hollywood musical, for example, while eliding the Brazilian *chanchada*, the (Bollywood) Bombay musical, the Mexican *cabaretera* film, the Argentinian tango film, and the Egyptian musicals with Leila Mourad.
>
> (Stam 2000: 129, emphasis in the original)

Whilst acknowledging the pitfalls associated with genre analysis, in the stimulating essay 'Rethinking Genre', Christine Gledhill (2000: 221), a critic well known for her work on melodrama, suggests that genre may 'once more [be] spiralling to the forefront of debate for contemporary film studies'. This is because, with the fragmentation of grand theory and its totalising tendencies, but the need to interrogate the relationship between films and their contexts undiminished, genre may provide a conceptual space in which the question of how to understand the life of films in the social. 'In this space, issues of texts and aesthetics – the traditional concerns of film theory – intersect with those of industry and institution, history and society, culture and audiences' (Gledhill 2000: 221).

This chapter – the first of three which, in different ways, are concerned with the question of genre – works between the positions set out by Stam and Gledhill. It explores the significance of this ubiquitous film mode in the Mexican cinema and in particular, seeks to address the question of how to understand melodrama in relation to the social. Mindful of Stam's warning about the provinciality of much genre criticism, it first sets out some of the problems associated with the insights offered by Euro-American melodrama study for an understanding of its Latin American counterpart. Then, focusing on the family melodrama, and more concretely on what Julianne Burton-Carvajal (1997: 198) terms the overlooked patriarchal melodrama, it offers analyses of three key examples: *Una familia de tantas* (One Family of Many, Alejandro Galindo, 1948), *El castillo de la pureza*

(The Castle of Purity, Arturo Ripstein, 1972) and *El Callejón de los Milagros* (Midaq Alley, Jorge Fons, 1994). By taking a transhistorical approach and weaving in and out of textual and contextual analyses, the chapter focuses on the representation of masculinity and patriarchal values at three distinct cultural moments: namely the 1940s, 1970s and 1990s. It argues for an understanding of masculinity as in crisis: a crisis that is registered in the spatial dynamics of melodrama and linked to broader themes in cultural history and developments in the socio-political sphere.

MELODRAMA AND MEXICAN CINEMA

In a review of *El Callejón de los Milagros*, a text that will be discussed in detail later in this chapter, Javier González establishes an intertextual relationship between Jorge Fons's 1994 film and the cinematic tradition to which it belongs:

> *El Callejón de los Milagros* [. . .] es una muestra excelente y revitalizada de que el melodrama corre por la sangre de los mexicanos. Y no lo decimos peyorativamente, al contrario. No se necesita un gran ejercicio de talento e imaginación para encontrar el hilo conductor que nos lleva de *Santa* al *Callejón* pasando por las realizaciones de los hermanos Rodríguez y Alejandro Galindo.

> *El Callejón de los Milagros* [. . .] is an excellent and revitalised demonstration that melodrama flows in the blood of Mexicans. And this is not meant pejoratively, quite the contrary. No great exercise of talent and imagination is required to discover the connecting thread that takes us from *Santa* to *Callejón*, passing through the productions of the Rodríguez brothers and Alejandro Galindo.
>
> (González Rubio 1995: 22)

As González Rubio's statement obliquely evinces ('revitalised' and 'this is not meant pejoratively'), melodrama languished for many years in a critical desert, accused of complicity with suspect ideological structures. More precisely, it was condemned on the grounds that it was perceived to be an excessively sentimental, escapist form of entertainment that appealed primarily to an 'uncultured' (especially female) mass audience. More recently, however, in light of critiques of the hierarchical divisions between high and popular culture and the rise of feminist film theory, this neglected film mode has become the subject of radical revision in the context of both Euro-American and Latin American film studies.

Renewed interest in screen melodrama arguably originated in the context of Euro-American film studies, in which Christine Gledhill's invaluable *Home is Where the Heart Is* provides a cogent historical overview of recent debates in the field, gathering together seminal essays on melodrama by prominent scholars such as Thomas Elsaesser, Geoffrey Nowell-Smith and Laura Mulvey. Charting the emergence of modern melodrama in Europe in the eighteenth century, Gledhill's own introductory chapter explores how the novel and drama came to reflect the familial, moralistic and sentimental concerns that evolved with the rise of the bourgeoisie and capitalist society. As a propertied middle class became established, particularly in the nineteenth century, the question of inheritance, of passing on the material possessions and cultural values of this ascendant social group through the patriarchal line, became a key concern that was increasingly played out in the cultural domain.

If melodrama developed in the context of eighteenth- and nineteenth-century Europe in the novel and drama, as Gledhill (1987: 24) argues, the genre's adaptation to the socio-political soil of the United States was transformative. Rather than an ascendant middle class pitted against a landed aristocracy, in its transatlantic passage melodrama was taken forward to express a nascent national tradition associated with the democratic sensibilities of the 'new' country. Class conflicts translated into urban versus rural oppositions in a move whereby the countryside was imbued with North America's founding ideology of egalitarianism and the frontier ethos. Despite key differences between European and North American contexts, by the time melodrama made its transition to screen, particularly in the American cinema, it is possible to discern a number of constants that were carried over into, and define, its cinematic development. The rise and popularity of melodrama, as Brooks (1976) asserted in the literary sphere, had become associated with periods of intense social and ideological change, and focused on the institution of the patriarchal family. Furthermore, it was often centred on conflicts with a class and/or sexual character and was played out in the interior, domestic spaces associated with this family, where *mise-en-scène* becomes charged with dramatic resonance. Early literary and theatrical melodrama both in Europe and the United States therefore laid the aesthetic and thematic foundations that would be carried forward in the cinema in the twentieth century.

When approaching the melodrama as a key mode in the overlapping spheres of Latin American and Mexican cultural production, it would be wrong to overlook the considerable corpus of work that has been generated in the arena of Euro-American film studies devoted to the re-evaluation of screen melodrama. However, at the same time as this brief overview of some of melodrama's key concerns, and particularly the cultural and historical conditions of its emergence, it would be problematic to assert that insights derived from a Euro-American context can be applied seamlessly to Latin American cinematic culture. For a start, to pinpoint the origins of modern European melodrama as co-extensive with the rise of the bourgeoisie in the eighteenth and particularly the onset of industrialisation in the nineteenth century, simply does not work for Latin America, where parallel developments did not take place. Thus Latin American film studies more generally, and Mexican film studies in particular, have certainly witnessed an upsurge in interest in melodrama that has developed apace with trends in Euro-American film studies. However, much of this work is concerned to chart the cultural and historical specificity of melodrama as a mode of cultural representation that at once overlaps in important ways with certain integral elements that are prominent in Euro-American studies of melodrama and, at the same time, is marked by significant breaks.

Let us return then to González Rubio's claim that melodrama somehow 'runs in the blood of Mexicans'. It is one thing to make such a claim; it is quite another to define what one means when referring to the label 'melodrama' in a Mexican context and what precisely might constitute the terms of its relationship to the national body politic. In the project of thinking across the treacherous terrain that separates Latin American and 'mainstream' Euro-American film studies, arguably the work of Ana López remains unsurpassed. In an important and often cited essay originally published in 1991, López subjects the status and significance of melodrama in what she terms the 'old' Mexican cinema to critical scrutiny. Attentive to developments in Euro-American film theory, in 'Tears and Desire', López (1993: 161) is nevertheless concerned to explore the different currency that melodrama holds in a Latin American context.

Like its Hollywood counterpart, until recently Latin American melodrama suffered a period of critical neglect: neglect that was, moreover, linked to the specific circumstances in which the various cinemas of the region developed. As López notes, 'old' Latin American cinema – consisting of films produced in the 1930s, 1940s and 1950s primarily in Argentina, Brazil and Mexico – in the 1960s became the 'other' against which the 'new' politically aware cinemas of this key decade defined themselves. In the eyes of this new generation of filmmakers and critics,

> [t]he old cinema's principal sin was its melodramatic proclivities. Making the melodrama synonymous with the Hollywood cinema, [Cuban critics Enrique Colina and Daniel Díaz Torres] argued that the Latin American films of the earlier period were little else than a poor imitation 'which opened the floodgates to a manifold process of cultural colonization'.
>
> (López 1993: 148)

In other words, in the eyes of the socially aware proponents of New Latin American Cinema, melodrama was doubly condemned. Not only was it a film mode associated with the debased cultural values of emotion and excess, but also it was a prime example of Latin America's subjugation to the cultural imperialism of Hollywood cinema and therefore redolent of the region's longstanding status as a derivative and second-rate entity.

López, however, takes issue with such short-sighted and dated critiques of melodrama, laying bare the elitism that underpinned this politically moti-vated attack on the 'old cinema' by proponents of the 'new'. Pointing to the mass popular appeal of the former – an appeal that the new cinemas simply could not and did not replicate – López argues that such popularity is more than grounds for a reappraisal of the 'old' cinema's cultural importance across the region.

Acknowledging that melodrama of the 1930s, 1940s and 1950s was indeed complicit with reactionary ideological structures and therefore undeniably derivative of Hollywood, for López, this ubiquitous film mode is, nevertheless, 'deeply embedded in Mexican and Hispanic culture and intersects with three master narratives of Mexican society: religion, nationalism, and modernization' (1993: 150). It is helpful to gloss López's definition of the historical and cultural specificity of melodrama in a Mexican context for her analysis, despite its emphasis on femininity, informs the discussion of the staging of masculinity in crisis in the film analyses below.

First, the kinds of narrative structure that characterise melodrama are similarly to be found as central components in the rituals of the Catholic religion that arrived in the 'New World' with the Spanish invasion and revolve around sin, suffering, abnegation and punishment. Second, melodrama invariably functions according to the logic of metonymy. That is to say, it focuses on the individual and/or the family unit which stand in for collective, national identity. Mexican national identity, in turn, is 'complicated by a colonial heritage that defines woman and her alleged instability as the origin of national identity' (López 1993: 150). More specifically, this female identity is associated with the 'defiled and abused' Malintzin/Malinche, the interpreter and lover of Hernán Cortés. Drawing on Octavio Paz's meditations on the Mexican national character set out in the classic 1950 text, *El laberinto de la soledad* (The Labyrinth of Solitude), López posits the defiled, abused and, crucially, 'open' maternal body as the site of origin of the modern nation. This 'open', maternal body is moreover a site 'which is simultaneously an altar of veneration and the place of an original shame. Victim of a rape, Malinche/la chingada, mother of the nation, carries the guilt of her victimisation. Deeply marked by this otherness, Mexican national identity rejects and celebrates its feminine origins' (López 1993: 151).

If the gendered violence of the colonial heritage made a profound impact on Mexican national identity, violence that is moreover played out in its cinematic culture, so too – as we saw in Chapter 2 – did the 1910 revolution:

> If we agree with Peter Brooks that the melodrama is a 'fictional system for making sense of experience as a semantic field of force' that 'comes into being where the traditional imperatives of truth and ethics have been violently thrown into question', then we should not be surprised by the cultural currency of the melodrama in post-revolutionary Mexico. [. . .] [T]he revolution changed the nature of public life, mobilized the masses, shook up the structures of the family without changing its roots and, as Carlos Monsiváis says, served as the inevitable mirror where the country recognized its physiognomy.
>
> (López 1993: 152)

In the aftermath of the upheavals wrought by the armed conflict, and the ensuing period of rapid social change, the kinds of narrative structure and identifications promoted by and through melodrama became important audio-visual vehicles through which to tell stories of cohesive nationhood. As we saw in Chapter 3, this was particularly true of the period of accelerated modernisation that occurred during the 1940s and coincided with the phase of increased cinematic production of the Golden Age of Mexican cinema.

To describe melodrama, à la González Rubio, as something that 'runs in the blood of Mexicans' may seem overstated. For all the problematic essentialism that subtends such a figure of speech, this statement may in fact find critical echo in the important recent work that has emerged on screen melodrama in the context of both the Mexican and Latin American cinema more generally. Despite the slipperiness of the term, the work of López demonstrates that as a key film mode, melodrama resonates with social and historical structures and narratives of identity that are deeply embedded in cultural modalities across the region. It is hardly surprising then, that with the growth of cinema in the 1930s and 1940s, melodrama should become a privileged meta-generic film mode through which new roles and models of conduct could be played out and new allegiances and identifications fostered.

The privileged status of melodrama in Mexico, whilst certainly indebted to the kinds of narrative structures that were prominent in the hegemonic cinema to the North, also partakes of elements that are profoundly marked by themes and issues pertaining to Mexican cultural history and identity. Therefore, even as melodrama was firmly linked to the new and to societal changes that accompanied the move towards modernisation, at the same time it inevitably harked back to older structures and narratives. And finally, if melodrama is concerned with both contemporary and historical identities, both are bound up with issues of gender which resonate in particular at the level of the family as the basic unit of the social structure.

UNA FAMILIA DE TANTAS

In her excellent study of constructions of femininity in Golden Age Mexican cinema *Mujeres de luz y sombra* (Women of Light and Shadows), Julia Tuñón has the following to say of the family as a social structure:

> La familia es una institución compleja que atañe a la esfera económica, social, ideológica y psicológica y que afecta tanto los temas de la sociedad en su conjunto como de los individuos en particular. Se trata de una instancia intermedia entre los unos y la otra, por lo que se ha considerado la unidad básica de la organización social. Lo es del melodrama mexicano.

> The family is a complex institution that overlaps with the economic, social, ideological and psychological spheres and that affects the themes of society as a whole as well as those of individuals in particular. It is an

101

organism that is half way between one and the other and for this reason has been considered the basic unit of social organisation. This is what the family of Mexican melodrama is.

(Tuñón 1998: 123)

If one of the constants of film melodrama is the way in which collective social and national identities are articulated metonymically via individual and/or familial stories, such a link between the macro and the micro is immediately evident in Alejandro Galindo's *Una familia de tantas*. Made in 1948, Galindo's film is one of a cluster of family melodramas made in this period, in which dramatic tension turns on old values, tied to a conservative, patriarchal order rooted in the past which are pitted against new values associated with the impact of modernity on the family unit. Other films in the same cluster include: *Cuando los hijos se van* (When Children Leave Home, Juan Bustillo Oro, 1941); *El cuarto mandamiento* (The Fourth Commandment, Rolando Aguilar, 1948); and *Cuando los padres se quedan solos* (When Parents Are Left Alone, Juan Bustillo Oro, 1948); *El dolor de los hijos* (The Children's Pain, Miguel Zacarías, 1948); *La familia Pérez* (The Pérez Family, Gilberto Martínez Solares, 1949); and *Azahares para tu boda* (Blossom for Your Wedding, Julián Soler, 1950).

Prompted by the formation of an emergent middle class, whose values were imitative to some large degree of North American cultural models, these films focused on the disintegration of traditional family bonds in the wake of modern social mores, displaying in so doing varying degrees of anxiety about the process.[2] As we have already seen, the 1940s constituted a period of accelerating industrialisation and urbanisation, coupled with strong economic growth and political stability which, by the late 1950s, was to be hailed as the 'Mexican miracle'.[3] And, as Joseph, Rubenstein and Zolov (2001: 10) state, 'In effect, the forties, fifties and sixties constituted a Golden Age of consumption.' In this period of rapid capitalist accumulation that accompanied the presidential *sexenio* of Manuel Ávila Camacho (1940–46) and especially that of Miguel Alemán (1946–52), such conspicuous consumption cannot be divorced from the sphere of official culture:

The market powerfully complemented the state in the production of social citizenship; indeed [. . .] it is difficult to discern where one domain begins and the other ends, so intertwined are the two. Mexicans' attachments to the patria grande were enhanced by the massification of culture and the commodification of everyday life, which increasingly bound rural and urban Mexicans together in common (if still unequal) rituals of consumption.

(Joseph *et al.* 2001: 10)

Whereas other films in the cluster that deal with the effects of the commodification of everyday life, and especially on the family, are on the whole deeply conservative, *Una familia de tantas*, by contrast, offers a more progressive narrative that endorses the positive benefits that modernity is implied to bring to the family and society more generally.

That the viewer is invited to draw a parallel between the family and the wider social realm is clearly signalled in the opening shots of Galindo's take on the dilemmas faced by this emergent social class. In addition to the title *Una familia de tantas* (One Family amongst Many), the film opens with an establishing shot of an anonymous cityscape (by extension, 'one city of many'), before panning horizontally to the left across the rooftops and in through a top-floor window of the Cataño family home. In this way, the opening moments set up a binary opposition between inside and outside that is to be a central structuring device throughout the film. This opposition is neatly figured in an exterior urban landscape that is equated with modernity and the interior of the Cataño home, a bastion of outmoded, traditional values which are to enter into conflict in the course of the film. This conflict is at once presented thematically in terms of gender relations within the family and also spatially, via the symbolic resonances of *mise-en-scène*, which on closer inspection reveal a surprisingly unconventional codification of gender and space.

Set almost entirely in the claustrophobic confines of the Cataño family home, *Una familia de tantas* is populated with stock melodramatic characters. At the head of the family stands Don Cataño, an authoritarian patriarchal figure of unyielding excess who exercises double standards towards his children with impunity. When Héctor's (Felipe de Alba) girlfriend falls pregnant out of wedlock, she is accepted into the family home, such is Don Cataño's desire to make of his feckless eldest son a man fit to carry on the family name and by extension the patriarchal social order. Yet when the eldest daughter Estela (Isabel del Puerto) is caught kissing her fiancé in the street, she is violently punished by her father, which impels her to run away. Similarly, Don Cataño is keen to marry off his middle daughter Maru (Martha Roth) to her rich and respectable but gawky provincial cousin Ricardo (Carlos Riquelme). Maru, however, is more attracted to the charms of vacuum cleaner salesman, Roberto del Hierro (David Silva), purveyor of modern, implicitly North American commodities (it is no coincidence that he works for the Bright O'Home corporation), who inveigles his way into the family home and who appears to offer a more egalitarian, modern relationship. She too abandons the family home to marry him, despite the lack of paternal consent. Finally, there is the mother figure, Doña Gracia (Eugenia Galindo), whose character conforms almost perfectly to the traits of self-abnegation and sacrifice, which were already firmly established in Mexican culture and cinema and nowhere better embodied than in the career of the actress Sara García, the Mexican cinema's maternal archetype *par excellence*.[4]

And yet Doña Gracia does not completely conform to type. After Maru has left the family home with Roberto in the closing moments, standing on the threshold of the family home, she finally challenges her husband's authority and establishes some ground rules of her own: 'De hoy en adelante a estos niños no se les prohibirá nada.'/ 'From today on, these children will not be forbidden

Figure 4.1 Un familia de tantas (Alejandro Galindo, 1948)

Source: Filmoteca de la UNAM

anything.' Whilst the viewer is left to speculate whether Don Cataño will be capable of embracing change, the closing scene of the two younger children playing happily certainly upholds this possibility as potential change for the better. By the same token, the viewer is encouraged to identify with Maru's choice of Roberto over her father's choice of Ricardo, as a husband with whom we might imagine she is to enjoy a 'modern' marriage of (relative) equality.

The viewer's condemnation of Don Cataño and sense of relief at Maru's escape from his tyranny is reinforced via the *mise-en-scène*, which in keeping with film melodrama, is charged with symbolic significance. Burton-Carvajal (1997: 217) notes that the distribution and representation of domestic space is integral to meaning in *Una familia de tantas*. She commments that: 'The majority of the film's sequences take place within the defined and confined spaces of the family home, a structure that is imposing without being grand, suggesting the decline of this Porfirian-style family.' Drawing on Tuñón's work, she continues:

> [I]n Mexican family melodramas the dining room is the setting of choice: 'In the dining room, the public and private converge [. . .], thus representing the family system by combining the consumption of

maternal sustenance in the space represented [and presided over] by the father'.

(Burton-Carvajal 1997: 217)

I suggest that we could take her analysis a step further to establish the whole house as tightly codified according to gender dynamics. This aspect of the *mise-en-scène* comes sharply into focus if we observe not only what kinds of activities are associated with each room, but also who is and, more interestingly, who is *not* seen in each of the various spaces.

We might start our investigation in the two spaces that appear most straightforward in terms of gender and representation: the kitchen and the daughters' bedroom, both of which are represented as feminine spaces *par excellence*. Not surprisingly, with one notable exception, men are conspicuous by their absence in those scenes set in the kitchen, for this space is reserved for Doña Gracia, the children and the comically audacious servant Guadalupe (Enriqueta Reza). Often, however, the kitchen is presented as an unruly place, as if it were not governed by the same authoritarian rules as the rest of the house. Thus it is at once a feminine space of containment and confinement, and at the same time, ironically, a space of relative freedom. The only (adult) male member of the household we do see in the kitchen, and then only once, is Héctor who enters it in great excitement to inform his mother that Roberto has come to ask for Don Cataño's permission to marry Maru. Héctor's incursion into the kitchen is, nevertheless, in keeping with the gendered codification of space, for by this stage in the film, Héctor's terror of his despotic father is tantamount to a form of symbolic emasculation. The daughters' bedroom similarly follows the same gendered spatial logic, in which Maru and Estela enjoy the sisterly intimacy of shared secrets. Like the kitchen, it too is a space of incarceration: Maru and Estela are frequently sent up to bed by their father at times that are clearly inappropriate for adolescents of their age. The bedroom is also a space of violence: this is where Don Cataño beats Estela having caught her kissing her fiancé. Indeed, Don Cataño enters his daughters' bedroom at will; so whilst it is a sanctuary of sisterly intimacy, it is also subject to policing by the authoritarian paternal presence.

It would be tempting to ascribe a rigid and wholly conventional gender dichotomy to the representation of space in *Una familia de tantas*, whereby femininity is equated with incarceration and containment, and masculinity with power, authority and freedom of movement. Although such a scenario holds true to some extent, it does not fully account for the spatial dynamics that inhere in Galindo's film, which are rather more complex when we take into account the exterior scenes that take place in the street beside the Cataño home. The street (in fact, it is patently a set) is associated with a freedom of sorts, with the kind of democratic relationships between men and women as expounded by Roberto and which he claims to enjoy with his own mother. In short, the street is allied to precisely the kinds of values and attitudes that are not tolerated within the house. Furthermore, whereas Estela, Maru, Doña Gracia and even the servant Guadalupe all appear in scenes (however, briefly) that take place outside in the street, there are significantly three characters who are not seen beyond the confines of the home. These characters are those men entrenched in authoritarian, traditional models of masculinity: Don Cataño, Héctor and Cousin Ricardo. This is not to argue that these three characters do not implicitly leave the house during the course of the film. The viewer is aware that both Don Cataño and Héctor have jobs as accountants that take them out of the house on a daily basis and indeed sees them leaving and arriving home. Rather, the point is that they are emphatically not seen in these exterior spaces. The only exception to this rule is the closing moments, in which we see Don Cataño on the threshold of the family home. In this scene, however, he is framed by a high-angle crane shot that places an emphasis on him as a diminutive figure, as if engulfed by exterior space.

On one level, this relationship between authoritarian masculinity and space is logical. The street and its values represent, after all, unequivocally the antithesis of those values that Don Cataño, and by association Héctor and Ricardo, espouse. On another, however, their exclusion from the exterior space of the street underlines a fundamental irony. That is, those characters that we would expect to move fluidly through spatial registers in that they are the most powerful, possess most control over what happens in the family home, and are paradoxically presented as those most incarcerated within the prison of traditional patriarchal values. Or, to put this slightly differently, *Una familia de tantas* is a film that places much visual emphasis on the confinement and containment of the female characters as subject to an unbending patriarchal law.[5] In the final analysis, however, it is not the women who are most trapped by tradition; rather it is the male characters who adhere to an outmoded model of masculinity. As the embodiment of a fundamentally *closed* masculinity, resistant to change, Don Cataño's crisis of masculine identity is symbolically signalled via the *mise-en-scène*: it is Cataño himself, and his son and heir Héctor, who are trapped in the patriarchal prison-home that is ultimately of their own making.

THE POLITICS OF MEXICAN MASCULINITY IN CRISIS

In her insightful reading of *Una familia de tantas*, Burton-Carvajal argues that the ending of Galindo's film is more than ambivalent. She takes issue with Emilio García Riera, who credits Galindo's film as having 'saved Mexican cinema from absolute social blindness, since it alludes in quite appropriate terms to the imminent replacement of an old and diminished middle class by a new and much larger one' (Burton-Carvajal 1997: 219). Rather, Burton-Carvajal challenges García Riera's socially progressive reading by pointing to the status of the pivotal female protagonist Maru, to whom the film concedes 'only one hard-won prerogative: choosing which man she prefers to belong to' (ibid.). Indeed, when viewed through a contemporary cultural optic, it is plain to see that in Galindo's film,

Figure 4.2 Una familia de tantas (Alejandro Galindo, 1948)

Source: Filmoteca de la UNAM

women are confined to the long-standing position as objects of cultural exchange; their presence is that of mediators linking men to one another.[6]

Noting that Martha Roth's performance borders on the hysterical – Maru is 'nervous', 'stressed out' and 'severely lacking in self-confidence' – Burton-Carvajal (1997: 219) concludes: 'Is it too carping to suggest that, in the heroine's case, she seems constrained to opt for hyperventilation over asphyxiation?' In so doing, she implicitly calls into question the degree to which modernity, as embodied in Roberto ('hyperventilation' as opposed to Don Cataño's 'asphyxiation'), might be considered 'progressive' for the film's female characters. Again, this assessment of Maru's choice is certainly correct.

Nevertheless, it is important to underline that *Una familia de tantas* is a piece with the ideological underpinnings of its context of production. It bears the imprint of discourses of the 1940s and 1950s: namely modernisation theory, the idea that 'underdeveloped' nations would achieve 'take-off' if they emulated the path of historical 'progress' of the 'developed' metropolis. In the process, gender relations would by necessity experience a degree of re-accommodation. Thus, if the film appears to uphold Maru's escape with sharp salesman Roberto, this is in keeping with the 'golden-age of consumption' that forms the ideological

107

backdrop to this particular union. Instead, therefore, it is helpful to shift the parameters of analysis, and explore the competing models of masculinity embodied in Don Rodrigo Cataño and Roberto del Hierro in terms of spatiality. Indeed, what makes *Una familia de tantas* such a compelling example of patriarchal family melodrama resides in the way it posits masculine identity as in crisis which, via the *mise-en-scène*, has strong associations with a notion of closed masculinity. Although closed masculinity has clear socio-temporal co-ordinates in the film, linked to the persistence of Porfirian values in the 1940s, as recent work on gender and national identity has shown, such a construction of masculinity has an older inflection in Mexican cultural history.

In a fascinating essay 'Power, Value and the Ambiguous Meanings of Gender', Marit Melhuus (1996) addresses the issue of how gender inflects formulations of *mestizo* imagery in contemporary Mexican society. She engages with critical reflections on the national character produced in the twentieth century, notably the work of Paz (1950) and Roger Bartra (1987) and, to a lesser extent, Claudio Lomnitz (1992), which is brought into dialogue with her own observations based on ethnographic field work. To some degree, Melhuus's analysis overlaps with Ana López's work on the cultural specificity of melodrama, for both scholars are concerned, albeit in different contexts, to probe the central but contested position that gender occupies in on-going debates on *mexicanidad*.

As we saw in López's analysis, debates on *mexicanidad* have been dominated since its publication in 1950 by Paz's *El laberinto de la soledad* (The Labyrinth of Solitude). For better or for worse, this study of the national character 'remains an obligatory touchstone' in Mexican studies (Bell 1992: 105) and has 'cast a tremendous shadow over the historiography and ethnography of Mexican and Latin American sexuality' (Nesvig 2001: 691). Paz located the origins of the nation in the conquest, when Mexico was forcefully opened up to the outside with the arrival of the Spanish in the sixteenth century. The symbolic burden of the forceful opening up of Mexico resides in the body of Malinche, who gives birth to the first *mestizo* child: a child that is the product of the ethnic violence of the conquest. Where López, following Paz, stresses female identity as a site of origin in this scenario of conquest and colonisation, Melhuus shifts the emphasis slightly in order to explore femininity and masculinity as mutually constitutive terms in national and nationalist myths of identity. More precisely, she is concerned to explore how gender relations have the power to create meaning 'not only *in* the world but also *of* the world' (Melhuus 1996: 231, emphasis in the original) and how such relations have been deployed in the process of legitimising state formation in the post-revolutionary period.

There are three elements of Melhuus's analysis to note here. First, that masculinity in Mexico is a contested category that is the result of a paradox. In a society in which there is a split between power and value, and in which the male is dominant, the highest value is nevertheless placed on the feminine as incarnated by the other dominant feminine archetype, the Virgin of Guadalupe. Men and women are classified differently: 'Whereas women appear to be classified discretely, as either decent or not decent, men are classified along a continuum, in positions relative to each other, as either more or less a man' (Melhuus 1996: 231). Second, if the origins of the nation are located, following Paz, in the myth of Malinche, in the open female body, this open (maternal) body is defined in opposition to the closed male body, whereby open is to closed as negative is to positive. Or, picking up on the analysis of Lomnitz, as Melhuus puts it:

> The value or aesthetics of 'closed-ness' is a kind of idiom of power where penetration stands for domination and 'impermeability' stands for power. The male (body) literally and symbolically embodies salient aspects of power and power relations. The imagery spills over into per- ceptions of homosexual relations, where it is the act of penetrating as opposed to being penetrated which distinguishes the true man from the 'homosexual'. Discourses of power are inherently male, explicitly sexual, and often conveyed in an idiom of violence.
>
> (Melhuus 1996: 240)

In short, the body is understood metaphorically in spatial terms, where the closed male body is equated with invulnerability, domination and power. And third, these myths of origins have further ramifications for an understanding of the structurally isomorphic relationship between the process of post-revolutionary state formation and the creation of a national body politic. Such myths of origin have not only featured prominently in intellectual codifications of national iden- tity, but also they have been mobilised in the legitimising processes of the Mexican state, where Melhuus (1996: 236) suggests, following Roger Bartra, these meta- discursive structures have hindered the development of modern democracy in Mexico. In a nutshell, the degree to which the virile 'aesthetics of closed-ness' and the impermeable body are linked to power stands in inverse relation to the state's capacity to embrace open, democratic structures and procedures of rule.

Having sketched out the metaphorical resonances of the male body as a potent site of socio-cultural meaning, it now becomes possible to engage more effectively with Maru's dilemma at the end of *Una familia de tantas* which, for Burton-Carvajal, is a source of disquiet. On the surface, Galindo's film posits the possibility of a new model of masculinity in the form of Roberto: a model that appears to be more egalitarian than the rigid inflexibility of Don Cataño's masculine embodiment. The family home becomes a metaphor for a closed and outmoded, traditional model of masculinity that Roberto penetrates by stealth. However, for all that he is presented with all the trimmings of a more 'open', democratic embodiment of masculinity, as his surname 'del Hierro' (iron) indicates, Roberto nevertheless represents a masculinity that is as hard, penetrating and closed as that which he displaces. Viewed through a metaphoric reading of the virile 'aesthetics of closed-ness', it may indeed not be 'too carping to suggest that, in the heroine's case, she seems constrained to opt for hyperventilation over asphyxiation'. Socially progressive insofar as its denouement questions and challenges Don Cataño's traditional paternal authority, *Una familia de tantas* nevertheless cleaves to a closed idiom of masculine power embodied in the penetrative force of Roberto.

In fact, to find a of critique of either the closed idiom of power that is masculinity or the concomitant discourse of modernisation, we must look to the 1972 and in particular Arturo Ripstein's *El castillo de la pureza* (The Castle of Purity). Indeed, there are many points of intertextual convergence between *El castillo de la pureza*, not least in David Silva's guest appearance in Ripstein's film. However, these points of convergence are undercut by one divergence of fundamental importance: the radically different socio-cultural context that forms the backdrop to *El castillo de la pureza*. For if Galindo's film was made against the backdrop of the optimism of a mid-century belief in the progress and prosperity that modernisation would bring, *El castillo de la pureza* was made at a very different moment in Mexico's social history.

SOCIETY, CINEMA AND THE 1970s

The economic boom which by the 1950s had been hailed as the 'Mexican miracle', was ultimately to prove illusory. In 1982, Mexico experienced a calamitous economic crisis, in which the peso suffered a 100 per cent devaluation, whereby its value in relation to the dollar declined tenfold. With its roots in the failures of modernisation in the form of uneven development and incomplete industrialisation, economic crisis was inevitably concomitant with social turmoil. And, not surprisingly, the 1982 crisis was the culmination of a longer process of decline that reached boiling point during the student demonstrations and infamous massacre of 1968.

Unlike many Latin American countries in the twentieth century, Mexico on the whole enjoyed relative political and social stability, owing in part to the fact that from 1929 until 2000, in effect, it was governed by a single political party. This party was known by a number of different names before acquiring the title of Partido Revolucionario Institucional (PRI) in 1946. The change in original title from Partido de Revolución Nacional was intended to mark the end of the years of foment of the properly revolutionary period and to signal a new phase in Mexico's political history. In this new phase, in theory at least, the nobler aims of the revolution such as land redistribution and social justice were to be institutionalised so as to become part of the social and political fabric. Yet as James Cockcroft notes, while the (party of) state played a pivotal role in the country's economic modernisation:

> It masked its often anti-Indian, anti-woman, anti-peasant, anti-worker, and anti-democracy policies behind the ideological banners of 'revolutionary nationalism' and 'directed democracy.' It presented itself as a defender of the 'revolutionary nationalist' ideals for which peasants, workers, students, and others had made great sacrifices and achieved

at least some advances. These ideals included national ownership of natural resources; agrarian reform; 'effective suffrage and no re-election'; 'autonomous' state universities and preparatory schools; 'Indianism' (*indigenismo*), and, long after women won the right to vote in 1953, 'women's equal rights.' Every government spokesperson and every PRI leader, right down to the local precinct, claimed to represent 'the poor' (*los pobres*) and 'the humble ones' (*los humildes*).

(Cockcroft 1998: 144)

Revolutionary in name alone, the PRI was a deeply conservative and profoundly patriarchal political entity, resolutely focused on pursuing a path of industrialisation and capitalist expansion, whatever the social cost. Moreover, as Mexico's economy started to falter in the 1960s, the PRI began to lose its legitimacy and found itself forced to resort to increasingly corrupt measures to ensure that its candidate won the six-yearly presidential elections.

Political repression of the late 1960s, which, as we saw in the introduction, culminated in the student massacre in the Plaza de Cuatro Culturas, gave way to the rhetoric of so-called *apertura democrática* ('democratic openness') associated with the *sexenio* of Luis Echeverría (1970–76). An astute political actor, Echeverría sought to distance himself from political violence of the past, courted the nation's intelligentsia, and took to the world stage in the promotion of a more left-leaning, democratic image. This entailed, for example a meeting with the socialist Chilean president Salvador Allende in 1972. Part of the political rhetoric of *apertura democrática* and Echeverría's programme of reconciliation with the intelligentsia was the promotion of a state-sponsored film sector. Echeverría's support of the national cinema was affirmed in public statements in which he emphasised the link between film and the nation.[7] And, as we saw in the introduction, Echeverría's *sexenio* is recorded as a particularly vibrant period in national cinematic history, in which socially and politically charged themes were no longer off limits and prominent directors of the period were able to make innovative films that challenged social, political and aesthetic orthodoxies. So, for example *Canoa* (Felipe Cazals, 1975) addresses the issue of political intolerance in its exploration of how the local priest is able to incite the isolated inhabitants of a small village in Puebla to murder a group of visiting students about to undertake a mountaineering trip. Arousing mob hysteria, the priest convinces the villagers that the students are communist agitators. In the wake of the Tlatelolco massacre, the cutting political resonance of *Canoa* cannot be ignored. Likewise, *El apando* (The Heist, Felipe Cazals, 1975), based on José Revueltas' novella written in the light of his own experiences, is a shocking indictment of the dehumanising brutality, corruption and exploitation of prison life.[8]

EL CASTILLO DE LA PUREZA

Forming part of the group of directors who became established in the 1960s and found official favour in the 1970s, Arturo Ripstein in *El castillo de la pureza* (Castle of Purity, 1972) eschews the social realism of other films of the period such as *Canoa* and *El apando*. Instead it is a highly stylised film that takes place mostly in the confines of the family home and draws heavily on the conventions of melodrama. Like *Canoa* and *El apando*, however, *El castillo de la pureza* is loosely based on a true story: of a man named Rafael Pérez Hernández, who locked up his wife and children in the family home in the 1950s. Focusing on Gabriel Lima's (Claudio Brook) spiral into madness, the film charts the tensions the family unit (comprising father, mother and three children) starts to manifest and which are the product of eighteen years of imprisonment.[9] The theme of the home as a site of incarceration that was metaphorical in *Una familia de tantas* has in *El castillo de la pureza* become literal.

Like Galindo's film, the dichotomy between interior and exterior space and the symbolically charged *mise-en-scène* are of central importance to our understanding of *El castillo de la pureza* and are signalled from the very first scenes. Where, however, *Una familia de tantas* opens with a horizontal panning shot that makes the interior/exterior dichotomy explicit from the outset, significantly, the camerawork of the opening of Ripstein's film places a firm emphasis on interior space, as if trying to deny the existence of an exterior. What is more, this audio-visual denial of exteriority and its ultimate failure mirrors Lima's obsession to maintain his family untainted by the 'contamination' that is the world outside the castle/home.

El castillo de la pureza opens with a blurred, extreme close-up of an object which, when it comes into focus, reveals one large and then four smaller, rusty cans that are clustered around the central can. As we later learn, these cans are connected to the external door and jangle in warning when the castle is to be penetrated from the outside. Dennis West notes that, as the first visual image, these cans

> furnish a symbolic key to [Lima's] authoritarian character and way of life: four small tins suspended around a larger one which, when it jiggles, forces the others to move. Gabriel Lima is the axis, the center, while the wife and three children are mere satellites directly, immediately, and necessarily subjected to that central force.[10]
>
> (West 1977: 120)

The first human figures to come into view are Lima's children, the portentously named Porvenir (Arturo Beristáin), Utopía (Diana Bracho) and Voluntad (Gladys Bermejo). Dressed in sombre prison-like uniforms, they are busy in the workshop, engaged in the production of the rat poison that is the family's source of income. When Voluntad accidentally knocks over one of the caged rats, Porvenir brutally

Figure 4.3 El castillo de la pureza (Arturo Ripstein, 1972)

Source: IMCINE

kills the escaped animal. Lima then takes Voluntad down into the basement of the house and locks her in a makeshift prison-cell, its outer door covered with barbed wire. The parallel between the caged rats and the incarcerated children is unmistakable. Rats are Lima's greatest fear and his livelihood; his very *raison d'être* is their extermination. In his campaign to prevent the spread of disease, we later learn that Lima's rat phobia is based upon a fear of their uncontrollable reproduction. In this configuration of rats, uncontrolled sexuality and Lima's children, the resemblance to *Una familia de tantas* is noteworthy. Both films revolve around the struggles of an unyielding patriarch to control his children's incipient sexuality: sexuality that is associated with the more promiscuous values of the world outside the home.[11]

In these opening scenes and throughout the film, narrative and *mise-en-scène* coalesce to emphasise Lima's increasingly frantic obsession to render impenetrable to the outside world his fortress-home. The inside of the home is a space of order and discipline, obedience and the iron will of paternal control. It is a utopian space in which a healthy mind makes for a healthy body and vice versa. The children's rigid home education is administered by their father and is complemented by a strict vegetarian diet and a regime of rigorous physical exercise. The flipside of discipline and obedience, however, is cruelty and punishment, as when Lima sheers off Utopía's hair, or locks his children up in the basement cell. And yet, like Don Cataño, Lima is the master of double standards, duplicity that becomes apparent in those scenes set in the exterior. Thus, despite the strict vegetarianism of his home, we witness Lima devouring meat tacos at a street stall; or, after accusing his wife Beatriz (Rita Macedo) of an infidelity many years in the past, he visits a prostitute.

The multiple similarities between *Una familia de tantas* and *El castillo de la pureza*, however, go beyond the merely thematic. The dialogue between the two becomes evident in a pivotal scene that figures the uninvited arrival of the inspector, played by David Silva in a clear reference to his role as Roberto in Galindo's 1948 film. The reference to Roberto, however, goes beyond the act of unwelcome penetration into the family home. The inspector, like Roberto, makes a pass at the middle daughter, Utopía, much to her father's fury. Similarly, the inspector chain-smokes, lighting one cigarette from the end of another, in an echo of Roberto's nervous habit at the end of *Una familia de tantas* as he awaits his bride-to-be. While there are important parallels between these two characters, there are also crucial differences that allow us to locate Ripstein's film in the social realm and, more precisely, to grasp something of its critique of that realm and also a shift in the valorisation of the earlier film's presentation of masculinity.

In Galindo's film it is abundantly clear that Roberto is upheld as a 'shiny', new example of progressive modern masculinity, the antithesis of Don Cataño's out-moded, bankrupt patriarchal embodiment rooted in the past. By contrast, Silva's performance as the inspector in Ripstein's film is decidedly seedy in his grubby raincoat. What is more, he is corrupt, exacting a *mordida* or bribe from Lima to guarantee that the authorities do not get to hear about Lima's illegal cottage industry in rat poison. In the earlier film, Roberto and Don Cataño are presented as antithetical to one another; the distinction between the inspector and Lima is, by contrast, not so clear-cut. As an emblem of the noisy, bureaucratic outside world, the inspector appears to embody the corruption and modernity against which Lima stands. And yet these distinctions collapse in the visual and behav-ioural parallels that are drawn between the two men: Lima, on his forays into the outside world, wears a raincoat, glasses and carries a case that are remarkably similar to those of the inspector. Like the latter, Lima also makes a pass at the shopkeeper's mini-skirt clad daughter. When the latter refuses, he denounces her to her mother who then beats her daughter. In other words, the 'shiny' new modernity of Silva's character in *Una familia de tantas* has metamorphosed into the ambivalent figure of the seedy and corrupt inspector. Yet the alternative, embodied in Lima and his utopian castle-fortress, is certainly no better.

The obvious parallels and crucial differences between *Una familia de tantas* and *El castillo de la pureza* are reinforced in the ending of Ripstein's film, which re-enacts the opening up of the interior to the exterior, as in Galindo's film; but casts this penetration in a radically different light. As in *Una familia de tantas*, it is again a woman who is responsible for the opening up of the Lima fortress-home. Although Utopía believes that the arrival of the police is a result of her desperate note begging for help, it is in fact the shopkeeper's daughter, keen for revenge, who alerts the police to Lima's poison-making activities. Where Galindo's film offers the viewer a linear narrative of progress, Ripstein's is resolutely circular. As Lima is removed by force from his fortress-home, an extreme close-up of the siren on the police-car invokes the opening image of the tin-bells that as we saw, for West, symbolise Lima's authoritarian relationship to his family. The resonances of the ending are stark: one form of masculine authority associated with a corrupt exterior which, by association with the inspector, has sold out to capitalist modernity, removes another form of unyielding patriarchal authority given to similar displays of double-standards. In the closing moments after Lima's removal, the viewer witnesses Beatriz's return home with the children. To the extra-diegetic sound of a slow, ominous drum beat that echoes the film's opening moments, the two elder children take care to lock and bolt the door, thereby ensuring the family's future incarceration despite the absence of the jailer. By establishing the exterior and interior, capitalist modernity and utopian idealism as embodied in competing masculinities as commensurate, *El castillo de la pureza* reveals that which *Una familia de tantas* conceals. Namely, one paradigm of masculinity that is bound by the penetrative aesthetic of closed-ness, simply displaces another. Arguably then, the ending suggests that until this paradigm of masculine embodiment has been subject to scrutiny, together with its feminine equivalent of openness, the cyclical narratives of enclosure are doomed to repetition. It is this open versus closed, feminine versus masculine dialectic that lies at the centre of Jorge Fons's film, *El Callejón de los Milagros*.

EL CALLEJÓN DE LOS MILAGROS

Released in May 1995, Jorge Fons's excellent take on the family melodrama, *El Callejón de los Milagros* (Midaq Alley), like its antecedents *Una familia de tantas* and *El castillo de la pureza*, coincided with a key moment in Mexico's political, economic and cultural history. A number of factors converge to make this juncture pivotal. First, the Ejército Zapatista de Liberación Nacional (EZLN) staged its dramatic uprising in the southern-most state of Chiapas on 1 January 1994. This unexpected event inaugurated the period and represented the forceful re-emergence of indigenous rights onto the national agenda and at the same time posed a challenge to the authoritarian system of the seven-decade, one-party rule of the PRI. Combining traditional indigenous beliefs and practices with ultra-modern technology and modes of communication, as many commentators have noted, the EZLN has rewritten the terms of engagement in political practice.[12] No coincidence, the North American Free Trade Agreement (NAFTA) was also implemented on 1 January 1994. Signed by the heads of state of Canada, the United States and Mexico, NAFTA was a trilateral agreement designed to bring down trade barriers between the participating nations. Demanding, amongst other things, autonomy from state and national governments, improvements in education and healthcare and the redistribution of agricultural land, the timing of the start of the EZLN's insurrection registered a powerful protest against the potential effects of NAFTA on the rights of Indian peasants.

Meanwhile, internal power struggles within the patriarchal '*familia revolucionaria*' of the PRI also started to erupt into the public domain with two high-profile political assassinations that accentuated the crises of legitimisation that had for years wracked the political system. Presidential candidate Luis Donaldo Colosio was gunned down in Tijuana; then PRI Secretary General José Francisco Ruiz Massieu fell victim to a similar, politically motivated murder in Mexico City. His reputation already tarnished by allegations of corruption, outgoing President Carlos Salinas de Gortari came under suspicion for involvement in the Ruiz Massieu affair and was forced to flee into exile.[13] And yet, despite his fall from grace, Salinas de Gortari was able to appoint his successor to leadership of the PRI, Ernesto Zedillo, in the time-honoured system known as the *tapado*. With distinct regal overtones, the outgoing president nominated his successor via the infamous *dedazo* (literally by pointing his finger at him). Thanks to Mexico's closed political system, the *dedazo*, up until the 2000 elections, at least, was a sure-fire way of guaranteeing the anointed candidate's accession to the presidential throne.[14]

In every sense antithetical events, the simultaneous emergence of the EZLN and NAFTA are, nonetheless, vectors of the same phenomenon of *apertura*, a crucially important discourse that entered into circulation in Mexico in the early to mid 1990s. Combined with the paroxysms of corruption and scandal which beset the PRI and which were seriously calling the political system's legitimacy into question, this was a very different moment from the stage-managed *apertura democrática* of the Echeverría *sexenio*.

An essentially spatial concept, insofar as it signifies the opening up of space within an already existing entity, as we have seen, *apertura* and its opposite 'closedness' are loaded terms within the context of family melodrama, particularly as they relate to the masculine. Set primarily in a working-class *vecindad* in the heart of Mexico City, from the opening moments of *El Callejón*, mise-en-scène, as is consistent with classic melodrama, comes saturated with contested meanings and impacts complexly on the viewing experience. The film opens with a ground-level establishing shot of 'El Callejón de los Milagros' that gives the film its title. Deep focus affords the viewer an image that emphasises depth and narrowness of space along which anonymous bodies circulate engaged in their daily activities, before the film cuts to the *cantina*, Los Reyes Antiguos, implicitly located at the centre of *El Callejón*.[15] The cantina's centrality and its name point up its status as a productive hub of patriarchal social and sexual organisation that will become apparent during the diegesis. Yet the cantina is also the hub of masculinity in crisis. Its owner Rutilio, like Don Cataño and Lima, asserts his authority through desperate performances of mastery through violence directed at his son and his wife. Moreover, the cantina is an enclosed, homosocial space, its defining characteristic being an intolerance of (sexual) difference. Those sexual others who do enter this space – Maru (Tiare Scanda), Susanita (Margarita Sanz), and Rutilio's lover Jimy

(Esteban Soberanes) – do so on terms that are marked as different from those who habitually frequent the cantina.

If the cantina is the site of masculinity *par excellence*, it finds its parallel in the feminised domestic sphere of Rutilio and Eusebia's (Delia Casanova) home, in which the fixed co-ordinates of gender relationships and their constitutive spatial registers that we have been exploring throughout this chapter are registered in an early sequence in which Rutilio violently beats Eusebia in retribution for her having sought advice from El Poeta (Óscar Yoldi) about her husband's homosexual affair. A deep-focus shot combined with the immobility of the camera serves to underline not so much the physical act of violence itself, as the domestic sphere as a (habitual) scene of violence. Spatial configurations in *El Callejón*, therefore, are determined by the connotations implicit in the masculine/feminine binary opposition, which are in turn articulated through and on the body as it circulates in space.

In an essay in which she seeks to tease out the specificities of the body–space relationship, Elizabeth Grosz (1998: 47) argues for an understanding of the body/city binary as one of 'congruent counterparts', whereby space is constitutive of the body and the body of space. According to the dynamics of gender in *El Callejón*, as in the other melodramas we have been exploring, space is also constitutive of the gendered body and the gendered body is constitutive of gendered space. However, the space/body relationship is even more complex in *El Callejón* than a notion of 'congruent counterparts' will allow. Indeed, the body that shapes and is shaped by space, must itself be understood according to the logic of spatiality. Reading the body spatially, it becomes possible to access the film's staging of *apertura*. This will come into sharper focus if we explore the second constant space of melodrama, namely the brothel, a liminal space occupied by a recurrent figure in Mexican melodrama: the prostitute, who in Fons's film goes by the name of Alma.[16]

The importance of the prostitute as an enduring figure in Mexican literature and culture cannot be overstated.[17] From *Santa* (Antonio Moreno, 1931) and *La mujer del puerto* (The Woman of the Port, Arcady Boytler, 1933) through *Aventurera* (Adventuress, Alberto Gout, 1949) to more recent productions such as Ripstein's *La reina de la noche* (The Queen of the Night, 1994) and of course, *El Callejón*, the prostitute has been a central and constant figure in national cinematic history. Given the privileged status enjoyed by the prostitute in its filmic intertexts, what is at stake in *El Callejón*'s re-presentation of the prostitute in Alma's narrative? Here it is instructive to return to López's seminal essay on melodrama and Mexico's 'old cinema'. This is because she suggests that the striking recurrence of the prostitute must be understood in the light of the charged and ambivalent position that 'Woman' occupies in Mexican cultural history.[18] That is to say, according to López, the enduring fascination with the prostitute in Mexican culture can be understood as a reworking of the myth of origins, whereby the origin of the nation is located at the site of the (violated) maternal body: that body, which as we have seen, was famously posited as 'open' by Octavio Paz in opposition to the closed male body.

What, however, are the resonances the Golden Age prostitute has for our understanding of her contemporary granddaughter? What relationship, moreover, does the prostitute enjoy with/as space?

If we turn now to Alma's narrative in *El Callejón*, we find that there are many ways in which her fall into prostitution resonates with the themes and issues sketched out above. In her relationship with Abel and the pimp José Luis, Alma embodies at once the myths of the eternal virgin and prostitute. With Abel, it is she who attempts to initiate sexual discourse. Yet he flatly rejects her advances, preferring to maintain her on an elevated pedestal which is signalled in an early scene in which he and Chava gaze up at Alma who is drying her hair in the window. Alma's betrayal of Abel in the denouement – that is to say, a betrayal by a prostitute – is heavily imbued with national symbolic significance. In her relationship with José Luis, it is Alma again who initiates the sexual act by returning to him despite discovering the truth about his '*amigos fiesteros*' (party-loving friends). The sinister scene in which he divests her of her virginity – turning her to take her from behind – is shot through with the violence of the *abierto/cerrado* (open/closed) binary signalled by Paz. Significantly, this key moment is immediately preceded and thereby presaged by the scene in which Alma and Eusebia cross paths as the latter is coming out of *misa* (the Mass). The virgin/prostitute dyad and its cultural ramifications are clearly encapsulated in this paradigmatic encounter between the long-suffering mother-figure, Eusebia and the fallen woman, Alma. With its presentation of stock characters, does *El Callejón* simply reinscribe tired melodramatic formulae?

This paradigmatic encounter between Eusebia and Alma is almost so obvious as to indicate that Alma's downfall that borders on parodic self-reflexivity. Indeed, elsewhere the status of Alma's trajectory as overtly cinematic is clearly signalled. For example, when Alma's elderly suitor Don Fidel (Claudio Obregón) visits Alma in her home, he attempts to strike up conversation with his future wife, a woman young enough to be his daughter. Struggling to make rapport with her, he asks what she likes to do: '¿Qué te gusta? ¿El teatro, la ópera, la música sinfónica . . . el ballet?' / 'What do you like? Theatre, opera, symphonic music . . . ballet?' Her response – 'El cine don Fidel.' / 'Cinema Don Fidel.' – serves to underline not only the chasm that separates them, but also Alma's association with the cinematic. This association is, moreover, overtly linked with sexuality. In the scene in which Alma and her friend Maru wait for the *pesera* (bus) that will take them to the cinema, Alma asks Maru which film they are going to see. Maru replies, 'Todas las que pasan en el Savoy son de puro sexo. Cabronsísimas . . .'/ 'All the films they show at the Savoy are all about sex. Brilliant . . .' It is no coincidence that this visit to the cinema coincides with José Luis's first introduction into the film; his flashy red car passes the two women as if kerb-crawling. Finally, during her seduction and subsequent initiation into prostitution, José Luis suggests to Alma: 'Una muchacha como tú puede aspirar a mucho más [. . .] podrías ser modelo, actriz de cine.'/ 'A girl like you can aspire to much more [. . .] you could be a model and film actress.' Within the logic of Mexican cinema, 'actriz de cine' and 'prostitute' are virtually coterminous.

That *El Callejón* draws attention to the cinematic status of Alma's trajectory (i.e. it flaunts its intertexts), and that Alma's body is charged with meanings which, following López, resonate on a national scale, would seem to suggest two things. First, *El Callejón* is self-reflexively replaying a time-honoured trope within Mexican cinema: that of the fallen woman. Second, in so doing, the film registers stasis in this national cinematographic narrative, which in turn is also signalled in the film's oppressive and restrictive structuring of space.

If Alma's narrative, in its overtly cinematic rendering, points ultimately to closure, then her narrative by association with that of another character, nevertheless opens up a differently configured understanding of bodies in/as space. This alternative understanding is embodied in the character Rutilio and his sexuality, a character who is associated with Alma via the violent etymological link – *puto/puta* (male/female prostitute) – (although not a direct equivalence, the homophobically charged *puto* derives its meaning through association with the equally stigmatised term *puta*); the tripartite plot that places Rutilio's narrative alongside that of Alma; and finally, the significance of the *puta*'s open body in Mexican cultural history.

There are a number of ways in which the film invites the viewer to read Rutilio, and particularly his relationship with Jimy, in national terms. On the one hand, the whole film is recognisably set in Mexico City's *centro histórico*, which Jerome Monnet describess in his cultural geography of this zone:

> Cuando se trata del centro de la capital de un gran país, cualquier discurso cualquier práctica entran en la arena política nacional, ponen en juego y manifiestan las tensiones que estructuran toda la sociedad mexicana y sus relaciones con el mundo.

> When the centre of a county's capital is at stake, any discourse, any practice enters into the arena of national politics. The tensions that structure all Mexican society and its relations with the world come into play and are manifest.

(Monnet 1995: 25)

Not only is Rutilio's cantina implicitly located at the centre of this heavily encoded filmic space; Rutilio and Jimy's first liaison takes place in the Zócalo, against the backdrop of El Palacio Nacional.[19] The camerawork of this sequence is worth noting. Jimy leaves the shop in which he works, which is recognisably situated in the arcades that line the south side of the Zócalo. In a shot that establishes Rutilio's point of view, Jimy walks down the arcades to meet his suitor; the two men start to converse and the camera pans around, bringing into view the cathedral and then the Palacio Nacional. Monnet has the following to say about this edifice:

> El Palacio es 'Nacional' y no 'presidencial' precisamente para subrayar que fue construido sobre los supuestos cimientos del palacio de los

Figure 4.4 El Callejón de los Milagros (Jorge Fons, 1994)

Source: IMCINE

emperadores aztecas, y que albergó a los virreyes de la Nueva España antes que a los presidentes de la República mexicana. Es, pues, por excelencia el lugar de la continuidad del Estado, el lugar de la Institución suprema.

The Palace is 'National' and not 'presidential' precisely to underline that it was built on top of the supposed foundations of the place of the Aztec emperors, and it accommodated the Viceroys of New Spain before the presidents of the Mexican Republic. It is, then, *par excellence*, the site of the continuity of state, the site of the supreme institution.

(Monnet 1995: 299)

Given that one of the defining characteristics of film melodrama is the symbolic use *mise-en-scène*, how are we to understand the contextualisation of Rutilio's homosexual transaction in 'el lugar de la Institución suprema'/ 'the site of the supreme institution'?[20] The answer again lies in the contrast and parallels with Alma's narrative.

In its presentation of Alma's story, *El Callejón* self-reflexively rehearses a reifying cultural narrative that links a violent heterosexual exchange with the origins of the nation. Such an exchange, to cite Paz, turns upon 'la dialéctica de "lo cerrado" y "lo abierto" [que] se cumple así con precisión casi feroz' / 'the dialectic of the "closed" and the "open" [which] fulfils itself with an almost ferocious precision'.

On another level, via Rutilio's story, which is also linked to the nation via *mise-en-scène*, the film posits the possibility of another kind of sexual economy and, at the same time another understanding of the male (homosexual) body. This homosexual body has been theorised by Elizabeth Grosz in the following way as:

> [a] body that is permeable, that transmits in a circuit, that opens itself up rather than seals itself off, that is prepared to respond as well as to initiate, that does not revile its masculinity . . . or virilize it . . . [this body] would involve quite a radical rethinking of male sexual morphology.
>
> (Grosz 1994: 2001)

Grosz's formulation has interesting ramifications when contextualised within Mexican cultural history. In *El Callejón*, Rutilo and Jimy's encounter, which takes place in front of 'the site of the supreme institution', contains the potential to subvert an established binary that posits the male body as closed and the female as open. Here again, it is instructive to note elements of *mise-en-scène* and camera-work related to this encounter. As the two men take leave of each other, the camera pans slightly to the right, thereby bringing into view the opening of the Zócalo metro station; a point-of-view shot then establishes Rutilio's gaze as he watches Jimy enter the opening of the underground space of the metro. To read Rutilio's body through queer theory as radically open is to insert another kind of body into the frame of national cinema, one that might offer the possibility of alternative inscriptions of sexual/cultural identity. That is to say, in the context of a film in which a violently closed patriarchal order prevails, such a reading presents the viewer with a glimpse of an alternative to the gendered dialectic of the 'closed' and the 'open': namely this reading presents the (albeit brief) possibility of radical openness.

But then again, to what extent is Rutilio's body really invested with subversive power? Let us not forget that it is his own (and only) son Chava who violently beats his lover (Jimy) almost to death; that, moreover, Rutilio is represented as desperate to ensure the future of his 'closed' patriarchal lineage through Chava. This desperation is voiced at a number of points throughout the film, but nowhere more potently as after Chava's violent outburst in the bathhouse. Here Rutilio, on learning of Chava's escape 'al otro lado' (to the other side, i.e. to the US), sobs pathetically into Eusebia's lap 'Mi único varoncito, hijo de la chingada' / 'My only male child, son of a bitch'. Our final glimpse of Rutilio, moreover, finds him behind the bar of 'Los Reyes Antiguos', nursing his grandson, baby Rutilio in his arms: business (almost) as usual.

CLOSING COMMENTS

By way of conclusion it is perhaps helpful to return to the idea that film melodrama tends to coincide with periods of intense ideological conflict. The three films that have provided case studies in this chapter were all produced at precisely such periods: accelerated modernisation associated with heightened patterns of capitalist consumption and shifting gender alignments in *Una familia de tantas*; political turmoil and corruption associated with the PRI in *El castillo de la pureza*; and finally, discourses of *apertura* and on-going political crisis in *El Callejón de los Milagros*. By reading the three films textually, contextually and comparatively, it is possible, following Gledhill (2000), to probe the life of melodrama in the social. Moreover, it is also possible to trace the emergence of a pattern underpinning the representation of masculinity and space, whereby the representation of a closed, sealed and violent male body gradually gives way to an albeit ambiguously configured, open male body.

Indeed, would it be a step too far to suggest that this dynamic also underpins the representation of masculinity in one of the recent Mexican movies to achieve major international success at the box office, *Υ tu mamá también* (And Your Mother Too, Alfonso Cuarón, 2001)? In the closing sequence, the deadpan third-person narrator (Daniel Giménez Cacho) informs the spectator of the historic defeat of the PRI in the election of July 2000. This is no melodrama, to be sure: *Υ tu mamá también* belongs to another genre altogether, the road movie, a genre that provides the point of departure for the discussion of the representation of rural and indigenous Mexico that is the subject of the next chapter. Before setting off on an exploration of the road movie, however, it is worth pausing briefly for reflection. Is it simply a coincidence that this road movie – a genre, like melodrama, that endows space with an excess of symbolic signification and which revolves around a coming-of-age story of its two adolescent male protagonists – has so much to say (indirectly) about contemporary Mexican culture and politics and also focuses on the homoerotically charged relationship of these protagonists?

5

SEEING THE OTHER THROUGH FILM

From *Y tu mamá también* to *¡Que viva México!* and Back Again

DEPARTURES

A film that traces a journey of sexual initiation from Mexico City to the Pacific coast, Alfonso Cuarón's extremely successful *Y tu mamá también* (And Your Mother Too, 2001) adheres to the codes and conventions of the road movie to a meticulous degree that render it in all but one dimension, generically exemplary. In the excellent introduction to the essays that comprise *The Road Movie Book* (1997), Steven Cohan and Ina Rae Hark enumerate these codes and conventions and explore their cultural and ideological freight that can be summarised as follows. First, they note that the road normally represents an open space, free from the hegemonic norms prevalent in the town/city, in which the protagonists (conventionally male) undergo various forms of transformative experience. Second, as archetypal quest narratives that are played out within the parameters of the nation space, the personal journey undertaken by the protagonists resonates on a national level and is inflected by the historical circumstances of a film's production context. Third, focusing on a mechanised mode of transport – the automobile, the motorcycle, etc. – the genre has also conventionally functioned as a device that brings modernity into dialogue with tradition. This dialogue, however, is rarely articulated via an antinomy; instead the road movie 'does not oppose so much as bring together the modernity of transportation on the twentieth-century road and the traditions still historically present in the settings that the road crosses' (Cohan and Hark 1997: 3).

Even a fleeting glance at Cohan and Hark's introductory comments confirms that *Y tu mamá también* displays a high degree of fidelity to generic convention. Taking to the open road in the presence of the older, and more sexually experienced Luisa (Maribel Verdú), but arguably more concerned with the sexual (and class) tensions that underpin Julio (Gael García Bernal) and Tenoch's (Diego Luna) relationship, the film follows the logic of the road movie as a vehicle for a male-centred escapist fantasy. What is more, the homoerotic charge to Julio and

Tenoch's relationship is not lacking in generic antecedents. Often focusing on the intimacy of a same-sex relationship with certain affinities with the buddy movie, as Cohan and Hark note, by the 1970s the queer subtext of the road movie had become increasingly apparent (1997: 9). The journey, with its associations with (self) discovery, is clearly an end in itself; indeed the protagonists' final destination – *Boca del Cielo* (Heaven's Mouth) – does not even exist. Iconographically, the camerawork privileges the rural landscape through which the road-protagonists pass, with a series of travelling and wide-angle crane shots characteristic of the genre. En route from the metropolis through the rural states of Puebla and Oaxaca, the film stages an encounter between its markedly modern, urban protagonists and a rural and implicitly traditional Mexico.

This encounter, moreover, takes place at a key moment in national history: as the non-character narrator informs the viewer, the official party of state, the PRI, has recently been defeated in the presidential elections. The quest for identity is unambiguously at once individual and collective. The national dimensions of this quest are not only enshrined in the characters' surnames, which are those of heroes and anti-heroes within the national pantheon: Julio *Zapata*, Luisa *Cortés*, Tenoch *Iturbide*, Chuy *Carranza* etc. In interview, Cuarón also makes this relationship explicit when he states: 'The film is about identity: two teenagers who are seeking their identity as adults, Luisa who is seeking an identity as a liberated woman and a country that is a teenage country trying to find its identity as a grown-up nation' (Smith 2002: 19). In short, *Y tu mamá también* is a paradigmatic coming-of-age road movie, in which the national inflections of the journey are impossible to ignore.

It is, of course, in this last detail that Cuarón's film goes against convention. For all *Y tu mamá también* is generically faithful, it is essential to foreground the national trajectory that is at stake, for it certainly requires further comment. This is because, as a genre, the road movie is synonymous with North American society and cultural values, ideologically rooted in the mythology of the frontier ethos that is projected onto a landscape traversed and bounded by the northern nation's highways (Cohan and Hark 1997: 1). From *It Happened One Night* (Frank Capra, 1934), *Sullivan's Travels* (Preston Sturges, 1941), through *Bonnie and Clyde* (Arthur Penn, 1967) and *Easy Rider* (Dennis Hopper, 1969), to *Thelma and Louise* (Ridley Scott, 1991) and *My Own Private Idaho* (Gus Van Sant, 1991), road movies abound in the North American cinema. This is not to say that other national industries have not produced road movies of significance, a fact that is reflected in Cohan and Hark's text in the section titled 'Alternative Routes', which includes contributions to this genre in the Australian and Italian cinemas, amongst others. As a producer of road movies, however, Mexico is absent from their volume; instead, it features as a final destination, offering refuge from the law or constituting an exotic playground for traveller-protagonists of the North American road movie.[1]

The road movie is, then, firmly linked to a North American cultural trajectory, with its roots in that country's nineteenth-century frontier ethos of westward expansion – expansion that came at the cost of the displacement and extermination of people who had lived there for centuries, not least Mexicans.[2] It should perhaps not surprise us that generically faithful examples of the road movie such as *Y tu mamá también* until recently have been difficult to track down either in the Mexican cinema, or in Latin American film culture more generally. Arguably, the closest the region comes to the genre may be what Ismael Xavier terms 'picaresque peregrinations', that share certain affinities with the conventions of the road movie – most notably of course the idea of travel – and are a feature in the cinemas of the region. Focusing on journeys of varying types,

> [they] explore the social experience of a continent whose modern history has been shaped by immigration and migration since the beginning of the European colonial enterprise. The displacement of human beings, the experience of the frontier, the building of new cities and the occupation of land has been an emblem throughout the Americas, and film production almost inevitably takes advantage of this historical background.
>
> (Xavier 1999: 358)

Two striking examples of the picaresque peregrination in recent years are *El viaje* (The Journey, Fernando Solanas, Argentina 1991) and *El norte* (The North, Gregory Nava, USA/UK 1983).[3]

Solanas's film centres on a fantastic journey undertaken by its adolescent protagonist Martín (Walter Quiroz), partly by bicycle, from Patagonia, through the Andes and Brazil to Mexico. Engaged in a symbolic search for his father and, by metonymic association, the region's origins and identity, from the outset it is clear that this film engages with the 'social experience of a continent whose modern history has been shaped by immigration and migration since the beginning of the European colonial enterprise'. Structurally, *El viaje* is divided into three sections, each of which is signalled by an inter-title superimposed upon a map of the subcontinent dating from the period of conquest and colonisation, suggesting that Martín's journey symbolises a form of contestatory remapping from a Latin American perspective. What is more, Solanas's film has embedded within it a critique of US media imperialism in the form of the recurrent scenes that feature the inclusion of a US-style, made-for-TV movie of oil exploitation that crops up in the most incongruous of places. Similarly, *El norte*, focusing on the enforced migration of siblings Enrique (David Villalpando) and Rosa (Zaide Silvia Gutiérrez) from the political violence of Guatemala through Mexico to California, offers a forceful condemnation of the banal reality that hides behind the illusion of the American Dream. Nava's film ends with Rosa's death of typhoid, a disease she contracted during the perilous border crossing through the sewage pipes that connect the powerful north with the impoverished south.

Viewed in tandem with these examples, it would be difficult to place *Y tu mamá también* within such a Latin American tradition of picaresque peregrinations with their vigorous anti-imperialist political critique. Indeed, in a review of the film, Paul Julian Smith notes that:

> [Cuarón] is eager to disassociate himself from what he calls a 'cinema of denunciation' – the explicitly political output of an earlier generation of engaged auteurs such as Felipe Cazal's *Los motivos de Luz* [Luz's Reasons] (1985), which explores poverty and exploitation amongst the underclass, or Paul Leduc's *Dollar Mambo* (1993), which attacks US imperialism.
>
> (Smith 2002: 16)

Despite Cuarón's declared distance from this strand of politicised Latin American cinema that emerged in the 1960s, and the film's unprecedented commercial success with its unabashed appropriation of a quintessentially North American genre, *Y tu mamá también* is not devoid of social comment. Nor do the genre's national affinities with specifically US cultural values prevent this film from dialoguing with an important debate in Mexican cultural history. On the contrary, in *Y tu mamá también* the road movie – as a genre that conventionally brings modernity into dialogue with tradition – becomes a perfect vehicle in which to travel through a terrain, namely rural Mexico with its *campesino* and indigenous inhabitants, which has occupied a privileged if ambiguous position within the national cultural imaginary.[4] The ambiguity of this position turns on a well-worn paradox. On the one hand, the ruling class has appropriated elements of *campesino* and indigenous 'folk' cultures as a site of authenticity to be harnessed to the myth of the modern nation. On the other, the exaltation of these subjects as national subjects has operated in tandem with the officially sanctioned marginalisation of 'real' Indians and *campesinos* who, in the words of Roger Bartra, are buried 'progressively deeper in the mud of modern society' (Bartra 2002: 7).

As will become clear later in this chapter, this is not to claim that the Indians and *campesinos* encountered (but often not seen) by the travellers are the key focus of *Y tu mamá también*. On one level, they are not. Instead, the film centres on the urban, adolescent male protagonists and their juvenile and often puerile banter that revolves almost exclusively around sexual experience past and present. Nevertheless, a combination of conspicuous camerawork and the non-character narrative voice-over works to foreground and thereby dramatise the protagonists' act of (not) looking at the indigenous, *campesino* others. And, in a nutshell, I wish to argue this is where the political charge of Cuarón's road movie lies: in its invitation to its viewer to take another look – that is to say, look critically – at the paradoxes that have conventionally underpinned the cinematic representation of indigenous and *campesino* Mexico, and in particular the role of the visual, of looking itself, within these paradoxes.

We cannot, however, grasp what is at stake in the invitation to take another look in this contemporary road movie, without first undertaking a major detour through the historical, ideological and cinematic traditions with which *Y tu mamá también* engages. In this way, the chapter rejoins a route already partially travelled in Chapter 3 in the detailed analysis of *María Candelaria*, which touched upon *indigenista* discourses in its discussion of spectatorship in the 1940s. However, in the current chapter and its detour, the most important destination on the itinerary is 1930: the year in which the Soviet director Sergei Eisenstein journeyed south to fail to complete the legendary film *¡Que viva México!* Eisenstein's film, itself a form of travelogue that has, rightly or wrongly, been posited as a mythical point of origin in the Mexican cinema, the moment at which the movie camera lens was turned upon the modern nation's 'archaic' indigenous culture. I do not wish to assert a direct path or road of influence from *¡Que viva México!* to *Y tu mamá también* – to so do would, after all, take some manoeuvring. Rather, in the first leg of my detour, I examine the impact of Eisenstein as international auteur within conventional accounts of Mexican film history, in which the Soviet director is alternately hailed as a founding father or decried as a pernicious presence. On the one hand, I examine the work of Mexican film and cultural scholars who have shown how Eisenstein was in fact as influenced by currents in Mexican cultural nationalism, as he was an influence on them. On the other, I am concerned with the way in which latterly Eisenstein's unfinished film has become a kind of degree zero for how *not* to represent Mexico – a shorthand for the clichéd, the stereo-typical, the reductive, particularly where the representation of rural, indigenous Mexico is at issue. Working through these critical positions, my aim is to show how the ethnographic discourses at large at a given historical moment inevitably permeate filmic production. In this way, I open a road back towards an under-standing of what is at stake in the invitation to take 'another look' in *Y tu mamá también*.[5]

EISENSTEIN'S ITINERARY

The circumstances of Eisenstein's travels to and around Mexico are well known. With a series of internationally renowned avant-garde films to his name – amongst them *Battleship Potemkin* (1925) and *October* (1927) – and having been granted a sabbatical by the Soviet authorities, the director and his entourage undertook a working tour of Germany, Switzerland, France, Belgium, the Netherlands and England, culminating in the United States. The US leg of the tour, however, did not work out as anticipated. Eisenstein's relationship with Paramount, to whom he was under contract, foundered in the face of difficulties when the Hollywood production company declared the director's scripts too expensive to develop. Casting around for funding, and unwilling to leave without undertaking a further project prior to the programmed return to Moscow, Eisenstein obtained funds of some $25,000 from the radical writer Upton Sinclair and his wealthy wife Mary Craig Sinclair to make a film about Mexico. To be called *¡Que viva México!*, the film was famously not finished in Eisenstein's lifetime.

The circumstances of the Mexican stay are well documented; what is more, the unfinished film has also attracted considerable critical attention. Nevertheless, commentators have been unable to agree on how to classify the film. Is *¡Que viva México!* a narrative or documentary film, a treatise on film form, or is it a type of ethnography?[6] Although these classificatory terms have their limitations – not least, because they set up false oppositions between say, narrative and documentary, or theory and practice – they are useful insofar as viewing *¡Que viva México!* can prove a quite bewildering experience; it is not always clear what you are watching. The crux of the matter and one of the major factors in the film's problematic status is that we can really only gain access to Eisenstein's Mexican film from two main sources: as it is sketched out in the script and through the multiple films that were derived from the forty hours' worth of material the director and his team filmed on their travels and sent back to the US for processing.[7]

From these sources, we know that *¡Que viva México!* was to consist of a prologue focusing on the cult of death in the pre-Hispanic past, followed by four novellas – *Sandunga, Fiesta, Maguey* and *Soldadera* – and an epilogue devoted to the day of the dead. Of the four, *Soldadera* was not filmed; on Sinclair's instructions, shooting was halted for the project had overrun both its budget and proposed duration. Each of the four novellas corresponded to different elements of Eisenstein's concept of the Mexican 'experience' of history, from the pre-Columbian 'primitive', through the feudal and Catholic colonial period, to the revolutionary and the modern, combining different orders of representation across the four. Despite this, the whole film was to hang together by a 'free aesthetic composition, and every part would be a variation on the theme of birth and death' (Karetnikova and Steinmetz 1991: 19). Filming required extensive travel – by road, automobile, plane, donkey and on foot – throughout the south of the Republic, to Taxco, Oaxaca, Acapulco, Tehuantepec, to locations in the Yucatán Peninsula, including the colonial city of Mérida and the Mayan ruins at Chichen-Itzá. En route, Eisenstein and his travelling companions encountered the rituals and customs of everyday life – from religious ceremonies to bullfights, and also came into contact with some of the cultures that made up the 'many Mexicos' of the country's complex ethnic mosaic.[8]

The incomplete status of *¡Que viva México!* and its attendant definitional problems notwithstanding, Eisenstein's visit to Mexico – accompanied by cameraman Eduard Tissé and assistant and co-scriptwriter Grigori Alexandrov – rapidly became the stuff of legend. Eisenstein and his aesthetic legacy have left an indelible, if controversial, mark on the historiography of the Mexican cinema as the following statement by Adolfo Fernández Bustamente signals:

> Ha sido el 'pionero'; el descubridor cinematográfico de todas estas bellezas. Detrás de él vendrán todos los demás, nacionales y extranjeros. Quiera el destino que siquiera sepan aprovechar la lección del maestro . . . que ha sabido seleccionar paisajes de embrujo.

He has been the 'pioneer'; the cinematic discoverer of all these beauties. After him will come all the rest, both nationals and foreigners. Let's hope that they are able to make the most of the lesson of the great master who has known how to select such bewitching landscapes.

(Cited in De los Reyes 1987: 114)

Heralded as a pioneer and 'forefather' of what was to become the aesthetic of the 'classical Mexican cinema', the Soviet director seems to have taught Mexicans – and others – how to see the nation. In fact, since Fernández Bustamante issued his laudatory statement in 1931, it has become a commonplace to underline the aesthetic impact that Eisenstein's vision of Mexico made on the development of the national cinema.

EISENSTEIN'S INFLUENCE

In recent critical work, Mexican film historians in particular have convincingly established that in the case of Eisenstein and Mexico, influence was in fact a two-way process. In turn, and of equal importance, the vibrant cultural renaissance of the post-revolutionary period made its mark on the Soviet director, as it did on the many foreign visitors who flocked to Mexico at this point.[9] Eisenstein enjoyed the support and friendship of many of the country's leading artists and intellectuals, including Diego Rivera (whom he had met during the latter's stay in the Soviet Union), David Alfaro Siqueiros, Adolfo Best Maugard, Jean Charlot, Gabriel Fernández Ledesma, Carlos Mérida, Pablo O'Higgins and Fernando Leal. And, as Eduardo de la Vega has demonstrated in his aptly titled book *Del muro a la pantalla* (From Wall to Screen, 1997), the state-sponsored muralist movement made a special impact on Eisenstein. The latter even conceived of his film as a 'cinematic mural' and intended to dedicate sections of his film to a different Mexican artist: the prologue to Siquieros; *Sandunga* to Charlot; *Maguey* to Rivera; and *Soldadera* to Orozco.

Fêted by the cultural elite, the Soviet's dealings with Mexican officialdom were, however, at times less than harmonious. In this sense, the influence that the Mexican context asserted on the director, whilst largely positive, also had decidedly authoritarian hues. At one point early on in the sojourn, Eisenstein and his team were arrested, accused of being agents of international communism and of portraying the Mexican working classes in ways that were 'altamente denigrantes para el país' / 'highly denigrating for the country' (De los Reyes 1987: 103). Once this contretemps was resolved and permission to film had been granted, the Mexican authorities kept a watchful eye on the development of the project. Keen to ensure that Eisenstein neither fell under the spell of stereotypical clichés, nor cast too critical a gaze on the social inequities that were, despite the revolution, still rife, Adolfo Best Maugard and Gabriel Fernández Ledesma were appointed as official guides working for the Secretaría de Educación. In this capacity, their

129

role was to ensure that 'no haya mixtificaciones, de que se usen las cosas auténticas, de que no aparezcan en esta película los charros de guardarropía a que nos tiene acostumbrados el cine americano' / 'there is no mystification, that authentic things are used, and the fake cowboys to which the American cinema has accustomed us do not appear in this film' (De los Reyes 1987: 110).

There is, however, more than a little irony in the fact that these official minders were charged with the duty of steering the Soviet visitors away from clichéd images of Mexico. This is because Eisenstein's stay in Mexico coincided with a cultural moment in which a series of stereotypes – albeit officially sanctioned stereotypes – were coalescing around the definition of *lo mexicano* and taking root in the popular imagination. Steered away from one form of stereotype, namely the Mexican cowboy à la Hollywood, Eisenstein nevertheless both gravitated and was guided towards another stereotype that was increasingly taking on national associations, namely the Indian.

Ricardo Pérez Montfort offers a detailed survey of the development of such stereotypes in the period 1920–40 in his excellent study of cultural nationalism *Estampas de nacionalismo popular mexicano* (1994) (Vignettes of Mexican Popular Nationalism). In particular, he highlights the way in which the architects of cultural nationalism – including government officials, archaeologists, artists, filmmakers and anthropologists – looked to the popular masses in search of unifying symbols of nationhood. And in so doing, 'se toparon de frente con que "lo mexicano" era imposible de entender sin contemplar que gran parte de los que formaba aquella masa popular – "esencia de la nación mexicana" – era "indígena" o "india"' / 'they came face to face with the fact that it was impossible to understand "Mexicanness" without contemplating that a great part of those who formed those popular masses – "essence of the Mexican nation" – was "indigenous" or "Indian"' (Pérez Montfort 1994: 161).

It must be emphasised that this process, whereby indigenous culture became hitched to constructions of national self-definition, was not a new, post-revolutionary phenomenon. Nor was it confined to post-independence constructions of a specifically national identity, although Stacie Widdiefield (1996) has observed that nineteenth-century nation-builders increasingly looked to the country's pre-Columbian past – particularly figures of indigenous nobility – as a site of origin. Nevertheless, as Enrique Florescano (1993) demonstrates, from as early as the seventeenth century, the elite of what would become Mexico started to claim the indigenous past as 'self', in the process of fashioning a Creole self, distinct from Spanish peninsular identity. However, if the Indian as a cipher for a proto-national identity was already in evidence in the seventeenth century, the debates around the significance of this figure for collective identity intensified significantly in the post-revolutionary era.

In a complex and suggestive essay, 'Racism, Revolution, and *Indigenismo*: Mexico, 1910–1940', Alan Knight brings to light a fundamental paradox about post-revolutionary *indigenismo* and its relationship to the concept of *mestizaje*. The paradox turns on the fact that while *indigenismo* emerged from the revolution

130

as a crucial and nation-defining cultural concept, the revolution itself was not fought in the name of race. Instead, the conflict was couched in terms of class. 'The Revolution that began in 1910 could be fought and was fought on the basis of considerable Indian participation [. . .] but in the absence of any self-consciously Indian project' (Knight 1990: 75). *Indigenismo* was, therefore, as it had been in the preceding centuries, an elite discourse deployed in the name of a nation-state struggling to consolidate and legitimate its identity. Born with the conquest, the Indian as a generic concept 'remained part of Spanish rather than Indian usage. It defined those who were not Spanish or *mestizo* and it lumped together the wide range of Indian groups, languages, and communities' (1990: 76).

In the immediate post-revolutionary period, the state set out to promote and foster a sense of identity that overcame such time-honoured binaries in which 'the old Indian/European thesis/antithesis [would give] rise to a higher synthesis, the *mestizo*, who was neither Indian nor European, but quintessentially Mexican' (1990: 85). In the final analysis, *indigenismo* was not really about incorporating a complex, pluralistic notion of the multiple indigenous ethnicities within national culture. Rather, as David Brading puts it in powerfully blunt terms:

> The ultimate and paradoxical aim of official *indigenismo* in Mexico was thus to liberate the country from the deadweight of its native past or, to put the case more clearly, finally to destroy the native culture that had emerged during the colonial period. *Indigenismo* was therefore a means to an end. That end was cultural *mestizaje*.
>
> (Brading 1988: 85)

Influenced by the state-sponsored renaissance in visual arts, which in turn mediated and promoted official *indigenista* discourses, Eisenstein's film similarly bears the imprint of the social and cultural trends of its context of making. Of all the sections of *¡Que viva México!*, arguably the prologue and *Sandunga* are the most redolent of post-revolutionary *indigenista* cultural discourse. The iconic montage sequence of the prologue mentioned above, in which contemporary indigenous people pose for the camera against of the remains of ancient pyramids, showing their status as the living 'descendants' of the pre-Columbian societies, the original architects of these artefacts, seems to aspire to the condition of photography. The only indication that these scenes are moving rather than still images comes, for example, in the form of a figure's garments that move in the wind. In so doing, the stasis of the prologue replicates the stock primitivist notion of time having stood still for these 'premodern' people.

In the 'tropical paradise' of matriarchal Tehuantepec, which is the focus of *Sandunga*, the indigenous Other is an overtly gendered construct, populated by exotic, bare-breasted women. Indeed, this is a classic trope in ethnographic discourse, whereby ethnography and pornography converge in the 'body of the woman [which] becomes the site of "primitive mastery," a sign of the uncivilized idea and object of desire within a discourse of colonial mastery' (Russell 1999:

Figure 5.1 ¡Que viva México! (Sergei Eisenstein, 1979)

Source: Mosfilm/BFI stills

124). What is more, within the terms of the period, there was nothing particularly pioneering in the visit to this 'tropical paradise'. Rather, Eisenstein and his team were simply following a well-trodden route:

> The women of Tehuantepec held mythic status among postrevolutionary *indigenistas* who idealized Mexico's cultural past. A popular narrative tells how the women of Tehuantepec maintained their traditional matriarchal social structure in which women held primary economic and political positions. In other words, according to myth, they represented a past that had escaped European rule, thereby sustaining a 'true,' uncorrupted Mexican society. The past was alive on the Isthmus of Tehuantepec, and it was brought to urban Mexico after the revolution when it became fashionable for women to wear Tehuana clothing.
>
> (Lindauer 1999: 126)

If there was nothing especially innovative either about Eisenstein's itinerary, his choice of subject, or the visual idiom in which he represented this subject, what then is at stake in Eisenstein's denomination as the 'father' and pioneer of Mexican cinematography? It is essential to stress here that it is not my intention to intervene

Figure 5.2 ¡Que viva México! (Sergei Eisenstein, 1979)

Source: Mosfilm/BFI stills

in debates regarding the issues of the 'originality' of Eisenstein as filmmaker, or the artistic 'merit' of his films. Rather, following De los Reyes, I wish to shift the emphasis towards value understood in terms of 'cultural capital' as a concept that sheds light on Eisenstein's status in Mexican film history. It is important to remember that the 1930s represent a period of aesthetic and generic experimentation in the history of the Mexican cinema, a period of transition – during which the foundations of what were to become the industry's infrastructure were also laid.

From early narrative films, such as *Tabaré* (Luis Lezama, 1918) or *Cuauhtémoc* (Manuel de la Bandera, 1919), to the names of film companies – Aztlán Films, Quetzal Films – the incipient national industry had clearly been influenced by *indigenista* discourses and official cultural policy (Pérez Montfort 1994: 165). Nevertheless, Eisenstein's visit proved pivotal, not because he necessarily saw indigenous Mexico afresh or even differently from Mexican cultural producers. Rather, as an avant-garde auteur of international standing, whose vision converged conveniently with official policy, Eisenstein's unfinished film, disseminated in the form of stills published in magazines and the various productions based on his footage, confirmed to international audiences that Mexico was worthy of contemplation. And, in attesting to Mexico's status as aesthetic spectacle, *¡Que* *viva México!* came to form part of the international machinery of cultural diplomacy that served an important internal legitimating function. Eisenstein's visit bestowed international prestige on Mexico and assured national cultural producers and audiences alike that the country's indigenous heritage – that 'buried and hidden part of [. . .] national being' (Bartra 2002: 5) – was indeed a sight to be acknowledged as self, and imagined as an integral part of that self.[10]

AFTER EISENSTEIN

The revisionist work of Mexican film scholars Aurelio de los Reyes and Eduardo de la Vega thus serves to bring a paradigm shift to emphasise the intercultural dimension of the Mexico–Eisenstein encounter. Their work notwithstanding, *¡Que viva México!* continues to occupy a central but contested position in its representation of the indigenous subject – a narration that echoes the views of Fernández Bustamante, who hailed Eisenstein as a pioneer. Thus, within standard accounts of the genealogy of the Mexican cinema, *¡Que viva México!* is positioned as an important precedent to the socially aware *Redes* (Nets, Fred Zinnemann, Emilio Gómez Muriel, 1934), a film that centres on the struggles of a group of Veracruz fishermen against exploitation. Like *¡Que viva México!*, Redes also featured non-professional, local actors and the collaboration of notable foreigners, namely the Austrian Zinnemann, and the North American photographer Paul Strand. In turn, Eisenstein's influence is traced through *Redes* to the creative partnership of director Emilio Fernández and cinematographer Gabriel Figueroa, whose films became synonymous with the so-called 'classical style' of Mexican cinema in the 1940s.

The Soviet director's presence is said to be registered in the emphasis that these films place: on the visual over the narrative potential of cinema; on the still, hieratic quality of the cinematic image; on the dominance of the landscape and its features (for example, trees and maguey); and on the romanticised, noble representation of Indians and their folkloric customs and rituals. More specifically, and as we saw in Chapter 3, Eisenstein's aesthetic influence may be evident, for example, in the opening sequence of *María Candelaria* (1943), in which a montage of shots juxtaposing a young Indian woman with the pre-Columbian past echoes the opening montage sequence of the prologue of *¡Que viva México!* An inventory of Fernández and Figueroa films purportedly inspired by the Eisensteinian aesthetic might also include: *La perla* (The Pearl, 1945), *Enamorada* (Woman in Love, 1946), *Río Escondido* (Hidden River, 1947), *Maclovia* (1948) and *Pueblerina* (1948), amongst others.[11] In fact, Fernández himself claimed to have had the opportunity to observe the Soviet director at work during the former's period of residence in Los Angeles: 'This is what I learned: the pain of the people, the land, the struggle for freedom and social justice. It was wonderful' (Tuñón 1995: 179).

It is questionable whether Fernández ever encountered Eisenstein at work and doubly debatable whether he saw fragments of the Mexican film. An expert myth-maker, 'Fernández took inspiration from men and monuments ranging from

Mexican Presidents Adolfo de la Huerta and Lázaro Cárdenas to foreign film-makers Sergei Eisenstein and John Ford' (Dever 2003: 24). Whatever the truth of the matter may be, in the eyes of Emilio Fernández, Eisenstein's influence may indeed have been positive: 'It was wonderful.' It would not be too much of an exaggeration to observe that for others, Eisenstein's legacy can only be described as pernicious. Jorge Ayala Blanco devotes a chapter of *La aventura del cine mexicano* to the filmic representation of *los indígenas*, which opens with the following observation:

Si consideramos que cerca de 10 por ciento de la población mexicana pertenece a diversas razas indígenas, y que más de la mitad son mestizos, no podrá menos que asombrarnos lo parcamente que el cine mexicano ha tratado el tema de los indígenas. [. . .]

La cintas indigenistas [. . .] incurren globalmente en los errores más comunes de la ideología de la clase media y de la retórica en turno. Fomentan una idea del indio como ser *sui generis*, sin analizar verdaderamente las causas de su marginalismo social, de su atraso, de su incultura, de su arraigo a tradiciones atávicas y de la explotación que habitualmente sufre.

If we consider that nearly 10 per cent of the inhabitants of Mexico belong to the diverse indigenous races, and that more than half are *mestizo*, it cannot but surprise us how infrequently the Mexican cinema has dealt with the theme of indigenous people. [. . .]

Indigenista films [. . .] across the board fall into the most common ideological errors of the middle class and the official rhetoric of the moment. They generate an idea of Indians as *sui generis* beings, without really analysing the causes of their marginalisation, their backwardness, lack of culture, their rootedness in atavistic traditions and the exploitation that they habitually suffer.

(Ayala Blanco [1968] 1993: 145)

What follows in Ayala Blanco's account is a catalogue of such films and details of their ideological and aesthetic shortcomings. Spanning 1912 through to 1965, these include: *La india bonita* (The Pretty Indian Girl, Antonio Helú, 1938); *Rosa de Xochimilco* (Carlos Véjar, 1938); *La noche de los mayas* (Night of the Mayas, Chano Urueta, 1939); Raíces (Roots, Benito Alazraki, 1953); *Macario* (Roberto Gavaldón, 1960); and *Animas Trujano: El hombre importante* (Animas Trujano: The Important Man, Ismael Rodríguez, 1961). Although Ayala Blanco makes scant reference to Eisenstein's film itself (he simply notes the aesthetic influence of *Thunder over Mexico* – one of the films that made use of Eisenstein's footage – on *Janitzio*), it is present nevertheless as a form of counterweight against which, for this critic, one of the Mexican cinema's most serious and successful treatments of indigenous culture works.

In *Tarahumara* (*cada vez más lejos*) (Tarahumara: Always Further On, Luis Alcoriza, 1965), Ayala Blanco finds a film that not only stands as a corrective to the folkloric excesses of what he colourfully terms 'el terrorismo plástico de la "escuela mexicana" de Figueroa y Fernández' / 'the expressive terrorism of the "Mexican School" of Figueroa and Fernández' (Ayala Blanco [1968] 1993: 152). More than this, '[E]n *Tarahumara* se evita sistemáticamente la tarjeta postal de lujo. Después de 30 años, el cine mexicano filmado en escenarios naturales empieza a liberarse del nefasto equívoco de herencia eisensteineana.' / '[I]n *Tarahumara* the glossy picture postcard is systematically avoided. After 30 years, the Mexican cinema filmed on location starts to free itself from the harmful mistake of the Eisensteinian legacy' (1993: 153).

It hardly requires stating that Ayala Blanco holds an unequivocally dim view of Eisenstein's cinematic bequest to Mexico. This view holds critical currency and finds echo in the work of other scholars. Thus, for example, whilst offering nuanced analyses of *¡Que viva México!*, Laura Podalsky and Joanne Hershfield both reach the conclusion that Eisenstein 'reduced rather than celebrated' (Podalsky 1993b: 37) Mexican culture and 'charted a cinematic allegory of Mexican history as a single "path through modernity," collapsing the heterogeneity of indigenous and mestizo populations into an orginary people, innocent in the tropical paradise of Tehuantepec' (Hershfield 1998: 66).

If, as Ayala Blanco claims, *Tarahumara* does indeed break with Eisenstein's aesthetic tutelage, how might it do so and what had changed in the intervening years since the Soviet's visit to effect such a shift? Focusing on the Tarahumara Indians who inhabit the sierra of the same name, and mixing real Tarahumaras and professional actors, Alcoriza's film tells the story of anthropologist Raúl's (Ignacio López Tarso) friendship with Corachi (Jaime Fernández), his wife Belén (Aurora Clavel) and their community. Having arrived in the sierra to conduct an anthropological survey, Raúl gradually becomes intimately involved in the problems facing the Tarahumaras. They are either exploited by white landowners when they agree to work for them, or their land is expropriated and they are forced to migrate when they attempt to continue in their traditional ways of living. The ending of *Tarahumura* is especially bleak. Having offered to accompany Corachi to the authorities to denounce the injustices suffered by the community, Raúl is shot dead. The film closes with an aerial shot of Corachi who runs after the light aircraft carrying away the body of his dead friend and implicitly one of the few whites who has managed, however imperfectly, to cross the ethnic and cultural divide between the two communities.

To be sure, *Tarahumara* differs significantly in its representation of indigenous culture from many of the films that preceded it. *¡Que viva México!* and those films that bear its 'picture-postcard' imprint register anthropological discourses of national origins of racial and cultural difference in circulation in the 1920s, 1930s, 1940s and 1950s. *Tarahumara* was made at the peak of the identification of national anthropology with official nationalism whose maximum expression, the National Museum of Anthropology, was completed in 1964 and incorporated

Figure 5.3 Tarahumara (Luis Alcoriza, 1964)

Source: Filmoteca de la UNAM

the National School of Anthropology on its top floor. Rather than endorse this official project, however, and focusing on the anthropologist in the field, *Tarahumara* prefigures an institutional crisis that was starting to beset the theory and practice of Mexican anthropology and that reached its height, like so many socio-political issues, in 1968. This crisis saw the emergence of a generation of anthropologists, the so-called *magníficos*, who called established anthropological traditions into question, and particularly their collusion with official discourses of state. More specifically, as Claudio Lomnitz argues:

> The 1968 generation complained that Mexican *indigenismo* had as its central goal the incorporation of the Indian into the dominant system, a system that was called 'national' and 'modern' by the *indigenistas*, but that was better conceived as 'capitalist' and 'dependent.' Mexican anthropology was described as an orchid in the hothouse of Mexico's authoritarian state, co-opted and entirely saturated by its needs and those of foreign capital.
>
> (Lomnitz 2001: 232)

Figure 5.4 Tarahumara (Luis Alcoriza, 1964)

Source: Filmoteca de la UNAM

In short, through its alliance with the state, for this generation of Mexican anthropologists, their discipline lacked critical distance from official policy and had effectively reneged on its political and moral duty to side with the popular classes that were its object of study.

Tarahumara aligns with the radical changes in the theory and practice of national anthropology that were emerging in the 1960s. Indeed, it emphatically eschews the exoticising tendencies of earlier representational paradigms that construed the Indian as a one-dimensional cipher, pristine remnant of an archaic culture on the point of extinction. Rather, conjoining narrative film with a documentary cum ethnographic style, *Tarahumara* works to expose the exploitative conditions in which its subjects live. It achieves this by endowing the characters with psychological depth, drawing the viewer into the Tarahumara community as witness to both its members' humanity and their suffering. In this way, it marks a decisive break with the ideological underpinnings of the aesthetic associated with Eisenstein and later, the Fernández–Figueroa partnership.

Alcoriza's corrective to the Eisensteinian legacy is not, however, without its own attendant problems. Not least among these is what James Clifford would term its 'anthropological humanism', which enshrines a will to knowledge in the convergence of the filmic and ethnographic look that ultimately seeks to render the other comprehensible. I shall return to the question of visual knowledge in my discussion of *Y tu mamá también* below. For now, however, I simply wish to note a tendency in critical debate surrounding the representation of the Indian that has polarised around two key positions – Eisenstein as purveyor of 'good' images to be emulated, versus Eisenstein as author of 'bad' images to be contested and, significantly, corrected. Although polarised, these positions nevertheless share common ground; Eisenstein's film becomes the yardstick by which to measure the accuracy of representations of indigenous cultures and peoples within the national cinema and indeed across other media such as photography and the plastic arts.[12]

END OF DETOUR: *Y TU MAMA TAMBIÉN*

Eisenstein resorted to a wealth of creative and cultural metaphors to denominate his Mexican film. In addition to 'cinematographic mural', he also described it as a 'film-symphony', a poem and perhaps most famously of all, a *sarape*. This traditional, brightly coloured, striped blanket was, as Eisenstein (1975: 251) explained in a letter to Sinclair, worn by Indians, *charros*, indeed, by *all* Mexicans. In a famous passage from *Film Sense*, he elaborates:

> So striped and violently contrasting are the cultures in Mexico running next to each other and at the same time being centuries away. No plot, no whole story could run through this serape without being false artificial. And we took the contrasting independent adjacence of its violent colors as the motif for constructing our film: 6 episodes [. . .] held together by the unity of the weave – a rhythmic and musical construction and an unrolling of the Mexican spirit.
>
> (Eisenstein 1975: 251)

The adjacency that Eisenstein adduced in Mexican pro-filmic reality was clearly still in existence in 1964 when Alcoriza made *Tarahumara*, in which the sierra landscape of the film's setting readily lends itself to the spatial and temporal metaphor of the *sarape* stripe. Moreover, set at the turn of the millennium, Cuarón's *Y tu mamá también* also travels through a terrain of equally startling contrasts. The urban protagonists of this road movie and the Indians and *campesinos* with whom they come into contact on their journey to the Pacific coast not only occupy different spaces, but could almost inhabit different time zones. Such is the radical disjuncture that separates the metropolitan values of the road protagonists and those of the rural world they traverse that on one level, some things at least appear not to have changed in the pro-filmic world in the intervening seventy years since Eisenstein's mythical journey through Mexico.

The persistence of a *sarape*-like social and ethnic structure in this film and its concomitant suggestion of stasis are, nevertheless, deceptive. If *¡Que viva México!* and *Tarahumara* bear the imprint of their ideological and historical context of production – namely, complicit and critical anthropological discourses – *Y tu mamá también* is similarly marked by cultural practices and theory in circulation at the end of the twentieth century, and in particular, experimental ethnography and film. This is not to suggest that *Y tu mamá también* is either 'experimental' or 'ethnographic'. After all, this feature film was a major commercial success both in its country of origin, in which it broke box office records, and also across Europe and North America. Financial success and transnational popular appeal are certainly not attributes one would automatically associate with experimental ethnography. However, as Catherine Russell observes in the opening paragraph of her wonderful book *Experimental Ethnography* (1999): 'In the last fifteen years, experimental film has diversified into a range of different media, styles, and practices, many of which impinge on both documentary and fiction.' In what sense then might experimental film and ethnographic theory impinge on the narrative and visual logic of *Y tu mamá también*? Russell provides a clue:

> Discussion of ethnographic film is often limited to content. One of the things that experimental film brings to ethnography is what Nichols [1994] describes as the ability to *see film* as cultural representation – as opposed *to seeing through* film. It is a difference between discourse analysis and content analysis, and it requires a selection of texts that are exemplary of particular configurations of culture and representation. We need to shift the emphasis from 'great works' to 'exemplary texts,' in keeping with the new role of art as it merges with culture, and discuss texts as historical productions with historically shifting experience.
>
> (Russell 1999: 22)

Following this line of argument, we could say that discussion of film featuring the ethnographic subject in the Mexican cinema has traditionally been limited to content. Eisenstein, Fernández and Figueroa *et al.* offer 'bad', politically suspect representations of Indians; Alcoriza produces 'good' images. If experimental ethnography foregrounds film as representation, self-reflexively drawing attention to the medium and its rhetorical strategies, the same logic inheres in *Y tu mamá también*, in which two elements in particular seem to allude to ethnography. These are the non-character explanatory voice-over and the interest in the subaltern figure.

To consider *Y tu mamá también* as an example of a fictional artefact on which the diversification of experimental ethnographic film has impinged is to return finally to the issue I raised at the beginning of this chapter – namely, to locate the political charge of this road movie. The political charge of *Y tu mamá también* lies, to quote Russell again, in 'its challenge to conventional forms of representation and the search for new languages and forms appropriate to a more pluralist social formation' (1999: 3). In what follows, and to conclude this chapter on seeing the Other in the Mexican cinema, I explore how this road movie dialogues with, and thereby poses a challenge to, cinematic traditions of representation that

140

precede it: from Eisenstein, through Fernández and Figueroa, to 'corrective' films such as *Tarahumara*. *Y tu mamá también* emphatically does not do this, I would argue, by proposing a different and, by extension, 'improved' form of representation to those that precede it. Rather, it focuses on *how* we see rather than *what* we see, where the practice of looking is bound up with historical configurations of power and knowledge. What is more, in this film, the practice of looking is inseparable from the pervasive theme of betrayal.

Indeed, on a purely thematic level, *Y tu mamá también* is all about betrayal. In the course of the diegesis, the protagonists Julio and Tenoch cheat on their absent girlfriends, despite adolescent promises of fidelity. The revelation by both of earlier sexual indiscretions with the other's girlfriend is a major source of conflict between the protagonists. Contravening their invented code of honour as *charolastras*, it also brings out unspoken class tensions between the wealthy and well-connected Tenoch and lower-middle-class Julio. A similar social divide separates former dental nurse Luisa and her aspiring writer husband Jano (Juan Carlos Remolina); his infidelity at first sight at least, appears to trigger Luisa's unlikely decision to embark on the journey with the boys to *Boca del Cielo*.

The theme of betrayal, however, cuts deeper than the deceptions that permeate the interpersonal relationships of the protagonists with their attendant social dimension. As an established genre, we observed in the introduction, the road movie invariably fulfils an allegorical function with national inflections. Also noted, *Y tu mamá también* is no exception: the combination of the characters' surnames – Zapata, Iturbide etc. – and Cuarón's own comments, insist that we read this film in national cultural terms. It follows then, that the theme of betrayal that subtends the interpersonal relationships is likewise to be read on a national level. In other words, this road movie invites its national audience to extend its understanding of the sexual and social betrayals that define the protagonists' relationships, to the tensions that underpin the divide that separates urban, modern Mexico and its rural, indigenous counterpart, which is tantamount to a form of betrayal. This betrayal is, moreover, presented in peculiarly visual terms, as urban Mexico's failure to see the Other – where the practice of looking is presented as the problem and the possibility of looking differently may provide a potential solution.

That this is the case is crystallised in the contradictions that permeate the Iturbide family's relationship with the nation's indigenous past and in the concrete example of Tenoch's relationship with his nanny Leo (Liboria Rodríguez). In an early sequence set in the luxurious home of the Iturbide family, the non-character voice-over informs the viewer as to how Tenoch acquired his name. Rather than the preferred 'Hernán', a name that invokes the conqueror of Mexico Hernán Cortés, his parents opt for the Aztec-inspired 'Tenoch'. This, the narrator informs us, is because: 'nació el año en que su padre entró al servicio público y, contagiado por un nacionalismo inusitado, bautizó Tenoch a su primer hijo' / 'born the year in which his father joined the ruling party and, affected by a sudden nationalism, he baptised his first born with [the name] Tenoch'. It is no coincidence that at this point the camera pans from the protagonists, occupied rolling a joint, to bring

*Figure 5.5 *Y tu mamá también* (Alfonso Cuarón, 2001)

Source: Anhelo Producciones

unobtrusively into view a cluster of ornamental pre-Columbian figurines. The implications could not be clearer. In time-honoured fashion, as members of the minority ruling elite, the Iturbide family arrogates to itself pristine elements of the indigenous national heritage at will to ensure and further its own social privilege. In this sense, it is simply putting into practice a politics of appropriation as members of the same social elite have done from the seventeenth century through to the present day. Insofar as the Iturbide family appropriates elements of the nation's indigenous heritage to ensure social and political advancement, the viewer is made aware that this wealthy family is oblivious to the vast social divide between it and the multitude of servants in its employ. So, for example, en route to *Boca del cielo*, as they travel past Tepelmeme, Tenoch refuses to acknowledge the birthplace of his Indian nanny. As the car speeds past the tiny rural village, the narrator takes us into Tenoch's thoughts:

> Tenoch pensó que nunca había visitado Tepelmeme, el pueblo natal de Leodegaria Victoria – Leo – su nana que a los 13 años emigró a la Ciudad de México. Leo encontró trabajo en la casa de los Iturbide y estuvo al cuidado de Tenoch desde recién nacido. Hasta los 4 años le decía mamá. Tenoch no hizo comentario alguno.

Tenoch realised that he had never visited Tepelmeme, the birthplace of Leodegaria Victoria – Leo – his nanny who migrated to Mexico City at the age of 13. Leo found work in the Iturbide home and looked after Tenoch from newly born. He called her mummy until the age of 4. Tenoch made no comment whatsoever.

In fact, to the degree that we as viewers respond to such visual and aural cues, we also become increasingly aware of the protagonists' inability to see beyond the circumscribed horizon of their own social and ethnic milieu. One of the first indications we have of the boys' metaphorical blindness occurs prior to the start of their journey to the coast and concerns the death of Marcelino Escutia. A migrant worker from Michoacán, as the voice-over tells us, Escutia was reluctant to walk the extra two kilometres to the building site where he worked by using the pedestrian bridge. Consquently he was knocked down by a speeding bus as he attempted to cross a busy Mexico City thoroughfare. As the boys drive past the scene of the accident, the camera pans 180 degrees within their vehicle, shifting through the boys' point of view through the front windscreen to a side view of the onlookers surrounding the blood-soaked body on the road, to a rear view of the scene. As the accident scene recedes into the background, testimony to the anonymity and alienation of the life of migrant workers in the metropolis, the narrator informs us that Escutia will be taken to the morgue, where it will take four days for his body to be claimed. If the camerawork positions us as a third pas-senger within the car, as throughout the film, the narrator shares his information with us alone. We look back and grasp something of the social implications of the scene we have just witnessed; Julio and Tenoch, it is implied, do not.

The technique of the straying camera is a recurrent motif throughout *Y tu mamá también*, underlining the gap between the audio-visual knowledge of the viewer and that of the protagonists. The viewer is constantly made visually to register the presence of the mostly anonymous subaltern figures that silently and almost unobtrusively go about the daily chores of cleaning, cooking and tending to the needs of those they serve, who largely remain oblivious to their presence. Slow pans offer glimpses into their world, but the glimpses are fleeting and unconnected.

At some points, the camera seems to stray to these silent figures in order to avoid overtly stereotypical spectacles, such as during the scene in the society wedding. In fact, whilst *Y tu mamá también* reveals the continuing co-existence of (at least) two different Mexicos – the rural and the urban – it gives short shrift to the kind of exoticising folkloric spectacle of which Eisenstein has been accused and with which the classical Mexican style of Fernández and Figueroa films of the 1940s is associated. This is evident, for example, in the sequence featuring the society wedding, as the *mariachi* musicians strike up in the arena at the centre of the opulent venue. Rather than linger on this potentially picturesque display – another stereotypical symbol of *mexicanidad* associated with the Bajío region that shed its regional affiliations to take on national connotations in the 1930s – the camera instead strays.[13] It cuts to follow an anonymous waitress taking refreshments to the squadrons of bodyguards waiting in the wings to protect members of the ruling elite present at the wedding and in particular, the guest of honour, the President of the Republic.

Indeed, the viewer of *Y tu mamá también* cannot fail to notice an imagery of the mundane and banal, the ordinary lives that are glimpsed, yet largely remain uncommented upon and unexplained throughout the film. From the small crowd gathered by the roadside collecting donations for the '*reina del pueblo*' (village queen); through the roadblocks at which soldiers interrogate peasants; to the Indian women cooking in the restaurant kitchen in which the main characters eat. The film is full of visual details of the incidental and the everyday. Although uncommented upon, this is not to say that these details are insignificant. Rather they are an integral part of meaning and should be read in conjunction with the commentary offered by the non-character narrator.

We have already noted that *Y tu mamá también* eschews folkloric spectacle à la Eisenstein, Figueroa and Fernández *et al*. At the same time, it is important to note that it also resolutely refuses what Russell terms the 'benevolence of humanism', which is 'ultimately a condescension toward the Other' (Russell 1999: 47). Here it is instructive to return to Luis Alcoriza's *Tarahumara*. This film, it will be recalled, for Jorge Ayala Blanco marked a definitive break with Eisenstein's aesthetic legacy in the Mexican cinema. Unlike *Tarahumara*, which gradually takes the viewer along with the anthropologist-outsider Raúl into the indigenous community, in the process claiming to give these characters psychological, 'human' depth, the camera in *Y tu mamá también* resolutely avoids adopting the Other's point of view. The viewer is not allowed to forget that she is always looking at the Other from the outside, another who refuses to look back. Who is the old woman in the restaurant? Where does she come from? And what is she doing? The viewer is denied access to the answers to such questions.

This is not to say that the viewing experience leaves us bereft of information. Far from it: for the non-character voiceover, with its disembodied, objective and measured tone – accentuated in the contrast with the male protagonists' marked *chilango* (Mexico City) slang – is excessively omniscient. It tells us what the characters are thinking and feeling and, in the case of Tenoch mentioned above, what they are not revealing. Furthermore, with all the trappings of conventional documentary style, the narrator tells us what is happening on screen and why it has happened with a precision bordering on the scientific. For example, the (no fewer and no more than) twenty-three pigs that destroy the protagonists' campsite have escaped from a nearby ranch. God-like, this narrator also knows and informs us of what will happen: that of the twenty-three pigs, fourteen will be slaughtered in two months' time for consumption at a local popular festival, whereupon their meat will provoke an outbreak of disease. On this level, the narration belies the neutrality associated with its tone, and acquires a distinct political charge, exposing the precariousness of the lives of the poor and also the human cost of advancing neo-liberal reform. Thus we learn that in one year's time, Chuy Carranza will be forced out of his traditional role as fisherman and that he and his family will have to abandon their home as a result of the construction of a luxury hotel on their community-owned land.

How, then, are we to reconcile these opposing tendencies in the narration: on the one hand, the incidental, banal visual detail of everyday life of the people passed on the road on which the narrator remains enigmatically silent; on the other, the occasional superabundance of information? The answer, I suggest, lies with the viewer of the film, who is set up by the narrator as equally omniscient, only to have this position undercut and undermined. Nowhere is the ambivalence of this viewing position more acute than in relation to the character of Luisa.

Throughout the film, a combination of the narrator and camerawork place the viewer in a position of superior knowledge – taking us onto a quasi moral high ground – *vis-à-vis* Julio and Tenoch and their grasp of Luisa's situation. As the film advances, the gap between their capacity to see and understand and that of the viewer appears to become ever wider. Unlike Julio and Tenoch, we know of Jano's infidelity, having witnessed the drunken telephone call in which he makes his confession. On a number of occasions, the camera adopts the point of view of one or other of the male protagonists as they spy on Luisa, catching glimpses

Figure 5.6 Y tu mamá también (Alfonso Cuarón, 2001)

Source: Anhelo Producciones

of her weeping alone. These shots serve to underline their incomprehension and to heighten our own status as knowing subjects, a discrepancy that is visually signalled in a bar scene towards the end of the film in which Julio and Tenoch play table football whilst Luisa telephones Jano to say goodbye. After an establishing shot focusing on Julio and Tenoch, the film cuts to two parallel telephone booths with glass panelled doors. Through one of the panels we see Luisa and hear her painful conversation with Jano; in the other darker panel, we see the male protagonists reflected in the glass, absorbed in their game and unaware of Luisa. The glass panels serve not only to bring the two scenes into parallel view, they also frame the viewer's gaze, drawing attention to the very act of looking itself and, most importantly, reinforcing the viewer's superior knowledge and sensitivity to the scene surveyed. We see and know; they do not.

In short, in their failure to see Luisa's predicament, the male travellers are presented to us as crassly insensitive, an insensitivity that parallels their blindness to the anonymous figures they encounter along the journey. The viewer, by contrast, registers their failure to see and acknowledge both Luisa's predicament and the subaltern subjects of rural Mexico along the way. And yet the film radically undercuts the viewer's omniscience and in so doing, the real political charge of Cuarón's film comes into focus, in its exposure of, and thereby challenge to the will to knowledge in looking and in the ethnographic look in particular. How does this work? At the end of the film, as Julio and Tenoch meet once again at their point of departure, Mexico City, the viewer is asked to revise her position of omniscience as the truth of Luisa's terminal illness is revealed. In the light of this knowledge, the viewer is forced to come to terms with the limits of her own visual understanding. Having enjoyed a position of visual mastery and even experienced moral superiority *vis-à-vis* the male protagonists, in the final analysis the viewer is obliged to acknowledge that to see is not after all to *know*. And in so doing, indebted to the reflexive tendencies of experimental film and ethnography, *Y tu mamá también* asks us to take another look – not so much at others, as at the whole question of looking itself.

6

THE POLITICS AND EROTICS
OF BORDER CULTURE

LOOKING ACROSS THE BORDER

A physical frame that mediates and constructs historical, social and economic entities, the 3,000-kilometre border that separates Mexico and the United States is structured according to the logic of what José Limón (1998: 4), following Sherry Ortner, terms 'the politics and erotics of culture'. For Limón, the politics and erotics of culture involve the complex interplay between, on the one hand, difference and hostility born out of a historical relationship of social inequality and, on the other, fascination with, and desire for, the Other. The border not only defines difference – i.e. where Mexico ends and the United States begins (or vice versa, depending on where you are looking from) – it also gives rise to a seemingly endless series of cultural binary oppositions: order/chaos; hard-working/lazy; active/passive; masculine/feminine; civilisation/barbarism; lawful/lawless; first/third, and so on. So widely disseminated and deeply ingrained are these cultural binaries, that it hardly needs stating that Mexico conventionally occupies the second position in each case.

At the same time, there exists a play of eroticism and desire in the relationship between Mexico and the United States that at once underpins and undercuts such stereotypes. In the US cultural imaginary, Mexico figures not only as a primitive, lawless hinterland, but also, as we saw in Chapter 5, as an exotic and liberating avenue of escape. In the Mexican imaginary meanwhile, the United States is both a hostile neo-colonialist power and site of a deeply coveted capitalist modernity. Furthermore, as the above parenthesised qualifier 'vice versa' indicates, the border is deeply implicated in the politics and erotics of looking: it delineates an ideo-logically located position from which viewing subject ('*de acá de este lado*'/on this side of the border) observes viewed object ('*al otro lado*'/on the other side).

Indeed, as the classic Mexican border movie *Espaldas mojadas* (Wetbacks, Alejandro Galindo, 1955) tacitly acknowledges, cinema has played an important role in the construction of such viewing positions and the propagation of meanings that circulate around the border and their attendant plays of difference and desire. Galindo's film opens with stock panoramic footage of Ciudad Juárez/El Paso accompanied by a pseudo-documentary voice-over informing the viewer:

147

Esto es Ciudad Juárez, ciudad fronteriza entre los Estados Unidos Mexicanos y los Estados Unidos de Norteamérica. En otros tiempos centro de vicio y crímenes de sangre [. . .] hoy en día Ciudad Juárez está dedicada al trabajo [. . .] Al otro lado del río está El Paso, ciudad fronteriza norteamericana en otros tiempos conocido como El Paso del Norte, puerto de entrada a ese país que *cuarenta años de cine han hecho aparecer como una nación donde todos sus habitantes son felices y donde todo se cuenta por millones.* [. . .] Este es Río Bravo del Norte [. . .] sus márgenes señalan la línea divisoria entre los dos países: de este lado es México donde todavía se habla en español y se canta a la Virgen de Guadalupe con guitarras. Allá del otro lado los rascacielos, símbolo arquitectónico del país más poderoso del mundo donde todos sus habitantes tienen automóvil, radio y televisión.

This is Ciudad Juárez, border city between the United States of Mexico and the United States of North America. In times gone by, a centre of vice and violent crime [. . .] nowadays Ciudad Juárez is dedicated to work. On the other side of the river is El Paso, North American border city, formerly known as El Paso del Norte, port of entry to the country which *forty years of cinema have made to appear like a nation in which all of its inhabitants are happy and where everything is counted by the million.* This is Río Bravo del Norte [. . .] its banks indicate the dividing line between the two countries: on this side is Mexico, where they still speak Spanish and sing to the Virgin of Guadalupe with guitars. There on the other side the skyscrapers, architectural symbol of the most powerful country in the world where all of its inhabitants have a car, radio and television.

Such a statement concerning forty years of cinema associated with the romance of the American dream (where 'everything is counted by the million') may be a gross over-simplification. It may also, as Claire Fox (1999: 109) suggests, represent a not so subtle dig at the US film industry. For all that it is lacking in subtlety, however, such a statement, embedded within a film narrative that aligns Mexico with tradition and the United States with modernity, attests to the powerful role that film has played in the construction of limiting binary oppositions of identity and nationhood. These oppositions crystallise in the border as a key trope within cinematic traditions both to its north and south.

Even as the border engenders limiting binary oppositions, however, it is important to remember that these are in circulation because the border is not an absolute, monolithic entity. Indeed, as the voice-over narrative that frames Galindo's film also implicitly signals, borders are historically contingent entities. That El Paso was once known as El Paso del Norte reminds the viewer that the border as it appeared to contemporary audiences of Galindo's film was in fact a relatively recent geo-political development. The line that currently bisects the two nations was established under the 1848 Treaty of Guadalupe Hidalgo, when Mexico sold the present-day states of California, Texas, New Mexico and Arizona and parts of Colorado, Nevada and Utah to the United States during the latter's period of westward expansion.

Borders, moreover, exist precisely because they can be crossed. The identities that they purport to define are never as stable as the sheer materiality of the border-as-frame would suggest. Indeed, in the contemporary age of transnational flows of citizens, consumers, capital and culture, the line that separates the United States and Mexico has recently generated a considerable critical literature devoted to the border as a compelling metaphorical construct. As a 'deracinated cultural myth' and the ultimate space of hybridity, the border has become *the* privileged trope that articulates the fragmentation of social realities in a globalising and fracturing world.[1] Indeed, for Néstor García Canclini, writing on the cusp of the twenty-first century:

> En la medida en que llegar a la globalización significa para la mayoría aumentar el intercambio con los otros más o menos cercanos, sirve para renovar la comprensión que teníamos de sus vidas. De ahí que las fronteras se vuelvan laboratorios de lo global.

> Insofar as arriving at globalisation for the majority signifies increasing exchanges with others who are more or less close by, it serves to renew the understanding we had of their lives. This is why borders become laboratories of globalisation.

> (García Canclini 2000: 34)

If the border has of late become a salient cultural myth, a 'laboratory' that encapsulates our current concerns with intercultural exchanges and flows, it is important to remember that it has not always enjoyed its contemporary status as a celebrated signifier of composite identities. Indeed, if we cast our gaze back a mere fifty years, the border as a negatively charged space of racially motivated violence and aggression comes starkly into view. With, according to Maciel and García-Acevedo (1998: 153), 'more features on immigration than any national cinema', unsurprisingly the border looms large as an imposing physical and thematic presence in the Mexican cinema.

The central focus of this chapter is then the border movie as a key genre in Mexican film culture. Although an imposing physical and thematic presence, as a generic constant, the border's meanings have, nevertheless, changed over time. My case studies in this chapter are two border movies that reflect these shifts: Galindo's classic *Espaldas mojadas* and María Novaro's updating and reworking of the genre *El Jardín del Edén* (The Garden of Eden, 1994). Locating my discussion within the broader context of the genre more generally, I am interested in tracing a series of convergences and divergences between the two films that chart the changes in the border's valences. On the one hand, I explore how these movies intersect with the broader socio-historical circumstances of their making.

In the case of Galindo's film, these are figured diegetically and involve the Bracero Program (1942–64), which regulated the supply of Mexican labour to the United States, and the heightened cultural nationalism that accompanied the ruling party's right-oriented politics of *desarrollo estabilizador* (stabilising development).[2] And on the other, Novaro's exploration of the border is played out against the backdrop of the infamous Proposition 187, a California law that sought to limit illegal immigrants' access to health and social services, and the negotiation and implementation of the North American Free Trade Agreement (NAFTA).

Interestingly, both directors encountered difficulties that ironically typify the kinds of dilemmas posed by the geo-politics of the border that their films to some degree lay bare. The release of *Espaldas mojadas* was delayed by two years at the request of the US State Department, during which time the film was amended in order to temper its critique of US immigration policy. Novaro and her team, on the other hand, ran into problems whilst filming on the US side of the border. In narrative terms, both films conform to a circular structure that is characteristic of the genre more generally in which the narratives open and close on the border. However, more than simple chronicles of attitudes towards cross-border flows of immigration, my focus will be on the visual presence of the border – its specularity – in each movie.[3] By exploring the border as a specular as well as material entity, my aim is to interrogate its potent presence within the Mexican cinema as an image-space that at once is structured by historically and culturally specific dynamics of looking and at the same time, structuring of such dynamics.

ESPALDAS MOJADAS

If we were to read *Una familia de tantas* as Alejandro Galindo's definitive take on the United States and its values, we might be forgiven for thinking that the director was an enthusiastic admirer of all things emanating from Mexico's power-ful northern neighbour. As we saw in Chapter 4, the film clearly embraces a notion of modernity and 'development' rooted in the United States and embodied in the figure of Roberto (David Silva), whom it pits against the hopelessly out-of-touch Rodrigo (Fernando Soler) with his overt associations with the traditional and outmoded values of *porfirian* Mexico. The coveted allure of US technological modernity, however, does not necessarily translate into a straightforward 'love' of the country or its citizens. García Riera (1992, vol. 7: 87) detects something of Galindo's deep-seated attraction to the USA in his extensive and unsubtitled use of English throughout *Espaldas mojadas*. Nevertheless, this attraction is deeply ambivalent and in this border movie, the United States is represented as a site of virulent racism and, as I shall demonstrate, is powerfully established via elements of narrative and *mise-en-scène* as a 'non-space' for Mexicans who have the mis-fortune to cross the Río Bravo.

Although arguably the most aesthetically accomplished and enduring of Mexico's border movies, *Espaldas mojadas* was certainly not the first film in its national cinematic context to focus on the issue of the flow of Mexican citizens across the border to the United States. As Fox (1999: 72) notes, the revolution provoked the first large-scale exodus of Mexican citizens at both ends of the social scale, including wealthy *Porfiristas* and rural poor fleeing the violence. A conflict that coincided with the rise of the visual mass media, and with many important battles fought on the Mexican sides of border twin cities, the dividing line between the two nations arguably gained heightened visual prominence at this point in its short history. In this process, there emerged an allegorical model of seeing the region, a model that continues to be invoked to the present day. Or as Fox puts it: 'the border is a synecdoche of the nations it divides [. . .] and the importance of border events is presented from the point of view of national actors rather than local inhabitants' (1999: 69).

Early precursors to *Espaldas mojadas* therefore include the silent film *El hombre sin patria* (Man Without a Homeland, Miguel Contreras Torres, 1922) and *La China Hilaria* (Roberto Curwood, 1938). Contreras Torres's silent film focuses on the migration of a wealthy upper-class protagonist, Rodolfo, who encounters racism and oppression in the USA, and returns to Mexico where he discovers true love. As the title indicates, *El hombre sin patria* serves as a cautionary tale about the loss of roots and identity experienced by Mexicans in the United States. Centring on a rural labourer Isidro, this theme is accentuated in *La China Hilaria*, which also ends with Isidro's homecoming, a much changed and morally diminished man. Culminating in their protagonists' return to Mexico, both films furthermore establish one of the key generic conventions of the border movie: the circular narrative involving the abandonment of and ultimate return to the Mexican homeland.

The second major wave of immigration occurred during the Bracero Program (1942–64), a bilateral agreement between Mexico and the USA to allow Mexican workers to migrate to participate in seasonal agricultural labour. During the period 1942–64, it is estimated that up to 4.5 million Mexican citizens headed north. The Bracero Program also spurred significant flows of illegal immigration of mutual benefit to both employees and employers. Illegal immigration obviated the need for both groups to comply with bureaucratic procedures that were both time-consuming and cost-incurring. Less scrupulous employers, willing to hire undocumented workers, also served to profit insofar as they could get away with paying lower wages. Although the Bracero Program formalised and legalised migratory flows, undocumented as well as documented Mexican workers were subject to prevailing economic conditions. Thus, with the economic recession of the mid 1950s, the US government set in motion 'Operation Wetback' in an attempt to bring illegal immigration under control with a campaign of mass deportation. Ostensibly targeting undocumented workers, 'Operation Wetback' also served to alter public attitudes towards Mexican workers more generally, as well as establishing 'a new benchmark in relations with immigrants; increased police surveillance and militarization became part of labor regulation' (Gómez-Quiñones and Maciel 1998: 40).[4]

With changes in the broader social fabric registered in mass media, it is hardly surprising that in the period coinciding with the Bracero Program, there ensued a wealth of films focusing on the phenomenon of migration. These include *Pito Pérez se va de bracero* (Pito Pérez Goes as a Wetback, Alfonso Patiño Gómez, 1947), *Yo soy mexicano de acá de este lado* (I'm a Mexican from This Side of the Border, Miguel Contreras Torres, 1951) and *Acá las tortas* (Juan Bustillo Oro, 1951).[5] Despite coming at the issue of border crossing from a variety of narrative angles, Maciel and García-Acevedo (1998: 154) observe that such productions are on the whole consistent in their negative representation of the experience. Many are overtly didactic; the migrant is frequently shown to encounter only hostility and racism; and the 'American Way of Life' is seen to pose a threat to 'authentic' Mexican identity and values. What is more, whilst border movies most certainly respond to transnational migratory flows, they are also intimately bound up with national cultural politics, which according to Fein, at mid-century turned on a 'frenetic search for "*lo mexicano*" that accompanied the boom to modernize in the post-war period' (Fein 1998: 159).

The didactic thrust that is a common feature of the genre is evident in *Espaldas mojadas*, even before the action has initiated. To the sound of melancholy guitar music, an 'important warning' scrolls down the screen, alerting the viewer to the director's intentions. The warning reads: 'Nuestro propósito es advertir a nuestros connacionales de la inconveniencia de tratar de abandonar el país en forma ilegal, con el riesgo de sufrir situaciones molestas y dolorosas que podrían hasta crear dificultades en las buenas relaciones que venturosamente existen entre ambos pueblos.'/ 'Our intention is to warn our compatriots of the problems associated with trying to leave the country illegally, which carries with it the risk of awkward and painful situations that could even cause difficulties for the good relations that fortunately exist between our two nations.' Although in keeping with the didactic thrust of the genre more generally, this warning is not as straightforward as it might at first appear. It was, in fact, added after pressure from the US State Department succeeded in persuading the Mexican government of Adolfo Ruiz Cortines (1952–58) to delay the film's release for two years. Emphasising the good relations that exist between the two nations is one thing, however. The warning does little to soften the harsh critique of the United States and its immigration policies that unfold in the main section of the fictional narrative.

Despite the fact that this 'important warning' is an external imposition, its didactic thrust is in keeping and indeed reinforced by the pseudo-documentary voice-over and establishing shots of Juárez/El Paso that follow, which lend the fictional story an objective, truth-like status. Chronicling the 'awkward and painful situations' experienced by one such 'wetback', Rafael Améndola Campuzano (David Silva), the movie serves as an unequivocal cautionary tale to the film's Mexican audience. After being shot at by North American border guards whilst swimming across the Río Bravo, Rafael, unlike most of his compatriots who attempt the illegal crossing, survives to make it to the other side. But there he encounters greed, exploitation, racism and cruelty in the neighbouring country.

Figure 6.1 Espaldas mojadas (Alejandro Galindo, 1955)

Source: Filmoteca de la UNAM

As he flees from one job to the next, the police in hot pursuit, Rafael is offered the pitiful wage of $1 per day to wash dishes by a Mexican American. The latter imperiously corrects him when he calls him a 'paisano': 'Yo no soy paisano, nací aquí de este lado.' / 'I'm not a compatriot, I was born here on this side.'

Working on the railroad for the aptly named Mister Sterling (Víctor Parra), Rafael encounters third-world conditions in the middle of the first. The only respite from the aggressive racism ('Don't touch me Mexican greaser, shut up dirty Mexican'), are the prostitutes who are bussed in en masse to service the workers, once Sterling and his foreman have selected the best for their personal gratification. And in case the film's warning message were not direct enough, as Rafael flees the law, in a series of shots, police officers blow their whistles and shout 'stop' straight to camera and, at the same time, to the audience. Finally, the film's circular narrative structure, culminating in the protagonist's return across the border back to Mexico in the company of Mexican American María del Consuelo (Martha Valdés) and the ex-patriot Luis Villareal (Óscar Pulido), is unequivocal. Rafael, it is implied, has performed a kind of patriotic rescue, delivering these characters from the alienating experience of the American Way of Life. Mexico, it is suggested, whatever its vicissitudes, is the best place for the Mexican citizen.[6] Such overtly patriotic didacticism is, moreover, reinforced with rather more subtlety at the level of the film's structuring of nationally codified spaces and the nationalistic gaze.

Fox (1999: 109) suggests that in visual terms, after the panoramic view of Juárez/El Paso in which the border is portrayed as a 'cultural trench', there is little to distinguish the US from the Mexican side of the river beyond props such as the Border Patrol watchtower and a rock with English graffiti 'God is watching'.[7] I would go further and argue that the 'Mexico' that the film upholds and celebrates is conspicuous by its physical absence in *Espaldas mojadas*. First, the majority of the action is supposed to take place on US territory (it was in fact filmed in Tepeyac studios). Mexico only features as a physical presence in the opening panoramic view, in the tracking shots of Rafael walking along a street in Juárez, in the form of the contracting office in which the protagonist's lack of documentation prevents him from obtaining work, and in the Big Jim Café. The cinematic resonances of this latter space are significant. Despite a careful emphasis in the opening voice-over on a Juárez that has parted company with its image as a den of violence and vice, a place now dedicated to work, in the final analysis, it nevertheless retains vestiges of its former reputation.

If Juárez had this reputation, it was more than familiar to its contemporary audience as such, thanks to the significant number of brothel melodramas made in the 1940s and 1950s set in the border city. Most saliently, this association is made abundantly clear in *Aventurera* (Adventuress, Alberto Gout, 1950), in which Ciudad Juárez is counterpointed with Guadalajara, which are established as twin sites of vice and sin and ultra Catholic conservatism respectively, around which the complicated and extravagant plot weaves. Other examples of this genre include *Allá en la frontera* (Over There on the Border, Juan Orol, 1943); *Los misterios del hampa* (Mysteries of the Underworld, Juan Orol, 1944); *La herencia de La Llorona* (La Llorona's Legacy, Mauricio Magdaleno, 1946); *Pecadora* (Sinner, José Díaz Morales, 1947); and *Frontera norte* (Northern Border, Vicente Orona, 1953). Although just a border staging-post in *Espaldas mojadas*, the seedier side of Juárez, which these films established in the minds of the national audience, lives on in the Big Jim Café, a haunt for prostitutes such as Margarita (Carolina Barret), who await the *braceros*, their pockets filled with dollars on their return from the United States.

It is another Mexico and other Mexican values which are a visually absent, but powerfully imagined presence in the film – that stand in stark contrast to both the border as a seedy thoroughfare and the negative values associated with the United States. Mexico is evoked nostalgically in the diegetic musical compositions that pepper the film which, as Hererra-Sobek has commented, are 'undergirded by nationalistic themes, love of country, homesickness, and desire to return to the motherland' (1998: 237). The film also upholds and celebrates the value of social bonds and commitment, which are thematised in the relationships between 'real' Mexicans (as opposed to inauthentic *pochos*, a derogatory term to denominate Mexican Americans). Instances of Mexico's status as a space of community include the dramatic opening border-crossing scene, in which the moribund Felipe

Quintanilla (José Chávez Trowe) urges Rafael to take his money, before requesting that he put him back in the river so that his body may reach its final rest in Mexico. This dying gesture of generosity stands in contrast to the material-istic individualism and greed associated with North American characters. Similarly, Rafael asks María del Consuelo to marry him in a scene that takes place imme-diately after the café's other waitress Agnes (Alicia Malvido) has just left with two male clients. Agnes, as María del Consuelo explains to Rafael, is to get married for a mere two months to Bud, a man who has 'won' her in a game of pinball for 30,000 points, so that they can cross the state border.[8]

If the nostalgically evoked vision of Mexico that the film espouses is (largely) physically absent but 'imaginatively' present, North American values are, by contrast, mapped onto a specific cultural geography whose co-ordinates are visually established from the outset of the film. Indeed, it is worth pausing to look more closely at the opening sequence which, as we have already seen, takes the form of a pseudo-documentary panoramic view of Juárez/El Paso. The camerawork that accompanies the panoramic view in this sequence establishes both the point-of-view of a simultaneously national and nationalistic gaze and also the semantic orientation of border and the identities that it engenders.

Espaldas mojadas opens with a sequence of panoramic shots of Ciudad Juárez/El Paso which, via a series of fades whereby the camera pans slowly to the left and downward, bring us down to street level on the Juárez side of the border. The Mexican city is a bustling space of trams, trains and people going about their daily business. In keeping with the logic of establishing shots more generally, this sequence allows the viewer to locate the ensuing action in a larger context before fragmenting that space into smaller units through close-ups and medium shots. However, as soon as the camera pans far enough left for El Paso to come into focus, the unimpaired panoramic view that has dominated in the shots of Mexico vanishes. Once El Paso, and by synechdocal extension the United States, come into the range of vision, the camera passes behind a series of pillar-like objects which partially obstruct our view.

There are a number of issues that need underscoring about this establishing sequence. Such panoramic shots draw attention to the act of looking. Here, the aerial, unhindered vision of Mexico at this point is emphatically replaced by a more structured, located gaze of the United States. This shift, which is also accompanied by a change in the tempo and style of music from melancholic to a 'modern' jazzier rhythm, serves to both foreground and ground the cinematic gaze. The locus of this gaze is established as resolutely on the Mexican side of the border, where 'they still speak Spanish and sing to the Virgin of Guadalupe with guitars'. Although at first sight, a seemingly insignificant visual detail, this shift nevertheless signals important thematic elements that the film will develop.

This device not only establishes the national locus of the gaze and, in con-junction with the voice-over, its ideological overtones, it also visually foregrounds two interrelated factors that are to be key tropes throughout the diegesis. First, it posits this cityscape, whose skyscrapers are later announced as an 'architectural symbol of the most powerful country in the world where all its inhabitants have a car, radio and television', as an object of desire. As object of desire, the United States as a site of capitalist modernity is presented as a distant and therefore ultimately unattainable sight for the nationally located subject, who would cross the other side of the border. And significantly throughout the rest of the film, the United States as urban landscape barely materialises as anything more than a remote backdrop, as for example, in the scene in which Rafael first meets the tramp Luis Villarreal/Louie Royalville in the railway yard. To the degree that this symbol of US power and modernity is established as a remote and ultimately unattainable object of desire, this framing device also prefigures what is to become a visually prominent trope: the United States that the Mexican subject is able to access is a liminal, or in-between space of alienation.

In fact, this representation of space is echoed throughout the sections of the film set north of the border. With the exception of the first scene featuring the military parade, where Rafael meets María del Consuelo and which is set in the café where María works, the United States is iconographically fixed as periphery and non-space for the Mexican subject. The visual impact of the United States as a barren and empty space is striking: from the railway yard in which Rafael

Figure 6.2 Espaldas mojadas (Alejandro Galindo, 1955)

Source: Filmoteca de la UNAM

meets Luis Villareal to the rubbish dumps in which he hides from the police; from the vast empty desert landscapes traversed only by trains headed for distant (and by extension unreachable) locations, to the dusty train tracks beneath whose carriages the Mexican labourers make their 'home'. Indeed, in a direct echo of the opening shot of the El Paso cityscape, throughout the action set in the United States, Rafael is constantly framed in spaces that are visually marked as in-between. Such framing is dramatically crystallised in the scenes set in the Mexican workers' pathetic makeshift home between the locomotives and the tracks, or when we see Rafael illegally riding the train ('*de mosca*'), perched precariously between two carriages.

At a narrative level, the United States as an in-between and ultimately non-space for both Mexicans and also Mexican Americans is echoed at a number of points during the film. On meeting up with Luis Villareal once again, after his escape from Mister Sterling, Rafael laments his loneliness to the tramp: 'Hay mucha gente que no cree que en un país tan grande, con tanta gente por millones se puede uno sentir tan solo.' / 'There are many people who can't believe that in such a big country, with millions of people, you can feel so lonely.' Even more poignantly, to the strains of a melancholic trio on the jukebox, María del Consuelo mourns the loneliness and alienation that her status as a Mexican American bestows on her:

> Me siento muy sola y me da miedo [. . .] Es miedo de verme aquí sola toda la noche con mis pensamientos. [. . .] Yo no soy mexicana, yo nací aquí. Soy pocha. [. . .] A nosotros la raza no nos quiere. Y los bolillos ya viste.

> I feel very alone and afraid [. . .] Afraid of finding myself here alone all night with my thoughts. I'm not Mexican, I was born here. I'm a *pocha*. Mexicans [la *raza*] don't like us. And the whites, well you saw.

It is clear that *Espaldas mojadas* posits Rafael's situation as an illegal 'wetback' and María del Consuelo's as a Mexican American as vectors of the same phenomenon of existential alienation. Living on the border between cultures is a negatively charged experience, tantamount to not living at all. Or as Rafael puts it: 'En una rueda de soledad [. . .] Tú en el centro, y no tienes ni un ruido, ni una mirada. Nadie te ve, nadie te oye. ¡No existes!' / 'In a wheel of loneliness . . . You in the centre and you don't even have a sound or a look. No one sees you, no one hears you. You don't exist!' This conflation of the border with no existence finds its most resounding echo in the movie in the very image of the physical border itself, in which the Río Grande/Bravo is established literally as a space of death. The river as border becomes the final resting place of those Mexicans, like Felipe, who fail the attempted crossing with Rafael at the beginning of the film; it is also where Mister Sterling is shot by the same border guards after Rafael throws him in, seeking revenge.

To the degree that the border is equated with death in *Espaldas mojadas*, it is also the site of the law. This association is made forcefully at the opening of the film. As the voiceover states: 'El puente internacional [. . .] se hizo para pasar [. . .] pero sólo para aquéllos que han jurado decir la verdad, sólo la verdad y nada más que la verdad.'/ 'The international bridge [. . .] was made to cross [. . .] but only by those who have sworn to tell the truth, the whole truth and nothing but the truth.' At the denouement however, whilst its status as a site of death is doubly reinforced with the shooting of Mister Sterling, the border as law nevertheless undergoes a change in meaning that is consonant with the brand of cultural nationalism that *Espaldas mojadas* endorses. In the closing scenes, the border as overzealous site of law is tempered and becomes rather a site of justice. Although riven with moral ambiguity – who is ultimately responsible for the death of Mister Sterling, the unseen US border guard who fires the shot, or Rafael who has thrown him into the river and to his death? – this scene affords the Mexican viewer one final frisson of nationalistic pleasure. The blonde, northern oppressor gets what he deserves; the traditional values of a nostalgically imagined Mexico triumph over the cruelty of the greed-driven United States.

In this way, *Espaldas mojadas* ultimately emphasises a vision of the border as an absolute marker of difference, as a fixed, immutable line. The border as viewing position that is established in the opening moments – resolutely on the Mexican side of the border – is forcefully re-entrenched in the closing scenes. As Fein (1998) points out, the manifest cultural nationalism of Galindo's film is consonant with the official rhetoric of the Mexican state of this period. The strident anti-Yankee message that *Espaldas mojadas* espouses is fraught with irony and ambivalence. In pursuing a policy of accelerating capitalist expansion, the Mexican state came to rely increasingly on an alliance with the United States. In short, the border as dividing line between Mexico and the United States was in the process of becoming more permeable: a permeability that not only involved the flow of Mexican labour north of the border, but also the southward influx of capital and culture.

At the same time, however, as its modernising project parted company with the nationalistic tenets that underpinned a politics rooted in revolutionary rhetoric, the Mexican state sought to distract popular attention from this project (Fein 1998: 166). Distraction came in the realm of the mass media, and especially in border movies such as *Espaldas mojadas*. By reinstating the border as an absolute marker of difference, one that structured a nationalistic gaze, Galindo's film meshed with official rhetoric by averting the popular gaze from the border's changing status, thereby disavowing its permeability.

EL JARDÍN DEL EDÉN

If Galindo encountered problems with *Espaldas mojadas* which delayed the film's release by two years, as a director engaged in the on-going cultural process of border construction, María Novaro ran up against the *realpolitik* of the border whilst making her third feature *El Jardín del Edén*. In a number of interviews and reviews that appeared at the time of the Mexican release of Novaro's border movie, the director comments on the difficulties that she and her team encountered during filming in August–September 1993 on the San Diego/Tijuana border. 'Filmar en la línea fronteriza fue "como estar en la guerra"'/ 'Filming on the border line was like "being at war"', Novaro states dramatically in *El heraldo* (Navarrete 1994: 31).[9] More specifically, the war that Novaro invokes centred on the infamous Proposition 187, presented in late September 1994 by California State Governor, Pete Wilson:

> Dadas las circunstancias políticas que se viven en la frontera, concreta-
> mente en California, María externó que el rodaje fue muy complicado:
> 'Cuando mi hermana y yo iniciamos la preparación todo parecía muy
> fácil. Todo parecía perfecto, pero el segundo día de rodaje llegó una
> orden de Washington de que nos retirarían el apoyo. De momento no
> lo entendí, hasta después, que se recrudeció la tensión por la propuesta
> 187 y la política en contra de los mexicanos, lo cual nos obligó a realizar
> el rodaje un poco en contra de ellos.'

> Given the political circumstances that the border is living through,
> particularly in California, María stated that filming was very complicated.
> 'When my sister and I started on the preparation, everything seemed
> very easy. Everything seemed perfect, but on the second day of filming
> an order arrived from Washington withdrawing support from us. At that
> time I didn't understand it, until later, the tensions caused by Proposition
> 187 got worse and the politics against Mexicans, which forced us to film
> kind of against them.'

> (Quiroz Arroyo 1995: 29)

Coming in the wake of the increased militarisation of the border zone in the 1980s, Proposition 187 sought to tackle the question of illegal immigration on another front. Parading under the acronym SOS, or 'Save our State', Wilson's Proposition aimed to stem the 'flow' of undocumented immigrants across the border by denying them access to essential services including medical, welfare and educational provision. It set out to do so by making it a legal requirement for health and education professionals to denounce any such undocumented immi-grants to the authorities.[10] Given California's geographical location and Wilson's declaration of a 'state of emergency' in San Diego county, Proposition 187 had alarming resonances for the Latino community in general and the Mexican community in particular.

El Jardín del Edén was therefore made against the backdrop of what Mancillas *et al.* (1999: 111) describe as 'the supercharged atmosphere of the San Diego–Tijuana social and political scene of the late 1980s and early 1990's. For Novaro, this supercharged atmosphere meant that the border crossing necessitated by the making of her movie – containing scenes set on both sides of the border, and concerned with border crossing in both real and metaphorical senses – became a troubled and fraught experience.

Novaro's film not only ran into difficulties north of the border during its making. Unlike Galindo's film, which was essentially well received, critical reception of the finished product south of the border was hostile, particularly on the part of influential Mexican film critics such as Jorge Ayala Blanco and Carlos Bonfil. The latter, in particular, questioned Novaro's status as doyenne of Mexican cinema on the international film circuits and accused the director of casting an exoticising and voyeuristic gaze at the border in her film. Drawing a comparison between *El Jardín del Edén* and Novaro's internationally successful 1990 feature *Danzón*, Carlos Bonfil states:[11]

> La saturación de signos visuales a la vuelta de cada esquina pronto desemboca en catálogo de clichés de fotogenia exportable. *Danzón* triunfa en el extranjero como paradigma de cine tercermundista de calidad. Con *El Jardín del Edén* sucede algo parecido, sólo que el fenómeno se acentúa. El binomio de la complacencia sentimental [. . .] y la efusiones [sic] de una fotografía autohipnotizada termina por aplastar un guión de sí ya bastante confuso.

> The saturation of visual signs at the turn of every corner soon ends up as a catalogue of exportable photogenic clichés. *Danzón* triumphs abroad as a paradigm of third world, quality cinema. With *El Jardín del Edén* something similar happens, only the phenomenon gets accentuated. The combination of sentimental complacency [. . .] and the effusion of self-hypnotised photography ends up distorting what is already a pretty confused script.

> (Bonfil 1995: 43)

At the risk of falling under the spell of 'una fotografía autohipnotizada', I want to pick up on Bonfil's comments as a starting point to explore the status and significance of the border in *El Jardín del Edén*. Specifically, I wish to examine two key elements of Bonfil's statement: first, his sense of the confused script; and second, his distaste for the proliferation of visual signs in the film.[12] It is my contention that the dramatic tension in Novaro's border movie is crystallised in the way in which it stages a conflict between the two elements that Bonfil identifies, namely narrative structure and visuality. On the one hand, therefore, I want to take issue with Bonfil in order to argue that *El Jardín del Edén*, in keeping with the border movie genre more generally, is a very tightly structured film indeed. Moreover, as is also consistent with the genre, and as we saw in the case of *Espaldas mojadas*, there is a link between the film's structure and the political conditions prevalent on the border at the time of its making that led to the accentuation of the border's physical presence as an absolute trope of difference.

Whilst it contains many elements that conform to the genre, at the same time, *El Jardín del Edén* parts company in significant ways with the cinematic tradition to which it belongs. Not least, as the case of *Espaldas mojadas* exemplifies, the border movie conventionally centres its narrative on a single male protagonist. Women feature as mere triggers to the plot: Rafael is forced to flee because of a relationship with a woman in Mexico; Margarita facilitates the crossing; and the 'rescue' of María del Consuelo gives him reason to return to Mexico. By contrast, the single, male-centred narrative is replaced in *El Jardín del Edén* by a multiple, woman-centred border narrative. Indeed, Novaro's film focuses primarily upon the way in which three women's lives loosely interweave in Tijuana: the North American Jane (Renée Coleman), in search of the exotic; the recently widowed Serena (Gabriela Roel), looking for a fresh start with her three children; the Chicana artist Elizabeth (Rosario Sagrav), in town to put on an exhibition of her work. The women's lives become interlinked by the presence of the Zacatecan, Felipe (Bruno Bichir), whom, after the violent failure of his first attempt to cross the border, Jane smuggles across, along with Serena's teenage son Julián. The plot, then, revolves around the border crossing, Serena and Elizabeth's search for Julián, and the deportation of both the latter and Felipe. Certainly, the narrative focus of *El Jardín del Edén* is diffuse. However, despite its multiple protagonists and, at times, meandering narrative, insofar as the film's plot is significantly perfectly circular, it conforms to its audience's generic expectations. As in *Espaldas mojadas*, this circularity becomes evident if we focus closely on the opening and closing sequences.

THE CIRCULAR BORDER

That Novaro ran into difficulties whilst filming on the border at a time in which it was in the process of being fortified, is registered in the high visual profile accorded to the physical frontier throughout the film. The opening of *El Jardín del Edén* presents the viewer with the spectacle of the border as seen from the Mexican side through a pair of binoculars. We learn that the character whose viewpoint is presented here is Felipe who, in the course of the film, is to cross the border in the boot of Jane's car only to be caught by the *migra* and deported back to Mexico. The film then cuts to Jane, whom we see arriving in Tijuana. A tracking shot follows Jane as she passes along the pavement, at which point a number of unobtrusive, but symbolically charged objects are visually fore-grounded: namely a row of birdcages, street musicians and Mexican curios set out on the pavement.

The closing sequences replicate the opening in reverse order. In the penultimate sequence, we see Jane, who is about to travel further south, at the bus station in Tijuana. Her exoticising gaze, one that we have witnessed throughout the film, fixes upon the Tabascan woman with birdcages strapped to her back. These cages are a clear visual echo of those that pass in front of the camera in the opening sequence in which Jane's screen presence is established. The film then cuts to Felipe, who stands at the border gazing fixedly ahead, *carnalillo* (buddy) at his side. Again, Felipe's location at the border mirrors his position in the opening sequence. The only differences here are in Felipe's physical appearance. With his hair gelled back, he has lost the innocent appearance of the country boy of the beginning. Like Rafael at the end of *Espaldas mojadas*, who has mastered a few words of English and is shown offering guidance to fellow wetbacks, Felipe has been disabused of his naivety and is wise now to the sophistications of border culture. Also, where in the opening sequence the border is figured as the corrugated iron fence viewed by night, in the closing scene Felipe views the border fence that runs up to the beach giving onto the Pacific Ocean and he does so by day and with the naked eye.

On one level then, the spectator is presented with a perfectly circular narrative structure that conforms to generic expectations. As far as coherence is concerned, narratives do not come much tighter than when they are circular, and their closure complete. But, given that Novaro's film reworks the genre in other ways, most notably in the multiple female protagonists, what are we to make of this narrative conformity? The tropes of repetition that inhere in Novaro's film and implicate its two central characters can be understood in the light of Roger Bartra's introductory comments to the work of the performance artist and writer Guillermo Gómez-Peña. Bartra has the following to say about the Mexico/US border:

> When we approach a border, the first thing that we worry about is how to cross it. A border tends to be a wall we can only cross if we have the necessary documents; it is a filter that is supposed to purify the passing flux. We can also approach a border wanting to transgress it, to cross it illegally, and to violate its rules. Whether we approach submissively with our passport and visa in hand, or as 'wetbacks' who scurry silently, protected by the night, the border stands waiting for us to cross, or to detain us [. . .] The border is a line that demands straightforward behavior; a red alarm lights if we 'approximate it tangentially' (as in *irse por la tangente*).[13]
>
> (Barta in Gómez-Peña 1993: 11)

Within the overall structure of *El Jardín del Edén*, both Felipe and Jane are characters who conform, albeit in different ways, to the border's demand for 'straightforward behaviour': behaviour that is vigorously upheld by Galindo's film. Felipe is cinematically descended from Rafael and represents the eternal 'wetback'. If we cast our gaze back to the opening scene, we will recall that the border – i.e. the corrugated iron fence – is presented from Felipe's viewpoint and, most importantly, through binoculars. This binocular viewpoint at once draws Felipe (and the viewer) closer to the border whilst at the same time underlining this character's physical distance from his object of vision. In suggesting both distance and proximity, the binocular vision in this opening scene is an effective device for articulating a notion of the border as an object of desire for Felipe. Or more to the point, this opening sequence articulates Felipe's desire for what lies on the other side: his own Garden of Eden.

Despite having been brutally attacked and deported from the United States in the course of the film, the closing scene suggests that the border, and what lies on the other side, continues to present the same allure for Felipe as he casts his gaze longingly across to the 'other side'. It suggests, as Carlos Monsiváis puts it, that he is one of the hundreds of thousands of Mexicans, Salvadorans and Guatemalans who:

> Year after year, in never diminished numbers [. . .] hurl themselves toward that obsessive goal (a modernity that is rooted in employment). They defy police brutality, the network of guides know as *polleros* (poulterers) who deceive and defraud undocumented workers, their peasant attachment to the soil, their feelings of inadequacy – cultural, linguistic, and technological. And in spite of everything, they persist.
>
> (Monsiváis 1997: 117)

Just as Felipe's persistent relationship to the border does not alter in any significant sense in the course of the film, Jane's attitude remains similarly static. If Eden for Felipe exists north of the border in the form of a modernity 'rooted in employment', Jane, as his mirror inverse, crosses the border into Mexico in search of the exotic and primitive. In fact, the Felipe/Jane dyad, and the quest narratives associated with each character, is underpinned by a series of binary oppositions including: man/woman; blonde/brown; south/north; poor/rich; work/pleasure and so on. Moreover, the desire of each for the other (side) is presented in overtly specular terms. Both Felipe and Jane are figured throughout the film as subjects of the gaze, whose object is in each case, what lies on the other side of the border. But to be the subject of vision – a spectator – implies a position from which that subject looks. In the case of both Felipe and Jane the position that each occupies is determined by the fixed co-ordinates of the border, which end up reproducing a reified notion of the other.

The specularity and fixed co-ordinates of Jane's search comes into sharp focus in the scene in which she encounters the Huavi women at work in the kitchen of the restaurant 'El Pescado Mojado'. Significantly, Jane's gaze alights upon these women as she opens a curtain, the camera presenting us with a point-of-view shot in the form of a slow-motion, idealised and romanticised vision of the women at work amongst their rustic cooking utensils. The curtains are deeply emblematic of the specularity and theatricality of this scene. They structure a stark spectator/spectacle binary, whereby Jane occupies the former, powerful position of subject of the gaze; the Huavi women the latter, powerless position of object of the gaze. It is worth noting that Jane is presented to us as the character who is able to cross the border with most ease and fluidity, even when 'violating its rules' when she crosses with Felipe and Julián in the boot of her car. And yet, the scene in 'El

Pescado Mojado', echoed in the slow-motion of Jane's vision of the Tabascan woman in the closing scene, bespeaks her ultimate failure to cross the border metaphorically and thereby part company with her own preconceived notions of Mexico as a 'Paradise Lost' (neatly figured in the scene immediately following that in 'El Pescado Mojado', in which the camera lingers over Jane's personal library, which includes Milton's text).

The circular narrative that I have traced can be associated with a particular attitude towards the border, one shared by Felipe and Jane and one which conforms to its binary logic and, importantly, to the conventions of the border movie genre. Borders frame national and cultural identities and, as such, their logic is predicated on the trope of difference: they define what is Mexico and what is not; what is the United States and what is not. The drive to heighten the border's visual presence as an absolute maker of difference – both diegetically and extra-diegetically, insofar as the film figures the militarisation of the border zone on the increase at the time of the film's making – is testimony to the profound anxiety, emanating from both sides of the border that subtends the potential erasure of that difference.[14] The extra-diegetic militarisation of the border in the 1980s culminating in Proposition 187, including the erection of corrugated iron fences (such as the 14 miles that run along the Tijuana/San Diego interface[15]), represents an insistence on the border's status as material object in the face of the ample proof of its permeability. Indeed, the border as an overwhelmingly physical and visually potent presence punctuates the whole film (starting with the first scene), whereby the border constantly reinstates itself into the viewer's field of vision as a fixed, immutable line. (When not visually represented in the film, it is never-theless frequently thematised aurally, through the menacing sound of border patrol helicopters.)

My point, in other words, is that a parallel can be established between the circular, closed nature of the film narrative as associated with Jane and Felipe; an approach to the border as an indelible marker of absolute difference between two geographical/cultural spaces; and the border-as-frame that determines who is looking at whom and how. These parallels are bound up with questions of visuality in that, as subjects of the gaze, neither Felipe nor Jane is able to transgress the fixed viewing co-ordinates established by the border-as-frame that determine the way in which each approaches the object of the gaze: the (exotic) Other. In this sense, it is important to underline that it is through the narratives of Felipe and Jane that *El Jardín del Edén* conforms to the generic conventions of the border movie so powerfully established in *Espaldas mojadas*. As Maciel and García-Acevedo (1998: 153) point out, one of the most important aspects of genre movies is that 'they contribute to the perpetuation of the status quo', which as we saw in Galindo's film, meshed with official state rhetoric. In what follows, however, I will suggest how Novaro's genre movie may indeed challenge the hegemonic status quo that determines relations between the two nations, and that this challenge revolves precisely around a more critical understanding of the border as specular frame and its attendant viewing positions.

THE SPECULAR BORDER

Having set up a link between Felipe and Jane's circular and generically conventional narratives and the conditions prevalent on the border at the time of the
film's making, it is helpful return to Bonfil's critique of Novaro's films. It will
be recalled that Bonfil complains 'the saturation of visual signs at the turn of
every corner soon ends up being a catalogue of exportable photogenic clichés'
(1995: 43). It is in the film's emphasis on the visual, however, that Novaro breaks
with the conventions of the border movie genre. Even as the border is staged as
a physically potent presence within the film – one that determines looking – the
potency of its visibility is undermined by the way in which the film plays on and
plays up the specularity of the border. To see how this might work, let us refocus
our gaze on the binoculars in the opening scene. If the opening sequence serves
to articulate Felipe's desire to cross over to '*el otro lado*', and is also the first of
many instances in which the border makes its presence felt as a tangibly physical
site/sight, then the binocular vision also lends itself to other readings.

From the start, an element of the carnivalesque is introduced in the film's
representation of the border. Within the context of the border movie genre,
Felipe's high vantage point and the binoculars themselves are determined by the
connotations implicit in the surveyed/surveyor binary, whereby Felipe would
conventionally occupy the former position. The power associated with the position
of the surveyor, it will be recalled, is neatly figured in *Espaldas mojadas*, in the
scene in which Rafael crouches beside a rock on which are inscribed the English
words 'God is watching'. The rock and Rafael are visually juxtaposed with the
border watchtower, from which the omnipotent guards survey all below them.
That Felipe is the surveyor suggests a reversal of sorts. According to the logic of
carnival, the reversal is, of course, temporary.[16] Nevertheless Felipe's momentary
positioning as powerful subject of the gaze and the subtending irony associated
with his position, serve to draw the viewer's attention to the very specularity of
the scene.

The specularity of the scene is reinforced by the kind of visual experience
that viewing through binoculars affords which, in the words of Fernando Celin
(1995: 7), 'produce imágenes aplandas, sin una referencia de espacio'/ 'produces
flat images, with no reference to space'. By displacing the illusion of three-
dimensionality and replacing it with an avowedly one-dimensional image, this
opening scene dramatises the border's status as image, precisely as visual representation. That the border is associated with visuality is further underscored by
a form of *mise-en-abîme* whereby, as spectators, our looking is foregrounded not
only in the presentation of Felipe's binocular vision, but also in the fact that the
figures he views on the border are also engaged in the act of looking: the first
figure perched on top of the fence is clearly looking over to the other side; another
at ground level is spying voyeuristically through a peep-hole in the fence.
Moreover, what Felipe sees from the vantage point of a balcony is presented to us
as pure spectacle: as his binoculars alight upon a group of Mexicans on 'this side',

one falls over, eliciting laughter from both the spectators on the balcony and the other performers on the scene. This performance is completed by the US border guards who faithfully follow the script of an everyday border dialogue – 'adiós amigos, see you tomorrow' – this bilingual exchange suggesting that this scene is played out on a regular basis between actors on both sides of the dividing line.

This opening sequence, then, promotes two notions of the border which are played out and off against one another throughout the film. The first is that of the border as an absolute dividing line that gives rise accordingly to absolute and monolithic definitions of identity and is associated with the characters Felipe and Jane. In the perspective of Roger Bartra, it involves seeing the border as a line that 'demands straightforward behaviour' (Gómez-Peña 1993: 11). The second notion is that of the border itself as image, as the site of specular performance. If the border is the site at which identity comes into sharp relief, I want to suggest, taking my cue from Bartra, that *El Jardín del Edén* 'approximates the border tangentially' by staging questions of identity precisely in terms of an engagement with issues of vision and visuality. In what follows, I briefly sketch out how various characters within the film engage with visual representation before finally focusing on a key moment in the film in which issues of the border, visual representation (both filmic and photographic) and identity converge. The point at which they converge is the frame.

With the exception of Felipe,[17] the remaining principal characters within the film engage in some capacity with visual images: Serena sets up in Tijuana as a professional portrait photographer; her son Felipe is to be seen throughout the film, camera in hand, making images of the border culture that he discovers in his new environment; finally, Elizabeth, the Chicana artist, has come to Tijuana to mount an exhibition of her work, which is very clearly concerned with a search for her Mexican roots and identity. Given that three of the five central characters are so overtly engaged in the production of images, it is perhaps unsurprising that, to return to Bonfil, the film is 'saturated with visual signs around every corner'. But, beyond merely stating the dominant role accorded to the visual throughout the film, just what is at stake in this insistent foregrounding of the visual domain?

To address this question, we must focus on the scene that occurs just after Jane introduces Elizabeth to Margarita Luna. We find Jane and Elizabeth looking through a book of photographs by the Mexican photographer Graciela Iturbide. Jane asks Elizabeth, 'Which one's you?', at which Elizabeth points to Iturbide's famous image, 'Nuestra señora de las iguanas' (Our Lady of the Iguanas). Jane's question, 'Which one's you?' emblematises in a straightforward manner the way in which cultural representations frame and produce identity through processes of (non-)identification. This particular iconic photographic image belongs to a series of images that Iturbide made in Juchitán and is imbued with a set of cultural signifiers, including Mexico as a rural, indigenous, southern, matriarchal entity. In order to understand this scene, it is important to view it within the context of an event that takes place just before Jane and Elizabeth sit down to flick through

Figure 6.3 El Jardín del Edén (María Novaro, 1994)

Source: IMCINE

Figure 6.4 El Jardín del Edén (María Novaro, 1994)

Source: IMCINE

Iturbide's photographs and which is a more buried trope of visual performativity within the film.

The film cuts from the restaurant to the 'Nuestra señora de las iguanas' scenes via a medium close-up shot of the bare, tattooed back of an incidental character, a cholo who then walks forward and turns to pose for a photograph with two small girls in front of a car. This incidental scene has no significance to the film's plot as such. As an unremarkable, if curious detail, however, it provides a potential clue to an understanding of the way in which *El Jardín de Edén* foregrounds issues of visuality and performativity, which are in turn linked to the theme of the border. To the photographically sensitive eye, the *cholo*'s tattooed back is a clear visual citation of another Iturbide photograph, 'The Frontier/Tijuana'. That is to say, the film performs this particular photograph. This is certainly not the only visual performance within the film. Others include Elizabeth watching Guillermo Gómez-Peña's 'Border Brujo' on video and her own performance with Maragarita Luna of Frida Kahlo's *Las dos Fridas* (1939). However, my interest here turns precisely on 'The Frontier/Tijuana' as photographic image and the way it emblematises other such visual performances that punctuate the film.

One possible reading of the inclusion of this photographic detail within the context of both this sequence and the film as border movie might revolve around a notion of the heterogeneity of Mexican cultural identity. That is to say, if

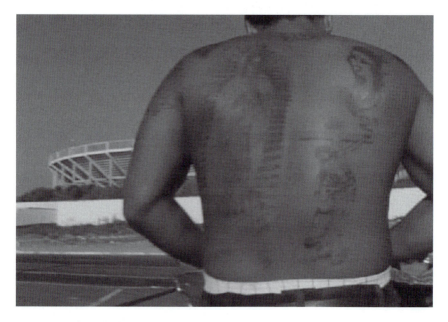

Figure 6.5 El Jardín del Edén (María Novaro, 1994)

Source: IMCINE

168

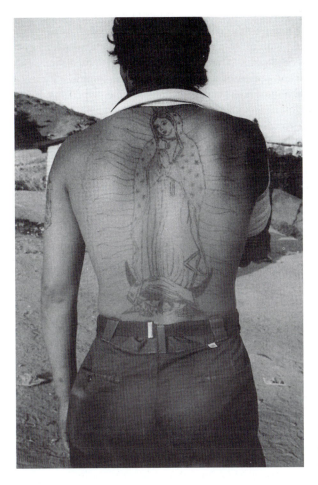

Figure 6.6
'The Border/La
Frontera' by Graciela
Iturbide (1990)

'Nuestra señora de las iguanas' signifies Southern identity, then 'The Frontier/
Tijuana' is imbued, amongst other things, with 'Northernness'. Moreover, as the
photograph's title both literally, and typographically, implies, the image represents
precisely border identity. The inclusion of two such signifiers of Mexicanness
within the same sequence counteracts any notion of monolithic Mexican identity
that the pervasive visible presence of the border might promote. This photograph
and its cultural connotations furthermore mesh with a host of other elements
within the film – from soundtrack (i.e. border music 'Hey baby, qué pasó'[18])
to Spanglish signs ('telephono') – that function as an insistent reminder as to the
permeability of the border.

The '*mise-en-film*'[19] as performance of Iturbide's photograph 'Frontier/
Mexico', however, is more complex, and this complexity turns not so much on
the content of the two 'photographs', as their form. Or, to put it another way,

169

not so much on what we see, as how we see it. 'Nuestra señora de las iguanas' is presented to the viewer *qua* photograph, that is, as a bounded, framed entity (i.e. the image is contained within the photographic frame itself, which in turn is framed within the pages of a book). 'The Frontier/Tijuana', on the other hand, is 'released' from its frame and presented as pure performance. James C. Faris has the following to say about photographs and their frames, which he claims:

> [W]hether still or moving – are bounded. That is, they are framed. As such, they inject another space – the limits, the edges – proscriptions, prohibitions of the image. These cannot be treated as arbitrary nor as artefact of technique. They define what is to be photograph what is not. They deny (what was not in the photograph).
>
> (Faris 1992: 255)

I would like to propose that for the 'photograph/frame' configuration in Faris's statement, we could equally substitute 'nation/border'. That is to say, the nation as a framed entity injects another space: the limits, the edges of the nation. It is these limits that *El Jardín del Edén* explores. However, the film is not concerned so much with the border as physical object, nor indeed with the traditional narratives associated with the border movie as a film genre (although elements of both – in the narratives of Felipe and Jane, and in the way in which the border is constantly reinstated as visible, physical presence – are present in the film). Rather, the limits with which the film is concerned are more accurately emblematised in the 'unframing' of the suggestively entitled 'The Frontier/Tijuana'.

This photograph has particular connotations within the context of this border movie. The photograph 'The Frontier/Tijuana' is an image about cultural identity – the tattoo inscribed upon the subject's back represents the Virgin of Guadalupe, symbol of Mexican national identity *par excellence*. If frames and borders contain and confine, then the unframing of this particular image is a gesture towards flux and fluidity, towards a notion of Mexican cultural identity as in-process, as performance. But gestures, unlike statements, are implicitly strategic. That the unframing is strategic cannot but be the case in the performance of 'The Frontier/ Tijuana'. This photograph is, after all, performed within the context of a film, which, in turn, is itself a series of framed photographic images. The point, in other words, is that there is no getting away from the contingency of the border/frame. The performance of this photograph within the film, however, is concerned with something more than a 'fotogenia exportable' predicated on a 'saturación de signos visuales', as articulated by Carlos Bonfil. It is also more than a gesture towards the freeplay of signifiers: in 'photography *mise-en-film*', the frame is after all emphatically always-already reinscribed by the medium itself.

I would suggest, in conclusion, what this something more might be, by returning firstly to Roger Bartra's idea of the border as 'a line that demands straightforward behavior; a red alarm lights if we "approximate it tangentially" (as in *irse por la tangente*)'. Bartra's transgressive notion of 'tangential approximation' finds resonance in Philippe Dubois' essay, 'Photography Mise-en-Film' in which he advocates a form of criticism based on a the notion of anamorphosis:

> To 'anamorphose' different image forms (a mobile point of view, one that hinges on moving) is often more penetrating and surprising than to observe prudently from the front, where though the image may appear to be fully visible, it also forms a screen (a static point of view, that of someone who does not see what is taking place behind him or her).
>
> The thing is to practice this kind of oblique, sideways approach deliberately. We might begin with this simple idea: that the best *lens* on photography will be found outside photography. Thus to grasp something of photography we must enter through the door of cinema.
>
> (Dubois 1995: 153)

To extrapolate: to grasp something of María Novaro's film, we must enter through the door of photography. For by entering through the door of photography it may be possible to avoid an immobile point of view, one that hinges on stasis and which in *El Jardín del Edén* is associated with the circular narratives of Felipe and Jane and each character's immobility to see the Other from anywhere other than 'prudently from the front'. To extrapolate further: to grasp something of the representation of the border, we must enter through the notion of the frame. The un/reframing of 'The Frontier/Tijuana' as photograph *mise-en-film*, on one level, functions as a structural *mise-en-abîme* and, as such, signals the status of *El Jardín del Edén* as (just) another discourse involved – like the border itself – in the framing of cultural identities. Beyond the self-reflexivity of the *mise-en-abîme*, however, by making the spectator aware of the logic of the border-as-frame, the film contains the potential, if not to erase the hierarchies which the border structures, then at least to formulate a tangential approach, one that might just cause the red alarm to sound.

171

AFTERWORD

In February 2001, incumbent presidents Vicente Fox and George W. Bush met at Fox's Guanajuato hacienda to discuss Mexico–US relations generally, and immigration policy in particular. The precise details of their negotiations remain unclear. Nevertheless, both leaders suggested that 'they were considering plans to "regularize" the status of undocumented workers currently living in the United States and bring additional Mexican guestworkers to the United States to fill labor shortages in the service sector' (Waslin 2001: 1). Seven months later, immediately after the terrorist attacks on the World Trade Center and Pentagon, legal border crossings between the two countries were dramatically suspended for 48 hours, preventing people and goods from entering or leaving the United States.

The closure of the border dramatically underlines the tension between, on the one hand, the border's potency as sheer material presence and site of absolute difference and, on the other, its status as celebrated signifier of hybridity. In the wake of the attacks, the border, inevitably, reopened. However, it is one thing to hold up the border as hybrid symbol *par excellence*; its material reality is another matter altogether. In short, the border's metaphorical status must always be anchored in and set against an understanding of its material reality. So, for example, most recently plans have been mooted to erect more protective fences and security at crossing points has been stepped up, stemming from a fear that terrorists may take advantage of the network of *coyotes* (or people smugglers) that operate there. As we saw in Chapter 6, the *realpolitik* of the border zone throws into sharp relief national tensions that have constantly been registered in film culture, from the revolution through the Bracero Program, to Proposition 187, and now seems set to refract the twenty-first century 'war on terror'.

Cinema's status as a quintessentially modern mode of representation with the potential to reach a mass audience means that the complexity of the inter-relationships that obtain between cinema, modernity and national culture cannot be overemphasised. As we saw in Chapter 3, cinema's gathering of community not only provides fertile ground for a study of nation as forged by spectatorship; detailed study of its texts can also afford an insight into how the practices of looking partici-pated in the process of modernisation. However, the border, and by extension the border movie, is a powerful instance of the way in which considerations of the national inevitably collide with issues of transnationalism.

Neither should we underestimate the ways in which Mexican culture and cinema are caught up in broader, transnational configurations of culture and power. The border is but one salient example that not only illuminates this dynamic, but also underlines Mexico's unique geo-political location to the south of the world's only remaining superpower. If the border movie as generic convention brings this dynamic into sharp focus, an understanding of the development of Mexican national cinema cannot be divorced from that of its northern neighbour. As the case study of Arcady Boytler's *La mujer del puerto* and its remake in Chapter 1 demonstrates, not only is Hollywood an important factor in any consideration of the Mexican cinema, but also this relationship must, in turn, be viewed in the light of broader transnational flows of culture and power and, moreover, in wider historical context stretching back to before the advent of the moving image.

La mujer del puerto represents a film that almost, but not quite, measured up to the international standards set by Hollywood. Made at a turning point in cinematic history, just as the national cinema's industrial bases were gaining solidity, Boytler's film continues to be evoked with nostalgia. Yet, as we have seen, if the Mexican cinema enjoyed a Golden Age during which its productions appealed to national and international audiences alike, those films that have been consecrated as popular classics are precisely those that focus on local themes and issues: the revolution; rural, folkloric and indigenous Mexico, etc. In short, the classics of this cinema are, to return to Alan Knight, those that deal in the idiom of the 'peculiarly' Mexican. Nowhere is this more evident than in the revolution as epoch-defining historical event that spawned multiple movies that participated in the process of installing the myth of the conflict in popular memory.

Nevertheless, as Catherine Russell (1999: 222) cautions, there is a difference between 'the ability to *see film* as cultural representation as opposed to *seeing through film*'. This difference is as fundamental to an analysis of films of revolution as it is to the transhistorical exploration of the representation of the internal Other in the Mexican cinema, the subject of Chapter 5. Russell's insights are, however, a guiding principle throughout the chapters that comprise this book. To note that this national cinema's (trans)national appeal resides in its emphasis on the local, the 'peculiarly' Mexican, is not the same as saying that this cinema offers a transparent window on Mexico. Rather, it is essential to view film as cultural representation and therefore to focus at once on the audio-visual narrative strategies by which film makes its meanings, and, at the same time, the historical contexts that shape these meanings. Here again it is important to stress the long view. A cultural-historicist approach to film is not only attentive to the immediate circumstances that give rise to a production, it is also alert to pre-cinematic structures, as we saw in the discussion of the specificities of spectatorship in Chapter 3.

Since the nostalgic days of the Golden Age when 'all the people' flocked to the movie theatres, the Mexican cinema has never regained its national audience.

Despite diminished viewing figures that have gone hand in hand with a retreat to the international art-house circuits, Mexican cinema nevertheless retains its ability to capture the national imagination. This capacity was manifest recently in two films that prompted calls for censorship and, in so doing, drew unprecedented numbers of viewers to the Republic's multiplexes.

El crimen del padre Amaro (The Crime of Father Amaro, Carlos Carrera, 2002), with its focus on an affair between a Catholic priest and a 16-year-old girl, was roundly condemned by right-leaning groups for its 'blasphemous' representation of the church as an institution. The controversy failed, however, to prevent the film's release and its wide reporting not only ensured that tickets to Carrera's film sold out on its opening weekend, but also that it went on to become the nation's biggest grossing movie at the box-office.

The other film, *La ley de Herodes* (Herod's Law, Luis Estrada, 1999), a hilarious political satire set in 1949, launched a direct attack on the corrupt capacity of the PRI to perpetuate itself in power. Drafted in by the party hierarchy to take over the mayoralty of the dusty backwater San Pedro de los Saguaros, comical non-entity Juan Vargas (Damián Alcázar) ventriloquises the political discourse of Miguel Alemán's regime, at first promising to bring 'modernity and social justice' to the village's indigenous inhabitants. Good intentions soon give way to 'Herod's law' of the film's title: 'O te chingas, o te jodes', which loosely (and politely) trans-lates as the law of survival of the fittest. Like the only other direct indictment of the PRI in national cinematic history, *La sombra del caudillo* (The Shadow of the Caudillo, Julio Bracho, 1960) – a film that deals with the violent paroxysms of the party of state's birth in the 1920s – *La ley de Herodes* at first struggled to gain commercial release. But if the regime successfully managed to censor Bracho's film for an astonishing thirty years, even its best efforts could not prevent its eventual release, for by 1999 Mexico was already experiencing what Matthew Guttman (2004) terms the 'romance of democracy'. And, as we saw in Chapter 4, with growing political openness came the demise of one-party rule in the presidential elections of 2000.

This is not to claim, as some commentators excitedly announced at the release of *La ley de Herodes*, a direct correlation between film and social reality. To put it bluntly, the PRI did not fall from power thanks to Estrada's film. Rather it is simply to assert the ongoing importance of retaining the national as a conceptual framework for the study of cinematic, and other forms of visual culture. A film such as *La ley de Herodes* demands to be anchored in the 'peculiarities' of the socio-historical context of its making.

The aim of *Mexican National Cinema* then has been to offer a selective account of the peculiarities of this regional cinema which is at once attentive to the speci-ficities of the national without, however, sacrificing the transhistorical and transnational contexts in which it is located. At the same time, this book has stressed another form of specificity – namely, medium specificity and the way in which this national cinema figures and reconfigures its subjects audio-visually. By placing an emphasis on practices of cinematic looking, both on what is seen and heard and how it is seen and heard, *Mexican National Cinema* subscribes to the notion that practices of looking are bound up with historical configurations of knowledge and power. Just looking, as Russell might say, is never *just* looking.

NOTES

INTRODUCTION

1 The *pachuco* is named after his trademark baggy zoot suit and is associated above all with the hybrid identity of Mexican Americans. On the origins of the word *pelado*, see Pilcher (2001: 8).

2 Throughout this book, I shall cite film titles in the original Spanish followed by the established translation, where such exists, or my own in the case of those films that do not have an English-language title. Similarly, when citing critical material in Spanish, I have opted to provide the Spanish followed by my own English translation.

3 For surveys of scholarship in the field, see Burton-Carvajal (1998a, 1998b), De la Vega (1994), García and Maciel (2001).

4 See the Bibliography for full details of Monsiváis's extensive body of work.

5 Mora brought out a second edition in 1989 and as I write, Macfarland Publishers are announcing a forthcoming new edition, spanning 1896–2004.

6 A version of *Mexican Cinema* was originally published in French to accompany a major retrospective exhibition devoted to the Mexican Cinema held at the Centre Pompidou, Paris from October 1992 to February 1993. It was revised, expanded, and translated into English by Ana M. López.

7 Owing to constraints of space, I have limited the items listed in this section to monographs. It would be an oversight, however, to omit to mention here the pioneering work of Ana M. López and Julianne Burton-Carvajal, whose research on Latin American cinema I draw upon throughout the body of this volume.

8 This is not to deny or downplay later periods in cultural and film history, which will equally be the subject of the chapters that follow. However, it is my belief that an understanding of the revolution as a pivotal event and process in Mexican history – including its precursors and aftermath – merits special attention here, for it sets the agenda for an understanding of cultural politics in the twentieth century.

9 In the compelling introduction to *Through the Kaleidoscope: The Experience of Modernity in Latin America*, Vivian Schelling points out that whilst historians generally connect modernity as a 'historical period of categorisation' to developments of the fifteenth and sixteenth centuries, 'it is the period of Enlightenment in the eighteenth century which is seen as crystallising different dimensions of modernity into a definite shape, what Habermas referred to as the "project of modernity"' (Schelling 2000: 4).

10 See Magali Carrera's excellent *Imagining Identity in New Spain* (2003) for a stimulating discussion of visual culture, race and the body politic in New Spain.

11 I use the dates 1910–20 for convenience only. I am, however, aware of the problems that surround the periodisation of the revolution: 'That "event" is variously described as having occurred between 1910 and 1917, 1910 and 1920, or 1910 and 1940, and the debates about how to periodize the revolution not only highlight its complexity as

a historical process during which popular resistance figured significantly, but also point to another process simultaneous in space and time: revolutionary and postrevolutionary state formation' (Joseph and Nugent 1994: 5).

12 See Garner (2001) for a profile of Porfirio Díaz.

13 In Obregón's case, it was a Catholic activist who gunned him down on 17 July 1928 in protest at the strong anti-clerical stance of the post-revolutionary regime.

14 As a political party, the PRI came into existence in the first instance in 1929 when it was known as the Partido Nacional Revolucionario (PNR); it became the Partido Revolucionario Mexicano (PRM) in 1938 before being re-baptised as the PRI in 1946.

15 See Castañeda (2000) on how Mexican presidents were chosen.

16 See especially the invaluable work of Ricardo Pérez Montfort (1994) on the emergence of national stereotypes.

17 See Koonings and Kruijt (1999) for a comparative study of political violence in Latin America. Knight's essay in this volume is, as always, particularly illuminating and makes a distinction between what he terms 'cupular' violence, which in Mexico, by comparison with say Argentina and Chile, remained low, yet nevertheless co-existed with violence and repression at a grass-roots level. Significantly, since the end of the PRI's hold over politics in 2000, Mexico's legacy of political violence has reasserted itself forcefully on the national agenda. In July 2001, the secret archives on politically motivated disappearances were opened to the Comisión Nacional de Derechos Humanos (CNDH, National Human Rights Commission) who calculate that 686 people were abducted, with a high incidence of disappearance from the state of Guerrero in the southwest of the Republic.

18 Himself a Spanish émigré, García Riera comments on the influx of Spaniards to Mexico between 1941 and 1945 (1998: 141–4). Chilean director Miguel Littín fled the 1973 coup that overthrew Salvador Allende to Mexico, where, in 1975 he made *Actas de Marusia* (Letters from Marusia), a film that won acclaim for the Mexican film industry. See Yankelevich (2002) on Mexico as a refuge for exiles.

19 Schnitman (1984: 3) divides the Latin American domestic film markets into three groups according to size: Argentina, Brazil and Mexico are the largest; Chile, Colombia, Peru and Venezuela are classed 'intermediate markets'; whilst the remaining countries are small. The size of the domestic film markets correlates with the relative strength of production. In this study, I am largely concerned with comparisons with Spanish-speaking regions of Latin America. I shall, however, make reference to Portuguese-speaking Brazilian cinema where relevant.

20 See Collier (1986) on the life, music and times of Gardel; Luciano Monteagudo and Verónica Bucich on Gardel and the first sound cinema; and Shaw (2003) on the *chanchada*.

21 See López (1994, 2000a) for detailed discussion of the continental impact of *Allá en el Rancho Grande*.

22 See the meticulous work of Seth Fein for detailed analysis of the relationship between the US and Mexican film industries in this period.

23 For more on the Ariel, including a history of the award and previous winners, see the Academia Mexicana de Artes y Ciencias Cinematográficas website at www.academiamexicana.com/.

24 Mora's *Mexican Cinema* (1989) provides a particularly useful overview of union issues in the Mexican cinema. Mora describes the schisms that took place in the mid-1940s as the 'skilled' members of the STIC – actors, directors of photography and directors – sought to form their own branch. Given that all workers in the film industry belonged to the STIC, from ticket-sellers to directors, with the former obviously by far in the majority, the minority skilled workers felt that their concerns were in danger of being overlooked. 'Thus, after a great deal of bitter recriminations and some threat of violence,

the Sindicato de Trabajadores de la Producción Cinematográfica (STPC), incorporating the seceding sections from the STIC was officially recognized [. . .] on March 14, 1945' (Mora 1989: 70).

25 See Anne Rubenstein's (2001) excellent essay on Infante's funeral in 1957, which provoked an outbreak of mass mourning from amongst the popular classes, culminating in a riot in which at least 140 people were injured.

26 See De la Vega (1999) for a detailed discussion.

27 López (1994: 10) explains how, in an attempt to avoid ever-increasing costs at home, Mexican filmmakers looked abroad for cheaper alternatives. With an established tradition of cultural exchange between the two countries (Cuban music and stars Ninón Sevilla and María Antonieta Pons were already popular) and lower production costs, in the 1950s, Cuba became Mexico's favoured co-production partner.

28 See Burton (1986) and Martin (1997) for detailed accounts of the New Latin American Cinema movements. See Guneratne and Dissanayake (2003) for a re-evaluation of the history and theory of Third Cinema.

29 See Cockcroft (1998: 254) for estimated figures for the dead, wounded and imprisoned. Films that deal with the student movement and political violence are scarce. In 1968, Leobardo López Aretche made *El grito*, a black-and-white documentary, but this film was never screened commercially. Jorge Fons's feature, *Rojo amanecer* (1989), set entirely in an apartment overlooking La Plaza de las Cuatro Culturas, is an effective and chilling exploration of the events of 2 October 1968. For a review of *Rojo amanecer*, see Vásquez Mantecón (1998). For a collection of essays on the year 1968 in Mexican cinema, which gathers together testimonies made by filmmakers, scriptwriters and critics, see Rodríguez Cruz (2000).

30 See Mora (1982), Ramírez Berg (1992a) and Maciel (1999) for a discussion of the influence of the Echeverría *sexenio* on the film industry.

31 The website can be accessed at: www.imcine.gob.mx.

32 On Cantinflas, see Pilcher (2001), Stavans (1998) and Monsiváis (1999). The literature on Buñuel is vast and expanding; see, for example, Evans (1995), Acevedo-Muñoz (2003) and Santaolalla *et al.* (2004).

1 REMAKING MEXICAN CINEMA

1 These alternative endings involve suicide, and abortion inflicted by Tomasa or self-inflicted by Perla herself, portrayed in gruesome, unflinching detail. Indeed, the visual idiom of the whole film is depressingly squalid.

2 Rotberg's film has an additional incestuous twist in that it contains what are within the fiction non-incestuous erotic scenes that are played by the brother and sister actors Evangelina and Roberto Sosa. Thanks to Dolores Tierney for pointing this out to me.

3 *El castillo de la pureza* features sibling incest, *Principio y fin* revolves around mother–son and sibling desire, and the murderous lovers in *Profundo carmesí*, whilst not related, masquerade as brother and sister.

4 For an excellent detailed account of early Mexican cinema, see De los Reyes ([1981] 1993a, 1984).

5 See Branston (2000) for a useful account of Hollywood's rise to supremacy in world markets.

6 More recently, approaches to globalisation and media imperialism have become rather more sophisticated. As Robert Stam and Ella Shohat (2000: 383) argue, 'the media imperialism thesis needs drastic retooling in the contemporary era. First, it is simplistic to imagine an active First World simply forcing its products on a passive Third World. Second, global mass culture does not so much replace local culture as coexist with it, providing a cultural lingua franca. Third, the imported mass culture can also be indigenized, put to local use, given a local accent [. . .] Fourth, there are powerful

reverse currents as a number of Third World counties (Mexico, Brazil, India Egypt) dominate their own markets and become cultural exporters [of soap opera].'

7 I focus on the cinema of the revolution in Chapter 2.

8 For a detailed discussion of the representation of Mexicans in North American film, see De Orellana (1991); García Riera (1987) and De los Reyes (1996a).

9 See Vasey (1997) for a detailed discussion of Hollywood's self-regulation of images of 'foreignness', which aimed to ensure maximum penetration of its products at a global level.

10 See Ramírez Berg (2002) on Latino stereotypes.

11 For examples of these tropes in European visual culture, see Honour (1976). Similarly, John J. Johnson's *Latin America in Caricature* (1993) is a rich source of images that depict US–Latin America relations in the print media.

12 This is not to deny that all cinemas are transnational; it is simply to recognise that some, or more to the point, one cinema is more transnational than others.

13 See Ramírez Berg (2000) for a detailed discussion of *El automóvil gris.*

14 In an essay on Sergei Eisenstein, Carroll and Banes (2000: 121) put the case of Soviet cinema and nation building in the following terms: 'The Soviet Union literally had to be invented. As is well known, cinema was expected to play a crucial role in this process. Surely it was for such a purpose that Lenin anointed cinema the premier socialist art-form.'

15 'Classical' Hollywood cinema refers to the dominant mode of narrative cinema during the studio era in Hollywood from the 1930s to 1960. See Bordwell *et al.* (1985), and Maltby and Craven (1995) for further discussion.

16 Sound, as a political issue in the Mexican cinema, is not limited to the early years. Discussing the politics of sound in the 1990s, Fox (1999: 18) notes, 'Even though the Mexican government attempts to limit the popularity of U.S. movies by dubbing only a select few "family entertainment" titles into Spanish while subtitling the rest, Hollywood productions are still extremely successful in Mexico.'

17 I discuss the representation of Mexico's internal indigenous other in Chapter 5, the revolution in Chapter 2, and I return to the figure of the prostitute in Chapter 4.

18 This statement is almost a direct quotation from a famous 1936 essay by Alfonso Reyes (Reyes 1960).

19 Jesús Martín-Barbero (1987: 205) identifies a fissure between mass and elite conceptions of culture and identity as part of an on-going debate in Latin American culture more generally.

20 For further discussion see Charney and Schwartz (1995) and Branston (2000).

21 Thanks to Catherine Grant for pointing this out to me.

22 In addition, in his notes on the film, García Riera (vol. 1, p. 108) brings to light what he calls a 'curious detail' about the film: that although the film's theme was considered scandalous, the Departamento de Diversiones (Department of Entertainment) did not prohibit men and women from seeing it in mixed-sex screenings. Cinema-going as social practice is discussed in Chapter 3.

23 This is a direct quotation from the original story in which Françoise declares to her brother Célestin 'Je vois tant d'hommes qu'ils me semblent tous pareils!'

24 See Hershfield (2000) for a discussion of Dolores del Río's star persona.

25 In the context of a discussion of the work of Brazilian director Ana Carolina, Laura Podalsky (2000: 116) notes: 'Latin American film criticism has on the whole overlooked the potential usefulness of psychoanalytically informed film theories. The critique of psychoanalysis in Latin American film studies often rests on the assumption of the region's break with "Western" traditions of the individual and the nuclear family that form the context behind the origin and applicability of psychoanalysis as articulated by Freud and Lacan.' As will become clear, like Podalsky, I find psychoanalytic theory that is attentive to historical context an illuminating interpretative tool.

26 My own cultural memory of Boytler's *La mujer del puerto* was formed during my first visit to the Filmoteca in Mexico City in 1997. An enormous poster of Andrea Palma as Rosario adorned the wall of the academic office, an image I then encountered repeatedly in the texts of Mexican film history.

2 THE MEXICAN REVOLUTION AS MOVING MEMORY

1 The Constitution of Aguascalientes took place in October 1914, after the resignation of Victoriano Huerta, an event that had given rise to the struggle to determine the direction that the revolution would take henceforth. It brought together representatives of the northern Carrancistas and Villistas, and the southern Zapatistas. The months between Huerta's political demise in July and the October Convention saw frantic to-ings and fro-ings, as both Villistas and Carrancistas attempted to broker a deal with Zapata, who adamantly refused to concede any compromise position on the Plan de Ayala. Finally, the three-way vying for power reached an accord of sorts at Aguascalientes, with the nomination of Eulalio Gutiérrez as provisional president and the forging of an uneasy and short-lived alliance between Villa and Zapata.

2 Marianne Hirsch (1997: 22) develops the term 'postmemory' with reference to the children of Holocaust survivors, although she suggests that 'it may usefully describe other second-generation memories of cultural or collective traumatic events and experiences.'

3 See Gutiérrez Ruvalcaba (1996) and Ortiz Monasterio *et al.* (2002) for more on the Casasola Archive.

4 See O'Malley (1986) and Benjamin (2000) for a detailed discussion of rituals and ceremonies. See Craven (2002) and Folgarait (1998) on muralism and revolution. On monuments, see Escobedo (1989).

5 In an essay on cinema's 'forgotten future, after 100 years of films', Gunning (2000: 317) notes that 'We now possess only a fragment of our film culture, with less than 20 per cent of silent cinema existing. No art form has ever been placed so directly in harm's way, the result of a combination of material fragility (the celluloid film base itself, as well as emulsion and color dyes) and institutional indifference.' The influential film critic is undoubtedly referring to 'mainstream' film output; the percentage of remaining Latin American film is likely to be lower than the 20 per cent quoted. See Ana López (2000b: 48) for an excellent discussion of early cinema in Latin America, where she notes that the 'early years of the silent cinema in Latin America, roughly 1896–1920, are the least discussed and most difficult to document in Latin American media history.'

6 For a detailed account of this phenomenon, see López (2000b), De los Reyes (1985) and De Orellana (1991, 2003).

7 Here, as elsewhere in this chapter, I am keen to avoid the term 'documentary' for, as noted below, the work of Nichols (2001) points out the problems associated with the indiscriminate use of what is a historically contingent category. For more on the correspondences between film and memory, see Turim (1989) and a fascinating essay by Susannah Radstone (2000). I examine this equivocal relationship between photographic realism and memory further in a discussion of still images of the revolution in Noble (2004).

8 Led by the former president Adolfo de la Huerta, the first uprising was in protest at Álvaro Obregón's choice of Plutarco Elías Calles as his successor. It was put down swiftly and represents an 'endpoint' in the jockeying for power that took place amongst members of triumphant Constitutionalist revolutionary faction. The *Cristero* rebellion, by contrast, was a popular uprising in response to the revolutionary government's anti-clerical policies, which seriously underestimated the power of religious feeling and faith harboured particularly by rural Mexicans.

9 It is important to note one exception to the virtual absence of the revolution for the nation's cinematic production: *El automóvil gris* (1919, produced by Enrique Rosas, directed by Rosas, Joaquín Coss and Juan Canals de Homes). Based on the true story of a series of robberies carried out by a notorious gang that took place in Mexico City in 1915, *El automóvil gris* is set against the backdrop of the chaos generated during the revolution. The success of the gang, whose getaway car gives the film its title, was widely held to be attributable to its contact with high-level government officials. And for this reason, according to Charles Ramírez Berg, the film represents 'an early expression of twin themes – the corruption of revolutionary ideals and the accompanying remorse over the loss of the unique opportunity the revolution afforded – that would haunt the nation's cinema for the next seven decades' (Ramírez Berg 2000: 4).

10 See Mraz (1999) for a detailed analysis of De Fuentes's anti-epic treatment of the revolution in these films.

11 Pérez Montfort (1994: 149) notes that throughout the 1930s, the stereotype of the revolutionary in both popular and academic discourse largely placed an emphasis on the negative side of this figure. Despite the constant efforts of post-revolutionary governments to promote a positive image, the revolution itself was represented with disappointment and bitterness.

12 Gustavo García usefully strikes a note of caution about the silence of silent cinema in the prologue to *Espacios distantes . . . Aún vivos*. Reminding his readers of the range of auditory devices deployed in early movies – from accompanying music to sound effects technicians who would, for example, splash water at the requisite moment, he states: 'el cine era mudo, pero no silencioso'/ 'cinema was mute, but it wasn't silent' (Álfaro Salazar and Ochoa Vega 1999: 12).

13 Carmen Toscano's presentation of the revolution as unified conflict is in fact in keeping with her father's filmmaking trajectory. Angel Miquel (1997: 83) notes that when, in 1920, Toscano put together a new version of his material, *Historia de la Revolución mexicana de 1910 a 1920*: 'Había en ella un cambio importante con respecto a las versiones anteriores: se abandonaba la consideración de las revoluciones parciales (maderista, orozquista, felicista) y se adjetivaba la revuelta como mexicana, es decir, como nacional. Se trataba, de hecho, de una de las primeras manifestaciones del concepto de la Revolución como un proceso unitario, que en las próximas décadas serviría al Estado como vehículo aglutinador.'/ 'In it there was an important change as regards the previous versions: the consideration of partial revolutions (the Madero, Orozco, Félix revolutions) was abandoned. Rather the struggle was modified as Mexican, that is to say, as a national struggle. In fact, what was at stake was one of the first manifestations of the revolution as a unitary process, which in the decades to come would serve the state as a unifying vehicle.'

14 His last significant new film was made in 1923, titled *Historia auténtica de Francisco Villa y su trágica muerte en Parral*, which featured old footage of Villa supplemented by material relating to his assassination in 1923. After this, Toscano made attempts in 1927 and 1935 to screen panoramic overviews of the Revolution (*Historia completa de la Revolución mexicana 1900–1927* and *La historia de la Revolución mexicana*), but neither was very successful due to their antiquated filmic language (Miquel 1997: 138). Unable to adapt to the demands of narrative filmmaking, from the 1920s onwards Toscano increasingly devoted himself to civil engineering, managing state-sponsored road-building projects.

15 Sklar (1993: 18) suggests that this technological development can be dated to the late 1920s.

3 THE FORMATION OF A NATIONAL CINEMA AUDIENCE

1 For a discussion of the intersection of radio broadcasting and nation building, see Hayes (2000).

2 Throughout this opening section, in order to avoid repetition, I have used the terms 'viewer', 'audience' and 'spectator' interchangeably. I understand these terms here in their broadest sense, as social practices that are located at the nexus between the act of movie-going and the positions that a given film text constructs for its viewers. I refine and clarify this understanding below.

3 Of the five categories, in the current chapter the second is arguably of less importance for I addressed the question of technical apparatus in the preceding chapter on the revolution and memory.

4 I shall return to these female viewers in my discussion of *María Candelaria* below.

5 See De los Reyes (1995b) for a detailed discussion of kissing in the cinema.

6 In *Mexico's Hope*, historian James Cockcroft (1998: 51) proposes the concept of 'intermediate classes' as more accurate than 'middle classes' 'because various groups compose the category. They are "intermediate" not because of supposedly "middle" levels of income, property, or power, but because they are situated in an intermediate position between major social classes [. . .] They are "caught in the middle," now siding with one pole, now with another, and almost always dividing among themselves, always "intermediate" to the central class conflict of the society in question.'

7 I return to these issues in my reading of *María Candelaria*.

8 Pilcher (2001: 23) notes that the conditions in the *carpas* were frequently deplorable, with inadequate sanitary facilities and dangerous lighting. Nevertheless, the authorities were prepared to turn a blind eye for 'better the *carpa* than the pulque shop and the tavern'. Here again, we see the official view of the role of popular entertainment as a means of controlling the masses.

9 For a general discussion of the role of comedy in the Mexican cinema, see Rafael Medina de la Serna (1995).

10 It is important to note in passing that melodrama is one of the favoured modes of the Mexican cinema and Latin American film culture more generally. It has also traditionally been one of the most maligned in critical circles and is a film mode to which I shall turn in Chapter 4.

11 In addition to the work of Monsiváis, with which I opened this chapter, a number of scholars have addressed issues of spectatorship, audience reception and cinema-going in Mexico from a range of perspectives. Representative work in the field includes: García Riera's generalised socio-cultural reflections in *El cine y su público* (1974); the rigorous historical work of De los Reyes ([1981] 1993) provides a fascinating insight into socio-cultural dimensions of movie-going; Norma Iglesias's *Entre yerba, polvo y plomo: Lo fronterizo visto por el cine mexicano* (1991) offers sociological case studies of viewers of border movies; Lauro Zavala's *Permanencia voluntaria: el cine y su espectador* (1994) is a Spanish-language synthesis of key debates in Euro-American film theory; Anne Rubenstein (1998b) provides a cultural-historical essay on the Cine Montecarlo; Francisco H. Alfaro and Alejandro Ochoa's *La república de los cines* (1998) is a socio-historical introduction to the film theatre in Mexico, with excellent photographic images; Rogelio Argrasánchez provides an array of film posters from the Golden Age (2001); and finally, works on Mexican film stars by Hershfield (2000), López (1999) and Paranaguá (1999) by necessity touch on questions of reception.

12 See the catalogue to the art exhibition *Iberoamérica mestiza*, coordinated by Miguel Leon-Portilla (2003), for a fascinating insight into issues of *mestizaje* in Spanish America.

13 See Nead (1992) for a detailed discussion of the status and significance of the female nude within Western iconographic traditions of visual representation.

14 As Hershfield (1996: 55) notes, there is no mistaking that this sequence is indebted to the prologue of Eisenstein's unfinished film *¡Que viva México!* For more on Eisenstein's aesthetic impact on muralism, see also De la Vega (1997).

15 In 1531, a dark-skinned Virgin Mary is supposed to have made an apparition to an Indian, Juan Diego, imprinting her image on his cape. In time, Juan Diego's vision was accepted by the Catholic Church and became consecrated as Mexico's very own dark-skinned virgin. See Lafaye (1974); Brading (2001) for a full discussion of the pivotal role of the Virgin of Guadalupe in Mexican history and culture.

16 If, in the period in question, movie-going in Mexico was primarily a family experience, I have nevertheless elected to use the masculine pronoun, given that I think that the (conventional) sexual politics of *María Candelaria* construct an implied male spectator.

17 I explore the representation of the Indian subject in greater depth in Chapter 5.

18 Rozado (1991: 19) echoes this point in his fascinating study, as does Monsiváis, who frequently uses religious metaphors in his discussions of the cinema audience, as for example: 'And if cinema brings ways of seeing the local, the national and the universal rapidly up to date, its does so through the *mystical feelings* of the spectators, who in the shadows construct a *sui generis* religion, which transfigures its followers and provides them with celestial visions' (Monsiváis 1995: 148, emphasis in the original).

19 The painter offers a realistic social characterisation of the Mexican muralists (especially Diego Rivera) who, in the post-revolutionary period, were busy establishing a celebratory iconography of the Indian across the walls of the nation's official buildings. See Craven (2002) for a detailed discussion of the relationship between art and revolution in Mexico. As Laura Podalsky (1993a) points out in her excellent discussion of the film that problematises the emergent tradition of Indian representation, the model in *María Candelaria* is none other than the one used by Rivera.

20 Rozado (1991: 84) argues that the painter is a well-intentioned lover of Indian beauty. Although Rozado's neglected study is extremely insightful and breaks the primarily historiographical mould of much Mexican film criticism, I find this reading of the painter difficult to sustain.

21 The word *populacho* means the masses but with a pejorative inflection (García Riera 1992, vol. 3: 67).

22 In an analysis of another Fernández film *Enamorada* (1946), which also contains an important narrative focus on a painting, Jean Franco (1989: 150) suggests that this particular scene involving the painting 'points to the importance of representation as a way of mediating conflicts. Indeed, portraits were commonly used in Hollywood film when emphasis was being placed on the work of representation.'

23 By one rather crude measure, it is possible to define the Golden Age of Mexican cinema in terms of film output. García Riera (1998: 121) has usefully quantified the rise in national production in the early 1940s. Out of 434 films that premiered in Mexico in 1941, 332 were North American, 27 Mexican, 35 European, 33 Argentine and 7 were of miscellaneous origin. By 1945, this had changed dramatically: out of a total of 363 films on exhibition, 245 were North American, 67 were Mexican, 20 were European and 31 were Argentine. By 1949, the number of Mexican features had risen to 108. As these figures demonstrate, given the enduring preponderance of North American films, it is essential to put the Golden Age in perspective. True, there were fewer North American films on exhibition; they still outweighed Mexican production by a significant ratio. If these figures put the Golden Age into perspective, however, so does a comparative glimpse at the output of Mexico's main rivals in the Spanish-language market, Argentina and Spain, which in 1949 produced 47 and 37 features respectively (García Riera, 1993, vol. 5: 7).

24 See the important work of Seth Fein for a detailed discussion of the relationship between the US and Mexican cinemas.

25 In 1996, for example Mexico had a total population of 93.7 million and 19.5 million households, of which 16 million had television sets, equating to a 91.7 per cent penetration. These figures are to be found in Getino (1998: 194). This places Mexico in third place in Latin America for television penetration after Argentina and Uruguay.

26 Thanks to Eduardo Alegría for sharing this childhood experience with me. In addition to Carro's book *El cine de luchadores* (1984), see also Rubenstein (2002) on the career and popularity of El Santo and Levi (2001) on *lucha libre* on the small screen.

4 MELODRAMA, MASCULINITY AND THE POLITICS OF SPACE

1 *Telenovelas* produced in Brazil, Mexico and Venezuela are consumed in countries as diverse as Ghana, the Ukraine, Italy, Slovenia and the Middle East. See Mato (1999) on the *telenovela* as transnational genre. Lillo (1994: 5) underlines the class associations of melodrama: 'En América Latina, y en México en particular, desde los veinte, el melodrama invade todos los espacios de la producción simbólica (radio, cine, televisión, historieta etc.) y se convierte en el producto más consumido por las clases populares'/ 'In Latin America and in Mexico in particular, from the 1920s on, melodrama invades all spaces of symbolic production (radio, cinema, television, comic book etc.) and it becomes the most consumed product of the popular classes.' For more on melodrama in Latin America, see Oroz (1995).

2 See Ayala Blanco ([1968] 1993), particularly his chapter on the family, for more detailed discussion of this social class. See also Ramírez Berg (1992a: 24).

3 See Cockcroft (1998) and Sherman (2000) for detailed analysis of the 'Mexican miracle' and its subsequent failure.

4 García's impressive career spans some six decades. The titles of the following films in which she appeared speak volumes about the particular maternal persona that García embodied: *Alma de sacrificio* (Soul of Sacrifice, Joaquín Coss, 1917); *No basta ser madre* (Motherhood Isn't Enough, Ramón Peón, 1937) *Mi madrecita* (My Little Mother, Francisco Elías, 1940); *La abuelita* (The Grandmother, Raphael J. Sevilla, 1942); *Mi madre adorada* (My Adored Mother, René Cardona, 1948).

5 In addition to those scenes already mentioned, such incarceration is dramatically foregrounded in the scene in which Maru and Estela eavesdrop on Roberto's first encounter with their father, where they are framed, as if behind bars, by the stair banisters.

6 This position, and particularly the association between women and commodities, is made explicit in the scene in which Roberto asks Don Cataño for permission to marry his daughter. With the refrigerator looming large in the living room, Roberto states to Cataño, 'Primero le vendí una barredora que probó serle útil [. . .] Después le vendí una refrigeradora. Usted comprenderá que este asunto es mucho más importante en mi vida.'/ 'First I sold you a vacuum cleaner that turned out to be of use to you. Then I sold you a refrigerator. You will understand that this business [i.e. marrying Maru] is much more important in my life.'

7 See Rashkin (2001) for more on Echeverría's film policies.

8 See García Tsao (1994) for more detail.

9 Prior to Ripstein's film, the story had inspired a play by Sergio Magaña, *Los motivos del lobo* (The Wolf's Motives) and a novel by Luis Spota, *La carcajada del lobo* (The Wolf's Laugh). See García Riera (1988) for further discussion of these literary antecedents.

10 As a first image, the cans not only symbolise the authority of Lima as father over the family unit. They also obliquely reference an auditory structural relationship between the interior and exterior: it is worth noting that one of key differences between inside and outside is auditory: the inside is eerily silent, whereas those scenes in which we

witness Lima's forays into the city outside the house are, by comparison, markedly noisy.

11 In Galindo's film, there are hints of incestuous desire, as when Don Cataño reprimands his children when Héctor and the three sisters enter the bathroom at the same time: 'Y tú ¿qué haces aquí? ¿Cuántas veces les tengo dicho . . .'/ 'What are you doing here? How many times have I told you?'. In *El castillo de la pureza*, these hints become an inevitable reality when Lima catches the adolescent Porvenir and Utopía, deprived of contact with others in the outside world, initiating a sexual relationship in the back of the old car in the courtyard.

12 Mignolo (2000: 185) conceives of Zapatismo as an example of what he terms 'border thinking'. Linked to other global experiences of coloniality, Zapatismo 'reflect[s] on the "double translation" allowing for an intersection of knowledge: Marxism modified by the Amerindian languages and cosmology and Amerindian epistemology modified by the language of Marxist cosmology in a cross-epistemological conversation that is rewriting and enacting a history of five hundred years of oppression.'

13 His brother and co-conspirator Raúl Salinas de Gortari was arrested on suspicion of involvement in the murder and also of laundering millions of pesos of drug money. He was indicted on the former charge and, in 1999, sentenced to fifty years in prison.

14 For a cogent historical overview of the period see Camp (2000) and Castañeda (1995). For an analysis of the origins and practice of the *tapado*, see Woldenberg (1995); and for a satirical graphic description of the *dedazo*, see Del Río (1982).

15 It is significant to note that in the original screenplay, the cantina is known as 'Las Glorias del Callejón'. See Leñero (1997).

16 See De la Mora (1992–93) for an excellent discussion of the status and significance of the brothel in Mexican film.

17 See Castillo (1998) for further discussion.

18 The prostitute has been read in socio-historic terms by Hershfield (1996) and in sociological/literary terms by Castillo (1998). Whilst I am aware of the nuances of these invaluable and insightful dimensions of the prostitute as national figure, I have chosen to focus here on elements of López's cultural/mythical analysis for reasons that will become apparent.

19 Also it is significant to note that the shop in which Jimy works is called 'Camisería Colón' or 'Columbus Clothing'.

20 I use the term 'transaction' deliberately, as many of the relationships between characters in the film are figured in terms of an economic exchange.

5 SEEING THE OTHER THROUGH FILM

1 Cohan and Hark (1997: 7) note that Jack Kerouac's *On the Road* (1957) had a decisive impact on the road movie as a genre and closes with a climactic trip to Mexico. David Laderman's *Driving Visions: Exploring the Road Movie* (2002: 1) opens with a verbal sketch of *Thelma and Louise* (Ridley Scott, 1991): 'They have been driving for days through the desert, with little sleep. They want to get to Mexico.' Thanks to Claire Lindsay for drawing my attention to these examples.

2 The border that bisects the USA and Mexico was established in 1848 under the Treaty of Guadalupe Hidalgo. The cinematic representation of the border is the subject of Chapter 6.

3 *El norte* is technically speaking a UK/US co-production and its director, Nava, is Mexican American. However, the cast (largely Latin American actors), theme and ideological stance of Nava's film make of it an exemplary 'picaresque peregrination' that justifies its inclusion here. Xavier's examples include, *Ajuricaba: The Rebel of the Amazon* (Oswaldo Caldeira, 1977), *Uirá: An Indian in Search of God* (Gustavo Dahl, 1972), and *Cabeza de Vaca* (Nicolás Echevarría, 1990).

4 John Mraz (2003: 195), taking his cue from John Womack (1968), suggests that the Spanish term *campesino* (denoting people from the campos or fields) is preferable to 'peasant' with its exoticist connotations.

5 I am indebted to Catherine Russell (1999) for the idea of taking 'another look'.

6 For work on questions of fiction and non-fiction, the real, realism and the referential, see Gaines and Renov (1999) and Margulies (2003).

7 Although the material filmed totalled some 200,000 feet, as Goodwin (1993: 130) states, this vast output also includes precautionary duplicate takes for, filming on location, the Soviet team was unable to review the rushes. King (1990: 45) notes that the British Film Institute holds some five hours of these rushes, edited consecutively.

8 See Geduld and Gottesman (1970); Karetnikova and Steinmetz (1991); De la Vega (1997) and Eisenstein (1983) for detailed accounts of the Soviet director's sojourn in Mexico.

9 See Delpar (1992) for an account of 'the enormous vogue of things Mexican' in the United States during this period. Other prestigious international visitors in the early decades of the twentieth century included Tina Modotti, Edward Weston, Paul Strand and D. H. Lawrence.

10 In this sense *¡Que viva México!* is but one example within a cultural process whereby national culture is validated on international cultural circuits in a gesture that confirms Mexico's legitimacy to itself. Although it could be argued that all nations are involved in this self-affirming pursuit of international cultural capital, the Mexican paradigm does seem to follow a particular pattern. This pattern is discerned in the geopolitical trajectory of two recent exhibitions of art originating in Mexico, namely 'Mexico: Splendors of Thirty Centuries' (1991) and 'Frida Kahlo and Tina Modotti' (1983). The former originally went on show at the Metropolitan Museum of Art, New York: the latter at the Whitechapel Gallery, London. Having been legitimated in the metropolis, both exhibitions subsequently returned to peripheral Mexico for consumption by national audiences. See Bartra (2002) and Wallis (1994) on 'Mexico: Splendors of Thirty Centuries', see Noble (2000) on the Whitechapel exhibition.

11 For a detailed discussion of the visual style in the Fernández–Figueroa partnership, see Ramírez Berg (1992b). In addition to Eisenstein, Ramírez Berg lists the creative influences on Fernández and Figueroa, including the engraver José Guadalupe Posada, the artist Dr Atl, the muralists, photographer Paul Strand, cinematographer Gregg Toland and directors Orson Welles and John Ford.

12 Eisenstein's film is often cited in studies of photographic representation. For example, see Mraz (2003).

13 Pérez Montfort (1994: 125) observes that *mariachi* music came to represent Mexican national identity particularly from 1930 onwards, with the foundation of the XEW radio station. For more on both XEW and regional/national musical traditions, see also Pérez Montfort (2000).

6 THE POLITICS AND EROTICS OF BORDER CULTURE

1 See for example, 'The Border Issue' of *Travesía*, 3 (1994).

2 My understanding of state intervention into the cultural politics of the mass media of the period is indebted to Fein (1998).

3 I use the terms 'specular' and 'specularity' here as defined by Kuhn (1994: 261): 'Relations of looking and seeing, often unconscious'.

4 See Gómez-Quiñones and Maciel (1998) for an overview of Mexican labour in the period 1890–1997.

5 See Iglesias (1991, vol. II) for a full survey of border movies ('*películas fronterizas*'). Iglesias's definition of what constitutes a border movie is broad and encompasses films

(1) that are set in a border city; (2) that refer to a border character; (3) that refer to people of Mexican origin who live in the United States; (4) that are filmed in a border city, whether or not that location is important to the plot; (5) whose plot refers to the border or to problems of national identity.

6 As Fein (1998) and Fox (1999) note, the 'push' factors that propel Mexican immigrants to the United States are paid scant attention in the film. We learn little of Rafael's need to leave Mexico beyond the fact that he is fleeing the son of a landowner with whom he is in dispute over a woman.

7 The irony of this graffiti is that the rock is juxtaposed with the watchtower manned by North American border guards who shoot indiscriminately at all those attempting to cross the river. Its visual impact finds echoes in the famous refrain 'pobre México: tan lejos de Dios, tan cerca de los Estados Unidos'/ 'poor Mexico: so far from God and so close to the United States' uttered by one of the musicians in the Big Jim Café at the beginning of the film. I return to the watchtower scene in the discussion of *El Jardín del Edén* below.

8 There is, however, more than a little irony to this contrast, given that it is only the second meeting between María del Consuelo and Rafael, the first having occurred in the street parade scene that takes place after the border crossing, when the former helps the latter to buy a hotdog.

9 Thanks to Miriam Haddu for sharing with me this and other press articles on *El Jardín del Edén*.

10 For a thorough account of Proposition 187 and its implications, see 'The Immigrant Backlash' issue of *NACLA* (1995). See also Castañeda (1995), particularly the cogent introductory chapter on relationship between Mexico and California.

11 According to Arredondo (2001: 120), '*Danzón* tuvo un éxito arrollador; las agencias internacionales de noticias la calificaron de "extraordinaria" y batió un récord de ventas' / '*Danzón* was phenomenally successful; international news agencies described it as "extraordinary" and it broke sales records.' Like *El Jardín del Edén*, *Danzón* takes up an established genre in the Mexican cinema – the brothel melodrama – which is reworked by feminising it.

12 Peña (1994) similarly argues that: 'La deficiencia principal de *El Jardín del Edén* se encuentra en la estructura de su historia, en la abundancia de caminos narrativos que emprende la directora'/ 'The principal deficiency of *El Jardín del Edén* lies in the structure of its story, in the abundancy of narrative paths on which its director embarks.'

13 It should be noted that the work of Guillermo Gómez-Peña is featured in the film: in the first sequence in which Elizabeth appears, a Gómez-Peña performance is playing on the video; and later we witness Elizabeth watching a video performance of Gómez Peña's character Border Brujo.

14 It is important to remember that the anxiety subtending the erasure of difference emanates not just from the US but also of course also from Mexico, where the fear of creeping Americanisation is equally strong. As Monsiváis (1997: 110) makes clear, the fear of Yankee imperialism south of the border has led, for example, to moves to protect the Spanish language from the colonising force of Spanglish.

15 Kraniauskus (1994: 7) underlines the militaristic associations of the border when he points out that 'the fence between San Diego and Tijuana [. . .] was made from the corrugated iron sheets used for temporary landing strips in Operation Desert Storm'.

16 I am using the notion of carnivalesque in the Bakhtinian sense.

17 Felipe is nevertheless linked with visuality in the opening scene as outlined above; he also becomes the object of Jane's ex/er/oticising photographic gaze in the scene in which they meet.

18 For a discussion of the use of music as a foreshadowing agent in the film, see Herrera-Sobek (Maciel and Herrera-Sobek 1998).

19 I borrow this term from Dubois (1995).

APPENDIX: FILMOGRAPHY

SYNOPSES

Mexican National Cinema is structured around case studies of some fifteen films which exemplify the central themes and issues explored in the book and which are discussed in the context of broader developments and in relation to similar films. The following synopses are designed to provide core information for each film discussed in detail and are listed alphabetically by title. They are derived from a combination of my own viewings of the films, information provided in Emilio García Riera's *Historia documental del cine mexicano* and the Internet Movie Database http://www.imdb.com/. The only film featured in the main body of the text not listed below is Sergei Eisenstein's *¡Que viva México!* This is because this unfinished film does not conform to the format of the filmography. In addition to the information provided in this book, the reader who wishes to learn more about a project to digitally restore Eisenstein's film may find it helpful to visit the following website: http://www.quevivamexico.com/site_home.htm.

El Callejón de los Milagros
(Midaq Alley)

Production: (1994) Alfredo Ripstein Jr., Alameda Films, IMCINE, Fondo de Fomento a la Calidad, Universidad de Guadalajara
Director: Jorge Fons
Script and adaptation: Vicente Leñero from the novel *Midaq Alley* by Naguib Mahfouz
Photography: Carlos Marcovich
Music: Lucía Álvarez
Cast: Ernesto Cruz (Rutilio), Delia Casanova (Eusebia), María Rojo (Doña Cata), Salma Hayek (Alma), Bruno Bichir (Abel), Daniel Giménez Cacho (José Luis), Luis Felipe Tovar (Güicho), Margarita Sanz (Susanita) Tiare Scanda (Maru), Juan Manuel Bernal (Chava), Estaban Soberanes (Jimy), Abel Woolrich (Zacarías), Óscar Yoldi (Ubaldo, 'El Poeta'), Claudio Obregón (Don Fidel)
Duration: 140 minutes

Further details

El Callejón de los Milagros won a total of forty-nine awards, including nineteen silver Ariels and a special mention at the Berlin International Film Festival in 1995.

Synopsis

Divided into four sections, named after the characters, Rutilio, Alma, Susanita and an epilogue 'The return', *El Callejón de los Milagros* is set in a working-class barrio of the historic centre of Mexico City. Each overlapping narrative opens with the same game of dominoes that takes place in the cantina of Rutilio.

1. Rutilio: this story focuses on his homosexual relationship with the younger Jimy – a liaison with violent consequences: Jimy is brutally attacked by Rutilio's son Chava, who then flees to the United States.
2. Alma: this story is launched in the first narrative (Rutilio), in which Alma initiates a relationship with the neighbourhood barber Abel. When Abel leaves Mexico for the United States in the company of Chava, she promises to wait for him to return. However, Alma is seduced by the opportunities that the wealthy José Luis appears to offer and ends up as a prostitute in a high-class brothel run by the latter.
3. Susanita: this story is the most lighthearted of the three and centres on spinster Susanita's relationship with and marriage to the unreliable younger barman Güicho.
4. The epilogue brings about a form of resolution. Abel and Chava return from the United States with Chava's wife and baby Rutilio, who after an initial rejection by his grandfather, is then accepted. On discovering that Alma has left the neighbourhood, Abel seeks her out in the brothel in which he provokes José Luis who stabs him. In the closing scene, Abel lies dying in Alma's arms.

El castillo de la pureza
(The Castle of Purity)

Production: (1972) Churubusco Studios, Angélica Ortiz
Director: Arturo Ripstein
Script and adaptation: Arturo Ripstein and José Emilio Pacheco
Photography: Alex Phillips
Music: Joaquín Gutiérrez Heras
Cast: Claudio Brook (Gabriel Lima), Rita Macedo (Beatriz), Arturo Beristáin (Porvenir), Diana Bracho (Utopía), Gladys Bermejo (Voluntad), David Silva (health inspector)
Duration: 110 minutes

Further details

Filming started on 3 July 1972 and was completed on 8 September at the Churubusco studios and locations in Mexico City. *El castillo de la pureza* premiered on 10 May 1973 at the Diana cinema with an opening run of eighteen weeks.

Synopsis

The action takes place in the fortress home of the Lima family, in which the patriarch, Gabriel Lima, has had his wife Beatriz and three children incarcerated for the past eighteen years. The family spend their lives manufacturing rat poison. Imposing a strict regime of physical exercise and vegetarianism within the home, outside Gabriel consumes meat, engages in a sexual relationship with a prostitute and propositions a young woman shop worker. On discovering Utopía and Porvenir in a sexual embrace in the battered old car that sits on the patio, Gabriel punishes his children severely. In revenge for the sexual advances made by Gabriel, the shop worker informs the police that he is producing rat poison without a licence. Gabriel is taken away by the police, and the final sequence of the film centres on Beatriz and the children who return alone to the 'castle of purity'.

El compadre Mendoza
(Godfather Mendoza)

Production: (1933) Interamericana Films, Rafael Angel Frías and José Castellot Jr., Producciones Aguila, Antonio Prida Santacilia
Director: Fernando de Fuentes
Script and adaptation: Juan Bustillo Oro and Fernando de Fuentes based on an idea by Mauricio Magdaleno
Cinematography: Alex Phillips
Music: Manuel Castro Padilla
Cast: Alfredo del Diestro (Rosalío Mendoza), Carmen Guerrero (Dolores), Antonio R. Frausto (Felipe Nieto), Luis G. Barreiro (Tenógenes), Joaquín Busquets (Colonel Bernández, Emma Roldán (María), José del Río (the child Felipe)
Duration: 85 minutes

Further details

Filming started on 17 December 1933 in the Nacional Productora studios and on location on El Rosario hacienda, Azcapotzalco, Mexico City. *El compadre Mendoza* premiered on 5 April 1934 at Palacio cinema with an opening run of one week.

Synopsis

During the revolution, landowner Rosalío Mendoza keeps in with each faction of the armed conflict, changing the portrait of Huerta or Zapata to suit the political stripe of visitors to his hacienda. During Mendoza's wedding to Dolores, a group of Zapatistas arrive to ambush the Federal troops who are at the celebrations. Mendoza is sentenced to death by firing squad, but Zapatista general Felipe Nieto saves him and the two men become friends and Nieto even becomes the godfather of Mendoza's son, Felipe. However, Mendoza finds himself in financial difficulties when a train loaded with his wheat is captured by revolutionaries. To save his family from financial ruin, Mendoza has to accept a role in a government plot to assassinate Nieto who is murdered as Mendoza, Dolores and Felipe Jr. flee from the hacienda.

Espaldas mojadas
(Wetbacks)

Production: (1955) ATA Films, José Elvira, Atlas Films
Director: Alejandro Galindo
Script and adaptation: Alejandro Galindo
Cinematography: Rosalío Solano
Music: Jorge Pérez H.
Cast: David Silva (Rafael Améndola Campuzano), Víctor Parra (Mister Sterling), Martha Valdés (María de Consuelo), Óscar Pulido (Luís Villarrea/Louie Royalville), José Elías Moreno (Frank Mendoza), Alicia Malvido (Agnes)
Duration: 116 minutes

Further details

Filming started on 4 May 1953 in the Tepeyac Studios. It premiered on 16 June 1955 in the Mariscala cinema with an opening run of five weeks.

Synopsis

Lacking the relevant documents, Rafael Améndola Campuzano negotiates with Frank Mendoza to cross the Río Bravo as an illegal 'wetback' in order to find work in the United States. The crossing proves dangerous: Rafael and his fellow wetbacks are shot at by North American border guards. Rafael survives to make it to the other side, only to encounter greed, exploitation, racism and cruelty in the neighbouring country. As he flees from one job to the next, the police in hot pursuit, Rafael is offered the pitiful wage of $1 per day to wash dishes by a Mexican American. Working on the railroad for the aptly named Mister Sterling, Rafael encounters third world conditions in the middle of the first. Rafael meets the ex-patriot Luis Villareal and Mexican American María del Consuelo, whom he helps to return to Mexico, with the promise to marry the latter. The film closes as

Rafael beats Mister Sterling and throws him into the river where he is shot by the North American guards who believe him to be another wetback attempting to make the crossing.

Una familia de tantas
(One Family amongst Many)

Production: (1948) Producciones Azteca, César Santos Galindo
Director: Alejandro Galindo
Script and adaptation: Alejandro Galindo
Photography: José Ortiz Ramos
Music: Raúl Lavista
Cast: Fernando Soler (Don Rodrigo Cataño), David Silva (Roberto del Hierro), Martha Roth (Maru), Eugenia Galindo (Doña Gracia Cataño), Felipe de Alba (Héctor), Isabel del Puerto (Estela), Alma Delia Fuentes (Lupita) Carlos Riquelme (Ricardo), Enriqueta Reza (Guadalupe)
Duration: 130 minutes

Further details

Filming started on 20 September 1948 in the Estudios Azteca at a cost of approximately 400,000 pesos. *Una familia de tantas* premiered on 11 March at the Cine Opera with an opening run of two weeks.

Synopsis

Set almost entirely in the family home of the Cataño family, which comprises the unyielding patriarch Don Rodrigo Cataño, his wife Doña Gracia and their five children Héctor, Estela, Maru, Lupita and unnamed youngest son. Don Cataño wishes to marry Maru off to her country cousin Ricardo. However, left alone at home one day, Maru receives a visit from vacuum-cleaner salesman Roberto del Hierro, who arranges to return and manages to convince Don Cataño that he should purchase one of the salesman's new-fangled gadgets. Maru and Roberto start up a relationship, meeting in secret on the street outside the Cataño family home whilst Maru is carrying out her domestic errands. Meanwhile, the girl-friend of the feckless Héctor falls pregnant out of wedlock and the latter is forced to marry her. Yet when Don Cataño catches Estela kissing her boyfriend, she receives a beating and decides to run away from home. Roberto asks Don Cataño for Maru's hand in marriage, the patriarch refuses, and Maru determines to follow through with the marriage against the will of her father. *Una familia de tantas* ends as Maru abandons the family home on her wedding day, receiving the blessing of all but her father.

Flor silvestre
(Wild Flower)

Production: (1943) Films Mundiales, Agustín J. Fink
Director: Emilio Fernández
Script and adaptation: Emilio Fernández and Mauricio Magdaleno from the novel
  Sucedió ayer (It Happened Yesterday) by Fernando Robles
Cinematography: Gabriel Figueroa
Music: Francisco Domínguez
Cast: Dolores del Río (Esperanza), Pedro Armendáriz (José Luis Castro), Miguel
  Angel Ferriz (Don Francisco), Mimí Derba (Doña Clara), Eduardo Arozamena
  (Melchor), Agustín Isunza (Nicanor), Tito Novaro (Esperanza's son)
Duration: 94 minutes

Further details

Filming started on 11 January 1943 in the CLASA studios. *Flor silvestre* premiered
on 24 April 1943 at the Palacio Chino cinema with an opening run of four weeks.

Synopsis

Narrated in the form of a flashback, Esperanza tells her military cadet son the story
of his origins as the offspring of her marriage with José Luis, who, hailing from a
rich landowning family, is disinherited when the family learn of his secret marriage
to Esperanza, a poor peasant woman. José Luis and Esperanza's liaison takes
place against the backdrop of the revolution, the egalitarian ideals of which José
Luis sympathises with and even puts into practice by marrying Esperanza. When
Esperanza and her son are kidnapped by false revolutionaries, José Luis is killed
whilst rescuing them.

El Jardín del Edén
(The Garden of Eden)

Production: (1994) Fondo de Fomento a la Calidad Cinematográfica, IMCINE,
  Macondo Cine Video, Ministère d'Affaires Exterieurs de France, Ministère
  de la Culture de la Republique Française, Société Générale des Industries
  Culturelles du Québec, Téléfilm Canada, Universidad de Guadalajara, Verseau
  International
Director: María Novaro
Script and adaptation: Beatriz Novaro, María Novaro
Music: José Stephens
Cast: Renée Coleman (Jane), Bruno Bichir (Felipe), Gabriela Roel (Serena),
  Rosario Sagrav (Elizabeth), Alan Ciangherotti (Julián), Angeles Cruz
  (Margarita Luna), Joseph Culp (Frank)
Duration: 104 minutes

Further details

Filmed on location in San Diego, California and Tijuana, Baja California, María Novaro won second prize in the 1994 Havana Film Festival.

Synopsis

El Jardín del Edén focuses primarily on the way in which three women's lives loosely interweave in Tijuana: the North American Jane is in search of the exotic; the recently widowed Serena is looking for a fresh start with her three children; Chicana artist Elizabeth is in town to put on an exhibition of her work. The women's lives become interlinked by the presence of Felipe, whom, after the violent failure of his first attempt to cross the border to the United States, Jane smuggles across along with Serena's teenage son Julián. The plot revolves around the border crossing, Serena and Elizabeth's search for Julián, and the deportation of the latter and Felipe back to Mexico.

María Candelaria

Production: (1943) Films Mundiales, Agustín J. Fink
Director: Emilio Fernández
Script: Emilio Fernández; Adaptation: Emilio Fernández and Mauricio Magdaleno
Photography: Gabriel Figueroa
Music: Francisco Domínguez
Cast: Dolores del Río (María Candelaria), Pedro Armendáriz (Lorenzo Rafael), Alberto Galán (Painter), Margarita Cortés (Lupe), Miguel Inclán (Don Damián)
Duration: 101 minutes

Further details

Filming started on 15 August 1943 at the CLASA studios. *María Candelaria* premiered in 1944 at the Cine Palacio where it had an opening run of four weeks.

Synopsis

Set in 1909, *María Candelaria* is narrated in the form of a flashback triggered by a conversation that takes place between a woman journalist and the unnamed painter, in which the latter explains to the former his motives for refusing to sell his famous nude painting of an Indian woman. The Indian woman in question is María Candelaria, ostracised by nearly all in her community (on the grounds that her mother was a prostitute), except Lorenzo Rafael. The idyllic but impecunious couple plan to marry. María Candelaria, however, falls ill with malaria and, denied the state-provided quinine by the villainous Don Damián, Lorenzo Rafael breaks into Don Damián's shop and steals the quinine along with a dress. Lorenzo Rafael is imprisoned and, in order to secure the money for his release, María Candelaria agrees to model for the painter who early in the film becomes enraptured by her 'indigenous beauty'. On discovering the painter wishes her to model for a nude study, María Candelaria refuses, leaving him to complete his image based on the body of another Indian woman. The villagers see the painting and, assuming that María Candelaria has indeed modelled for it, burn her home and stone her to death.

Memorias de un mexicano
(Memories of a Mexican)

Production: (1950) Carmen Toscano de Moreno Sánchez from materials from the archives of Salvador Toscano Barragán.
Editing and script: Carmen Toscano de Moreno Sánchez, narrated by Manuel Bernal
Music: Jorge Pérez H.
Duration: 100 minutes

Further details

Premiered on 24 August 1950 at the Chapultepec cinema with an opening run of three weeks.

Synopsis

Memorias de un mexicano comprises a panoramic overview of events and personages from early twentieth-century Mexican history in the form of a chronologically ordered series of actualities presented as filtered through and therefore a visualisation of the Mexican of the film's title. Based on material made by the first Mexican to import film equipment to Mexico, Salvador Toscano (1872–1947), the footage was filmed between 1897 and 1923, incorporating scenes from the presidential reign of Porfirio Díaz, through the revolutionary years to the immediate post-conflict period. This footage was selected and edited by the film pioneer's daughter, Carmen Toscano, who also scripted a fictional narrative voiceover to add dramatic force to scenes from the turbulent early years from national history.

La mujer del puerto
(The Woman of the Port)

Production: (1933) Eurindia Films, Servando C. de la Garza
Director: Arcady Boytler
Script: Guz Aguila, based on the short story 'Le port' by Guy de Maupassant; Adaptation: Guz Aguila and Raphael J. Sevilla
Photography: Alex Phillips; special effects: Salvador Pruñeda
Music: Max Urban

Cast: Andrea Palma (Rosario), Domingo Soler (Alberto Venegas), Joaquín
 Busquets, Fabio Acevedo (Don Antonio), Antonio Polo (Don Basilio)
Duration: 76 minutes.

Further details

Filming started on 24 November 1933 in the México Films studios. *La mujer del
puerto* premiered on 14 February 1934 at the Regis cinema with an opening run
of one week.

Synopsis

Divided into two, the first part of *La mujer del puerto* takes place in Córdoba,
Veracruz State and focuses on the events that will lead to the protagonist
(Rosario's) descent into prostitution. Betrayed by her boyfriend, Rosario's mis-
fortune increases when her ailing father dies before she is able to get medicine to
him. Set in the port of Veracruz, the second part centres on Rosario's encounter
with the sailor Alberto who rescues her from a drunk who is accosting her in the
brothel in which she works. After making love, Rosario and Alberto discover that
they are brother and sister, and Rosario commits suicide by throwing herself into
the sea.

La mujer del puerto
(1991)

Production: (1991) Dos Producciones, Chariot 7 Production.
Director: Arturo Ripstein
Script and adaptation: Paz Alicia Garcíadiego
Photography: Juan José Urbini
Music: Lucía Alvarez
Cast: Evangelina Sosa (Perla), Damián Alcázar (Marro), Patricia Reyes Spíndola
 (Tomasa), Alejandro Parodi (Carmelo), Ernesto Yañez (Eneas).
Duration: 110 minutes.

Synopsis

The same story is told from the perspective of three protagonists: Marro, Perla
and Tomasa, who are brother, sister and mother respectively.

1. Marro: On disembarkation from ship in the port of Veracruz, Marro ends up
    in a seedy brothel in which, unknown to him, his sister works as a prostitute
    and his mother as a washerwoman. The house specialty is '*el acto inter-
    nacional*' in which Perla performs fellatio on a member of the audience in
    competition with Carmelo at the piano, the latter attempting to hold a note
    for longer than it takes Perla to make her client reach his climax. Marro is

selected to perform in the act, but suffering from a fever collapses before the act is over. Later Marro and Perla have sex and then discover their familial relationship. Despite the incest, Perla wants to stay with her brother. Marro returns to his ship; Perla follows, committing suicide by slitting her wrist and throwing herself into the sea.

2. Perla: As in Marro's story, Perla's version starts with the siblings' encounter in the brothel during the '*acto internacional*' and their relationship. Perla argues with her mother Tomasa, wishing to continue her relationship with Marro. The latter leaves for sea; Perla tries to commit suicide but fails. Tomasa makes her daughter abort the foetus she is carrying as a result of the incest.

3. Tomasa: Tomasa's story includes a flashback which contextualises Marro's escape to sea as a young child. Charged with the responsibility of protecting his younger sister from the inappropriate attentions of their drunken father, Marro fails and his mother asks him to help her tackle the drunk. Marro kills his father and escapes. At the police station, Tomasa encounters Carmelo who has been charged with theft; she denounces her son as the murderer and trades sexual favours with the police chief to free Carmelo. Tomasa, Carmelo and Perla start work at Eneas's brothel. At the end of Tomasa's story, the brothel is set to close.

Tarahumara

Production: (1964) Producciones Matouk, Antonio Matouk
Director: Luis Alcoriza
Script: Luis Alcoriza
Cinematography: Rosalío Solano
Music: Raúl Lavista
Cast: Ignacio López Tarso (Raúl), Jaime Fernández (Corachi), Aurora Clavel (Belén), Eric del Castillo (Tomás), Alfonso Mejía (Roniali), Berta Castillón (Nori), Pancho Córdova (Ceredonio), Regino Herrera (Muraca), Carlos Nieto (Pedro), Luis Aragón (Rogelio), Alvaro Ortiz (doctor).
Duration: 115 minutes

Further details

Filmed on location in the Sierra Tarahumara between 20 October and 24 December 1964, *Tarahumara* premiered on 9 September at the Roble cinema with an opening run of seven weeks.

Synopsis

Anthropologist Raúl travels to the Sierra Tarahumara in north-east Mexico to study the problems encountered by the Tarahumara Indians who live there. He befriends Corachi and his wife Belén and becomes increasingly involved in the

Tarahumaras's problems: they are both exploited by white landowners when they agree to work for them, or their land is expropriated and they are forced to migrate when they attempt to continue in their traditional ways of living. Raúl offers to accompany Corachi to the city to denounce the injustices suffered by the community, but before he can do so, he is shot dead.

¡Vámonos con Pancho Villa!
(Let's Go with Pancho Villa!)

Production: (1935) CLASA films, Alberto J. Pani
Director: Fernando de Fuentes
Script and adaptation: Fernando de Fuentes and Xavier Villarrutia from the novel by Rafael F. Muñoz
Cinematography: Jack Draper
Music: Silvestre Revueltas
Cast: Antonio R. Frausto (Tiburcio Maya), Domingo Soler (Pancho Villa), Manuel Tamés (Melitón Botello), Ramón Vallarino (Miguel Angel del Toro), Rafael F. Muñoz (Martín Espinoso), Raúl de Anda (Máximo Perea), Carlos López *Chaflán* (Rodrigo Perea).
Duration: 92 minutes

Further details

Filming started in November 1935 in the CLASA studios at a (for the time) record cost of $100,000. *Vámonos con Pancho Villa* premiered on 31 December 1936 at the Palacio cinema with an opening run of one week.

Synopsis

Set in 1914, six friends – Melitón, Miguel Ángel, Tiburcio, Martín and the Perea brothers, Máximo and Rodrigo – form the group known as *Los Leones de San Pablo* and join the revolution to fight with Pancho Villa. One by one, Los Leones are killed in the conflict. Máximo, Martín and Rodrigo die in separate incidents. The remaining Leones become part of Villa's personal guard. Melitón dies in a game of Russian roulette. Miguel Angel contracts cholera, and Tiburcio is forced to kill him and burn his body. Tiburcio, disappointed with Villa's cowardice in the face of the cholera epidemic, abandons Villa's army and returns to his village.

Y tu mamá también
(And Your Mother Too)

Production: (2001) Producciones Anhelo, Bésame Mucho Pictures
Director: Alfonso Cuarón

Script: Alfonso Cuarón and Carlos Cuarón
Cinematography: Emmanuel Lubezki
Cast: Gael García Bernal (Julio Zapata), Diego Luna (Tenoch Iturbide), Maribel
    Verdú (Luisa Cortés), Juan Carlos Remolina (Alejandro 'Jano' Montés de
    Oca), Daniel Giménez Cacho (Narrator), Liboria Rodríguez (Leodegaria 'Leo'
    Victoria), Diana Bracho (Silvia Allende de Iturbide), Silverio Palacios (Jésus
    'Chuy' Carranza), Mayra Serbulo (Mabel Juárez de Carranza), Andrea López
    (Lucero Carranza).
Duration: 105 minutes

Further details

Filmed on locations in Mexico City, Huatulco and Puerto Escondido, *Y tu mamá
también* won a host of awards, including the prize for Best Foreign Language
Film by the following institutions: Boston Society of Film Critics, Broadcast
Film Critics Association, Chicago Film Critics Association, Dallas-Forth Worth
Film Critics Association Awards, Film Critics Circle of Australia, Florida Film
Critics Circle, Ft. Lauderdale International Film Festival, London Critics Circle,
Los Angeles Film Critics Assocation, New York Film Critics Circle, San Francisco
Film Critics Circle.

Synopsis

After the departure of their girlfriends on a trip to Europe, Julio and Tenoch
embark on a journey to the fictitious 'Boca del Cielo' (Heaven's Mouth) in the
company of Luisa who, unknown to the boys, has recently been diagnosed with
cancer. Luisa has sex with Tenoch and then Julio, which triggers rivalries between
the two and confessions about previous sexual infidelities. On arriving at the coast,
the trio spends some time in the company of fisherman Chuy Carranza, before
Julio and Tenoch return to Mexico City. Luisa remains behind and the boys learn
of her death at the end of the film.

REFERENCES

Acevedo-Muñoz, E. R. (2003) *Buñuel and Mexico: The Crisis of National Cinema*, Berkeley: University of California Press.

—— (2004) 'Sex, Class, and Mexico in Alfonso Cuarón's *Y tu mamá también*', *Film and History*, 34(1): 39–48.

Agrasánchez Jr., R. (2001) *Cine Mexicano: Carteles de la Época de Oro 1936–1956/ Posters from the Golden Age 1936–1956*, San Francisco: Chronicle Books.

Alfaro Salazar, F. H. and Ochoa, A. (1998) *La república de los cines*, Mexico City: Clío.

Alfaro Salazar, F. H. and Ochoa Vega, A. (1999) *Espacios distantes . . . Aún vivos: Las salas cinematográficas de la ciudad de México*, Mexico City: Universidad Autónoma Metropolitana-Xochimilco.

Anderson, B. ([1983] 1991) *Imagined Communities: Reflections on the Origin and Spread of Nationalism* (revised edn), London: Verso.

Arredondo, I. (2001) *Palabra de mujer: Historia oral de las directoras de cine mexicanas (1988–94)*, Madrid/Frankfurt/Aguascalientes: Iberoamericana, Vervuert, Universidad Autónoma de Aguascalientes.

Aumont, J. (1987) *Montage Eisenstein*, trans. Hildreth L., Penley, C. and Ross, A., Bloomington, IN: Indiana University Press.

Ayala Blanco, J. ([1968] 1993) *La aventura del cine mexicano en la época de oro y después (1931–1967)*, Mexico City: Grijalbo.

—— ([1974] 1986) *La búsqueda del cine mexicano (1968–1972)*, Mexico City: Editorial Posada.

—— (1986) *La condición del cine mexicano (1973–1985)*, Mexico City: Editorial Posada.

—— (1991) *La disolvencia del cine mexicano: Entre lo popular y lo exquisito*, Mexico City: Grijalbo.

—— (1994) *La eficacia del cine mexicano: Entre lo viejo y lo nuevo*, Mexico City: Grijalbo.

—— (2001) *La fugacidad del cine mexicano*, Mexico City: Océano.

Barker, F., Hulme, P. and Iversen, M. (eds) (1998) *Cannibalism and the Colonial World*, Cambridge: Cambridge University Press.

Bartra, E. (1999) 'Faldas y pantalones: El género en el cine de la Revolución mexicana', *Film-Historia*, 9(2): 169–80.

—— (1987) *La jaula de la melancolía: Identidad y metamorfosis del mexicano*, Mexico City: Grijalbo.

Baptra, R. (2000) 'Paradise Subverted: The Invention of the Mexican Character', trans. Hall, C. J., in Camayd-Freixas, E. and Gonzáles, J. E. (eds) *Primitivism and Identity in Latin America: Essays on Art, Literature and Culture*, Tucson: University of Arizona Press.

—— (2002) *Blood, Ink, and Culture: Miseries and Splendors of the Post-Mexican Condition*, trans. M. A. Healey, Durham, NC, and London: Duke University Press.

Bell, S. M. (1992) 'Contexts of Critical Reception in *El laberinto de la soledad*: The Contingencies of Value and the Discourse of Power', *Siglo XX/20th Century: Critique and Cultural Discourse*, 10(182): 101–24.

Benjamin, T. (2000) *La Revolución: Mexico's Great Revolution as Memory, Myth, and History*, Austin: University of Texas Press.

Beverley, J., Oviedo, J. and Aronna, M. (eds) (1995) *The Postmodernism Debate in Latin America*, Durham, NC: Duke University Press.

Bhabha, H. K. (1994) *The Location of Culture*, London: Routledge.

Bonfil Batalla, G. ([1987] 1994) *México profundo: Una civilización negada*, Mexico City: Grijalbo.

Bonfil, C. (1995) '*El Jardín del Edén*', *La jornada*, 15 October: 43.

—— (1997) 'El patrimonio fílmico' in Florescano, E. (ed.) *El patrimonio nacional de México*, vol. II, Mexico City: Consejo Nacional para la Cultura y las Artes/Fondo de Cultura Económica.

Bordwell, D., Staiger, J. and Thompson, K. (1985) *The Classical Hollywood Cinema*, New York: Columbia University Press.

Brading, D. A. (1988) 'Manuel Gamio and Official *Indigenismo* in Mexico', *Bulletin of Latin American Research*, 7: 75–89.

—— (2001) *Mexican Phoenix: Our Lady of Guadalupe: Image and Tradition across Five Centuries*, Cambridge: Cambridge University Press.

Branston, G. (2000) *Cinema and Cultural Modernity*, Buckingham/Philadelphia: Open University Press.

Brooks, P. (1976) *The Melodramatic Imagination: Balzac, Henry James: Melodrama and the Mode of Excess*, New Haven, CT: Yale University Press.

Burton, J. (1986) *Cinema and Social Change in Latin America: Conversations with Filmmakers*, Austin: University of Texas Press.

—— (1990) *The Social Documentary in Latin America*, Pittsburgh: University of Pittsburgh Press.

Burton-Carvajal, J. (1994) 'La ley del más padre: melodrama paternal, melodrama patriarcal, y la especificidad del ejemplo mexicano', *Archivos de la Filmoteca*, 16: 51–63.

—— (1997) 'Mexican Melodramas of Patriarchy: Specificity of a Transcultural Form', in Stock, A. M. (ed.) *Framing Latin American Cinema: Contemporary Critical Perspectives*, *Hispanic Issues*, 15: 186–234.

—— (1998a) 'The String of Pearls or the Bibliographer's Recompense', *Studies in Latin American Popular Culture*, 17: 233–54.

—— (1998b) 'De la pantalla a la página: taxonomía y periodización de la bibliografía sobre cine latinoamericano' in Burton-Carvajal, J., Torres, P., and Miquel, A. *Horizontes del segundo siglo: Investigación y pedagogía del cine mexicano, latinoamericano y chicano*, Guadalajara: Universidad de Guadalajara/Instituto Mexicano de Cinematografía.

Burton-Carvajal, J., Torres, P. and Miquel, A. (1998) *Horizontes del segundo siglo: Investigación y pedagogía del cine mexicano, latinoamericano y chicano*, Guadalajara: Universidad de Guadalajara/Instituto Mexicano de Cinematografía.

Burton-Carvajal, J., Montiel Figueiras, M. and García, G. (2002) *Matilde Landeta: Hija de la revolución*, Mexico City: IMCINE/CONACULTA.

Camayd-Freixas, E. and González, J. E. (eds) (2000) *Primitivism and Identity in Latin America: Essays on Art, Literature and Culture*, Tucson: University of Arizona Press.

Camp, R. A. (2000) 'The Time of the Technocrats and Deconstruction of the Revolution', in Meyer, M. C. and Beezley, W. H. (eds) *The Oxford History of Mexico*, Oxford: Oxford University Press.

Carrera, M. M. (2003) *Imagining Identity in New Spain: Race, Lineage and the Colonial Body Politic in Portraiture and Casta Paintings*, Austin: University of Texas Press.

Carro, N. (1984) *El cine de luchadores*, Mexico City: Universidad Nacional Autónoma de México.

Carroll, N. and Banes, S. (2000) 'Cinematic Nation-Building: Eisenstein's *The Old and the New*', in Hjort, M. and Mackenzie, S. (eds) *Cinema and Nation*, London: Routledge.

Castañeda, J. G. (1995) *The Mexican Shock: Its Meaning for the U.S.*, New York: The New Press.

—— (2000) *Perpetuating Power: How Mexican Presidents Were Chosen*, New York: The New Press.

Castillo, D. A. (1998) *Easy Women: Sex and Gender in Modern Mexican Fiction*, Minneapolis: University of Minnesota Press.

Castro Ricalde, M. (2002) 'Violencia y género: El cine mexicano de la década de los ochenta', in De Diego, F. and Schwartz, A. (eds) *Repensando la violencia y el patriarcado frente al nuevo milenio: Nuevas perspectivas en el mundo hispánico y germánico*, Ottawa: University of Ottawa.

Celín, F. (1995) 'Comparta nuestros sueños', *Novedades*, 5 November.

Charney, L. and Schwartz, V. R. (eds) (1995) *Cinema and the Invention of Modern Life*, Berkeley, LA: University of California Press.

Cien años de cine mexicano: 1896–1996, (CD ROM), Mexico: Conaculta/IMCINE/Universidad de Colima.

Ciuk, P. (2000) *Diccionario de directores del cine mexicano*, Mexico City: CONACULTA/Cineteca Nacional.

Clifford, J. (1988) *The Predicament of Culture: Twentieth-Century Ethnography, Literature and Art*, Cambridge, MA: Harvard University Press.

Cockcroft, J. D. (1998) *Mexico's Hope: An Encounter with Politics and History*, New York: Monthly Review Press.

Cohan, S. and Hark, I. R. (eds) (1993) *Screening the Male: Exploring Masculinities in Hollywood Cinema*, London: Routledge.

Cohan, S. and Hark, I. R. (eds) (1997) *The Road Movie Book*, London: Routledge.

Collier, S. (1986) *The Life, Music and Times of Carlos Gardel*, Pittsburgh: University of Pittsburgh Press.

Contreras Magaña, M. (1996) *Ciudad abierta: Los años de oro*, vol. I, Mexico City: Análisis y Evaluación de Prensa.

Craven, D. (2002) *Art and Revolution in Latin America, 1910–1990*, New Haven, CT: Yale University Press.

Dawson, A. S. (1998) 'From Models for the Nation to Model Citizens: Indigenismo and the 'Revindication' of the Mexican Indian, 1920–40', *Journal of Latin American Studies*, 30: 279–308.

De la Mora, S. (1992–93) 'Fascinating Machismo: Toward an Unmasking of Heterosexual Masculinity in Arturo Ripstein's *El lugar sin límites*', *Journal of Film and Video*, 44: 3–4.

—— (1999) 'A Career in Perspective: An Interview with Arturo Ripstein', *Film Quarterly* 52(4): 2–11.

De la Peza, C. (1998) *Cine, melodrama y cultura de masas: Estética de la antiestética*, Mexico City: Consejo Nacional para la Cultura y las Artes.

De la Vega Alfaro, E. (1987) *Juan Orol*, Guadalajara: CIEC/Universidad de Guadalajara.

—— (1988) *Alberto Gout (1907–1966)*, Guadalajara: CIEC/Universidad de Guadalajara.

—— (1989) *Raúl de Anda*, Guadalajara: CIEC/Universidad de Guadalajara.

—— (1992a) *José Bohr*, Guadalajara: CIEC/Universidad de Guadalajara.

—— (1992b) *Arcady Boytler. 1893–1965*, Guadalajara: CIEC/Universidad de Guadalajara.

—— (1994) 'Evolución y estado actual de la investigación sobre cine mexicano' in De la Vega Alfaro, E. and Sánchez Ruíz, E. E. (eds) *Bye Bye Lumière: Investigación sobre cine en México*, Guadalajara: Universidad de Guadalajara.

—— (1997) *Del muro a la pantalla: S. M. Eisenstein y el arte pictórico mexicano*, Guadalajara: Universidad de Guadalajara/ Instituto Mexiquense de Cultura. Instituto Mexicano de Cinematografía.

—— (2000) 'The Decline of the Golden Age and the Making of the Crisis', in Hershfield, J. and Maciel, D. R. (eds) *Mexico's Cinema: A Century of Film and Filmmakers*, Wilmington, DE: S. R. Books.

De los Reyes, A. [1981] (1993a) *Cine y sociedad en México: Vivir de sueños, 1896–1930*, vol. 1, Mexico City: UNAM.

—— [1981] (1993b) *Cine y sociedad en México: Bajo el cielo de México, 1920–1924*, vol. 2, Mexico City: UNAM.

—— (1984) *Los orígenes del cine en México*, Mexico City: Fondo de la Cultura Económica/SEP.

—— (1985) *Con Villa en México: Testimonios de los camarógrafos norteamericanos en la Revolución*, Mexico City: UNAM.

—— (1987) *Medio siglo de cine mexicano (1896–1947)*, Mexico City: Editorial Trillas.

—— (1995a) 'The Silent Cinema' in Paranaguá, P. A. (ed.) *Mexican Cinema*, London: BFI.

—— (1995b) 'Los besos y el cine', in Estrada de Guerlero, E. (ed.) *El arte y la vida cotidiana*, Mexico City: UNAM/Instituto de Investigaciones Estéticas.

—— (1996a) 'El gobierno mexicano y las películas denigrantes. 1920–1931', in Durán, I., Trujillo, I. and Verea, M. (eds) *México–Estados Unidos: Encuentros y desencuentros en el cine*, Mexico City: Filmoteca de la UNAM/IMCINE/CISAN.

—— (1996b) *Dolores del Río*, Mexico City: Grupo Condumex.

De Luna, A. (1984) *La batalla y su sombra (La Revolución en el cine mexicano)*, Mexico City: Universidad Autónoma Metropolitana – Xochimilco.

De Orellana, M. (1990) 'The Voice of the Present over Images of the Past: Historical Narration in *Memories of a Mexican*', in Burton, J. (ed.) *The Social Documentary in Latin America*, Pittsburgh: University of Pittsburgh Press.

—— (1991) *La mirada circular: el cine norteamericano de la Revolución Mexicana, 1911–1917*, Mexico City: Joaquín Mortiz.

—— (1993) 'The Incursion of North American Fictional Cinema 1911–1917 into the Mexican Revolution' in King, J., López, A. M. and Alvarado, M. (eds) *Mediating Two Worlds: Cinematic Encounters in the Americas*, London: BFI.

—— (2003) *Filming Pancho: How Hollywood Shaped the Mexican Revolution*, trans. King, J., London: Verso.

De Toro, A. and De Toro, F. (1999) *El debate de la postcolonialidad en Latinoamérica: una postmodernidad periférica o cambio de paradigma en el pensamiento latinoamericano*, Madrid: Iberoamericana/Frankfurt am Main: Vervuert.

203

Del Río, E. (Rius) (1982) *Su Majestad el PRI*, Mexico City: Grijalbo.

Delpar, H. (1992) *The Enormous Vogue of Things Mexican: Cultural Relations between the United States and Mexico, 1920–1935*, Tucaloosa: University of Alabama Press.

Dever, S. (2003) *Celluloid Nationalism and Other Melodramas: From Post-Revolutionary Mexico to Fin de Siglo Mexamérica*, Albany: State University of New York Press.

D'Lugo, M. (2003) 'Authorship, Globalization, and the New Identity of Latin American Cinema', in Guneratne, A. R. and Dissanayake, W. (eds) *Rethinking Third Cinema*, New York and London: Routledge.

Dubois, P. (1995) 'Photography Mise-en-Film: Autobiographical (Hi)stories and Psychic Apparatuses', in Petro P. (ed.) *Fugitive Images: From Photography to Video*, Bloomington and Indianapolis: Indiana University Press.

Durán, I., Trujillo, I. and Verea M. (eds) (1996) *México–Estados Unidos: Encuentros y desencuentors en el cine*, Mexico City: Filmoteca UNAM/IMCINE/CISAN.

Dyer, R. (1998) *Stars*, London: BFI.

Egan, L. (2001) *Carlos Monsiváis: Culture and Chronicle in Contemporary Mexico*, Tucson: University of Arizona Press.

Eisenstein, S. (1975) *Film Sense*, ed. Leyda, J., San Diego: Harcourt, Brace, Jovanovich.

—— (1983) *Immoral Memories: An Autobiography*, trans. Marshall, H., Boston: Houghton Mifflin.

Elena, A. and Díaz López, M. (eds) (2003) *The Cinema of Latin America*, London: Wallflower Press.

Ellis, J. (1982) 'The Literary Adaptation: An Introduction', *Screen* 23: 1.

Elsaesser, T. (ed.) (1990) *Early Cinema: Space, Frame, Narrative*, London: BFI.

Escobedo, H. (ed.) (1989) *Mexican Monuments: Strange Encounters*, New York: Abeville Press.

Evans, P. W. (1995) *The Films of Luis Buñuel: Subjectivity and Desire*, Oxford: Oxford University Press.

Fabian, J. (1983) *Time and the Other: How Anthropology Makes its Object*, New York: Columbia University Press.

Faris, J. C. (1992) 'A Political Primer on Anthropology/Photography', in Edwards, E. (ed.) *Anthropology and Photography, 1860–1920*, New Haven, CT: Yale University Press, 1992.

Fein, S. (1996) 'La imagen de México: La segunda guerra mundial y la propaganda fílmica de Estados Unidos', in Durán, I., Trujillo, I. and Verea, M. (eds) *México–Estados Unidos: Encuentros y desencuentros en el cine*, Mexico City: IMCINE/UNAM.

—— (1998) '*Dicen que soy comunista*: Nationalist Anticommunism in the Mexican Cinema of the 1950s', *Nuevo Texto Crítico*, 11 (21/22): 155–72.

—— (1999a) 'Everyday Forms of Transnational Collaboration: US Film Propaganda in Cold War Mexico', in Joseph, G., LeGrand, C. and Salvatore, R. (eds) *Close Encounters of Empire: Writing the Cultural History of U.S.–Latin American Relations*, Durham, NC: Duke University Press.

—— (1999b) 'From Collaboration to Containment: Hollywood and the International Political Economy of Mexican Cinema after the Second World War', in Hershfield, J. and Maciel, D. R. (eds) *Mexico's Cinema: A Century of Film and Filmmakers*, Wilmington, DE: S. R. Books.

—— (1999c) 'Transcultured Anticommunism: Cold War Hollywood in Postwar Mexico', in Noriega, C. (ed.) *Visible Nations: Latin American Cinema and Video*, Minneapolis: University of Minnesota Press.

Florescano, E. (1993) 'The Creation of the Museo Nacional de Antropología of Mexico and its Scientific, Educational, and Political Purposes', in Hill Boone, E. (ed.) *Collecting the Pre-Columbian Past*, Washington DC: Dumbarton Oakes Research Library and Collection.

—— (ed.) (1995) *Mitos mexicanos*, Mexico City: Aguilar/Nuevo Siglo.

Folgarait, L. (1998) *Mural Painting and Social Revolution in Mexico, 1920–1940*, Cambridge: Cambridge University Press.

Foster, D. W. (1999) *Gender and Society in Contemporary Brazilian Society*, Austin: University of Texas Press.

—— (2002) *Mexico City in Contemporary Mexican Cinema*, Austin: University of Texas Press.

Foucault, M. (1970) *The Order of Things: An Archaeology of the Human Sciences*, trans. Sheridan Smith, A. M., London: Tavistock.

Fox, C. F. (1999) *The Fence and the River: Culture and Politics at the U.S.–Mexico Border*, Minneapolis: University of Minnesota Press.

Franco, J. (1989) *Plotting Women: Gender and Representation in Mexico*, London: Verso.

Freud, Sigmund (2000) *Totem and Taboo*, trans. Brill, A. A., New York: Prometheus Books.

Gaines, J. M. and Renov, M. (eds) (1999) *Collecting Visible Evidence*, Minneapolis: University of Minnesota Press.

Galindo, A. (1985) *El cine mexicano: Un personal punto de vista*, Mexico City: EDAMEX.

Gamboa, F. ([1903] 2002) *Santa*, Madrid: Cátedra.

García, G. (1994a) *No me parezco a nadie: La vida de Pedro Infante*, Mexico City: Clío.

—— (1994b) 'Tengo una tumba donde llorar. Ismael Rodríguez contra el melodrama', *Archivos de la Filmoteca*, 16.

—— (1995) 'Melodrama: The Passion Machine', in Paranaguá, P. A. (ed.) *Mexican Cinema*, London: BFI.

—— (1999) 'In Quest of a National Cinema: The Silent Era' in Hershfield, J. and Maciel, D. R. (eds) *Mexico's Cinema: A Century of Film and Filmmakers*, Wilmington, Delaware: Scholarly Resources.

García, G. and Aviña, R. (1997) *Época de oro del cine mexicano*, Mexico City: Editorial Clío.

García, G. and Coria, J. F. (1997) *Nuevo cine mexicano*, Mexico City: Editorial Clío.

García, G. and Maciel, D. (2001) *El cine mexicano a través de la crítica*, Mexico City: UNAM/IMCINE/Universidad Autónoma de Ciudad Juárez.

García, S. (2003) 'Immigration Reform Key to Border Security', Americas Program Silver City, NM: Interhemispheric Resource Center.

García Canclini, N. (1989) *Culturas híbridas: Estrategias para entrar y salir de la modernidad*, Mexico: Grijalbo.

—— (1994) *Los nuevos espectadores: Cine, televisión y video en México*, Mexico City: IMCINE/CNCA.

—— (1995) *Consumidores y ciudadanos: Conflictos multiculturales de la globalización*, Mexico City: Grijalbo.

—— (1997) 'Will There be Latin American Cinema in the Year 2000? Visual Culture in a Postnational Era', in Stock, A. M. (ed.), *Framing Latin American Cinema: Contemporary Critical Perspectives*, Minneapolis: University of Minnesota Press.

—— (2000) *La globalización imaginada*, Mexico City: Paidós.

García Riera, E. (1974) *El cine y su público*, Mexico City: Fondo de Cultura Económica.

—— (1987) *México visto por el cine extranjero*, vols 1–6, Mexico City: Ediciones Era & Guadalajara: Centro de Investigaciones y Enseñazas Cinematográficas.

—— (1988) *Arturo Ripstein habla de su cine con Emilio García Riera*, Guadalajara: Centro de Investigaciones y Enseñzas Cinematográficas.

—— (1992) *Historia documental del cine mexicano*, vols 1–18, Guadalajara: Centro de Investigaciones y Enseñazas Cinematográficas.

—— (1998) *Breve historia del cine mexicano: primer siglo, 1897–1997*, Mexico City: Ediciones Mapa/IMCINE.

García Tsao, L. (1994) *Felipe Cazals habla de su cine*, Guadalajara: Universidad de Guadalajara/Centro de Investigación y Enseñanza Cinematográficas.

Garner, P. H. (2001) *Porfirio Díaz*, Harlow: Longman.

Geduld, H. M. and Gottesman, R. (eds) (1970) *Sergei Eisenstein and Upton Sinclair: The Making and Unmaking of ¡Que viva México!* Bloomington: Indiana University Press.

Geertz, C. (1988) *The Anthropologist as Author*, Stanford, CA: Stanford University Press.

Getino, O. (1998) *Cine y televisión en América Latina: Producción y mercados*, Santiago: LOM Ediciones/Ediciones CICCUS.

Gledhill, C. (1987) *Home Is Where the Heart Is: Studies in Melodrama and the Woman's Film*, London: BFI.

—— (2000) 'Rethinking Genre', in Gledhill C. and Williams, L. (eds) *Reinventing Film Studies*, London: Arnold.

Gómez-Peña, G. (1993) *Warrior for Gringostroika*, intro. by Bartra, R., trans. Fusco, C., Minnesota: Graywolf Press.

Gómez-Quiñones, J. and Maciel, D. R. (1998) '"What Goes Around, Comes Around": Political Practice and Cultural Response to the Internationalization of Mexican Labor' in Maciel, D. R. and Herrera-Sobek, M. (eds) *Culture Across Borders: Mexican Immigration and Popular Culture*, Tucson: University of Arizona Press.

González Rubio, J. (1995) '*El Callejón de los Milagros*', *Revista Dicine*, 63.

Goodwin, J. (1993) *Eisenstein, Cinema and History*, Urbana, IL: University of Illinois Press.

Grant, C. (2002) 'Recognizing Billy Budd in Beau Travail: Epistemology and Hermeuneutics of an Auteurist "Free" Adaptation', *Screen* 43(1): 57–73.

—— (2003) 'Still Moving Images: Photographs of the Disappeared in Films about the "Dirty War" in Argentina', in Hughes, A. and Noble, A. (eds) *Phototextualities: Intersections of Photography and Narrative*, Albuquerque: University of New Mexico Press.

Grimshaw, A. (2001) *The Ethnographer's Eye: Ways of Seeing in Modern Anthropology*, Cambridge: Cambridge University Press.

Grosz, E. (1989) *Sexual Subversions*, St Leonards: Alan & Unwin.

—— (1994) *Volatile Bodies: Toward a Corporeal Feminism*, Bloomington and Indianapolis: Indiana University Press.

—— (1998) 'Bodies–Cities', in Nast, H. J. and Pile, S. (eds) *Places through the Body*, London: Routledge.

Gruzinski, S. (2001) *Images at War: Mexico from Columbus to Blade Runner (1492–2019)*, trans. by Heather MacLean, Durham, NC: Duke University Press.

Guneratne, A. R. and Dissanayake, W. (eds) (2003) *Rethinking Third Cinema*, New York and London: Routledge.

Gunning, T. (1990) 'The Cinema of Attractions: Early Film, its Spectators and the Avant-Garde', in Elsaesser, T. (ed.) *Early Cinema: Space, Frame, Narrative*, London: BFI.

—— (2000) '"Animated Pictures": Tales of Cinema's Forgotten Future, after 100 years of films', in Gledhill, C. and Williams, L. (eds) *Reinventing Film Studies*, London: Arnold.

Gutiérrez Ruvalcaba, X. (1996) 'A Fresh Look at the Casasola Archive', *History of Photography*, 20(3): 191–96.

Gutmann, M. C. (1996) *The Meanings of Macho: Being a Man in Mexico City*, Berkeley, CA: University of California Press.

—— (2003) (ed.) *Changing Men and Masculinities in Latin America*, Durham, NC: Duke University Press.

—— (2004) *The Romance of Democracy: Compliant Defiance in Contemporary Mexico*, Berkeley, CA: University of California Press.

Guzmán, M. L. ([1928] 1991) *El águila y la serpiente*, Mexico City: Editorial Porrúa.

Hansen, M. B. (2000) 'The Mass Production of the Senses: Classical Cinema as Vernacular Modernism', in Gledhill, C. and Williams, L. (eds), *Reinventing Film Studies*, London: Arnold.

Hayden, T. (ed.) (2002) *The Zapatista Reader*, New York: Thunder's Mouth Press/ Nation Press.

Hayes, J. E. (2000) *Radio Nation: Communication, Popular Culture, and Nationalism in Mexico, 1920–1950*, Tucson: University of Arizona Press.

Herrera-Sobek, M. (1998) 'The Corrido as Hypertext: Undocumented Mexican Immigrant Films and the Mexican/Chicano Ballad', in Maciel, D. and Herrera Sobek, M. (eds), *Culture Across Borders: Mexican Immigration and Popular Culture*, Tucson: University of Arizona Press.

Hershfield, J. (1992) 'The Construction of Woman in *Distinto amanecer*', *Spectator*, 13(1): 43–51.

—— (1996) *Mexican Cinema/Mexican Woman, 1940–1950*, Tucson: University of Arizona Press.

—— (1997) 'Women's Pictures: Identity and Representation in Recent Mexican Cinema', *Canadian Journal of Film Studies/Revue canadienne d'études cinématographiques*, 6: 1.

—— (1998) 'Sergei Eisenstein's ¡Que viva México! as Ethnography' in Grant, B. K. and Sloniowski, J. (eds) *Documenting the Documentary: Close Readings of Documentary Film and Video*, Detroit: Wayne State University Press.

—— (2000) *The Invention of Dolores del Río*, Minneapolis: University of Minnesota Press.

Hershfield, J. and Maciel, D. R. (1999) *Mexico's Cinema: A Century of Film and Filmmakers*, Wilmington, DE: S. R. Books.

Higson, A. (2000) 'The Limiting Imagination of National Cinema', in Hjort, M. and Mackenzie, S. (eds) *Cinema and Nation*, London: Routledge.

Hirsch, M. (1997) *Family Frames: Photography, Narrative and Postmemory*, Cambridge, MA: Harvard University Press.

Hjort, M. and Mackenzie, S. (eds) (2000) *Cinema and Nation*, London: Routledge.

Honour, H. (1976) *The New Golden Land: European Images of America from the Discoveries to the Present Time*, London: Allen Lane.

Horton, A. and Macdougal, S. Y. (1998) *Play It Again, Sam: Retakes on Remakes*, Berkeley: University of California Press.

Hymes, D. (1974) *Reinventing Anthropology*, New York: Vintage.

Iglesias, N. (1991) *Entre yerba, polvo y plomo: Lo fronterizo visto por el cine mexicano*, 2 volumes, Baja California: El Colegio de la Frontera del Norte.

Isaac, A. (1993) *Conversaciones con Gabriel Figueroa*, Guadalajara: Universidad de Guadalajara/CIEC.

Johnson, J. J. (1993) *Latin America in Caricature*, Austin: University of Texas Press.

Johnson, R. and Stam, R. (1995) *Brazilian Cinema*, New York: Columbia University Press.

Joseph, G. M. and Nugent, D. (1994) *Everyday Forms of State Formation: Revolution and the Negotiation of Rule in Modern Mexico*, Durham, NC: Duke University Press.

Joseph, G. M., Rubenstein, A. and Zolov, E. (2001) *Fragments of a Golden Age: The Politics of Culture in Mexico since 1940*, Durham, NC: Duke University Press.

Joseph, G. M. and Henderson, T. J. (2002) *The Mexico Reader: History, Culture, Politics*, Durham, NC: Duke University Press.

Kaplan, E. A. (1992) *Motherhood and Representation: The Mother in Popular Culture and Melodrama*, London: Routledge.

—— (1997) *Looking for the Other: Feminism, Film and the Imperial Gaze*, London: Routledge.

Karetnikova, I. and Steinmetz, L. (1991) *Mexico According to Eisenstein*, Albuquerque: University of New Mexico Press.

King, J. (1990) *Magical Reels: A History of Cinema in Latin America*, London: Verso.

Knight, A. (1986) *The Mexican Revolution*, 2 vols, Lincoln, NB: University of Nebraska Press.

—— (1990) 'Racism, Revolution, and *Indigenismo*: Mexico, 1910–1940', in Graham, R. (ed.) *The Idea of Race in Latin America, 1870–1940*, Austin: University of Texas Press.

—— (1992) 'The Peculiarities of Mexican History: Mexico Compared to Latin America, 1892–1992', *Journal of Latin American Studies*, 24: 99–144.

—— (1994) 'Popular Culture and the Revolutionary State in Mexico, 1910–1940', *Hispanic American Historical Review*, 74(3): 393–444.

—— (1999) 'Political Violence in Post-Revolutionary Mexico', in Koonings, K. and Kruijt, D. (eds) *Societies of Fear: The Legacy of Civil War, Violence and Terror in Latin America*, London: Zed Books.

Koonings, K. and Kruijt, D. (eds) (1999) *Societies of Fear: The Legacy of Civil War, Violence and Terror in Latin America*, London: Zed Books.

Kraniauskus, J. (1994) 'Border Issues', *Travesía: Journal of Latin American Cultural Studies*, 3(1–2): 5–13.

Kuhn, A. (1994) *Women's Pictures: Feminism and Cinema*, 2nd edn, London: Verso.

Laderman, D. (2002) *Driving Visions: Exploring the Road Movie*, Austin: University of Texas Press.

Lafaye, J. (1974) *Quetzalcoatl and Guadalupe: The Formation of Mexican National Consciousness, 1531–1813*, trans. Keen, B., Chicago: University of Chicago Press.

Larrain, J. (2000) *Identity and Modernity in Latin America*, Cambridge: Polity.

Leñero, V. (1997) *El Callejón de los Milagros*, Mexico City: Mexico City: Ediciones El Milagro.

León-Portilla, M. (2003) (coord.) *Iberoamérica mestiza: Encuentro de pueblos y culturas*, Spain/Mexico: Fundación Santillana/SEACEXEspaña/CONACULTA-INAH, Ayunt amiento de Madrid/Centro Cultural de la Villa.

Levi, H. (2001) 'Masked Media: The Adventures of Lucha Libre on the Small Screen' in Joseph, G., Rubenstein, A. and Zolov, E. (eds) *Fragments of a Golden Age: The Politics of Culture in Mexico since 1940*, Durham, NC: Duke University Press.

Lillo, G. (1994) 'Melodrama mexicano', *Archivos de la Filmoteca*, 16.

Limón, J. E. (1998) *American Encounters: Greater Mexico and the United States, and the Erotics of Culture*, Boston, MA: Beacon Press.

Lindauer, M. A. (1999) *Devouring Frida: The Art History and Popular Celebrity of Frida Kahlo*, Hanover: Wesleyan University Press/University Press of New England.

Lomnitz, C. (1992) *Exits from the Labyrinth: Culture and Ideology in the Mexican National Space*, Berkeley, CA: University of California Press.

—— (1999) *Modernidad indiana: Nueve ensayos sobre nación y mediación en México*, Mexico City: Planeta.

—— (2001) *Deep Mexico, Silent Mexico: An Anthropology of Nationalism*, Minneapolis: University of Minnesota Press.

López, A. M. (1991) 'Tears and Desire: Women and Melodrama in the "Old" Mexican Cinema', *Iris*, 13.

—— (1993) 'Tears and Desire: Women and Melodrama in the "Old" Mexian Cinema', in King, J., López, A. M. and Alvarado, M. (eds) *Mediating Two Worlds: Cinematic Encounters in the Americas*, London: BFI.

—— (1994) 'A Cinema for the Continent', in Noriega, C. A. and Ricci, S. (eds) *The Mexican Cinema Project*, Los Angeles: UCLA Film and Television Archive.

—— (1999) 'Hollywood–Mexico: Dolores del Río, una estrella transnacional', *Archivos de la Filmoteca*, 31: 12–35.

—— (2000a) 'Facing up to Hollywood', in Gledhill, C. and Williams, L. (eds) *Reinventing Film Studies*, London: Arnold.

—— (2000b) 'Early Cinema and Modernity in Latin America', *Cinema Journal*, 40(1): 48–78.

López Aranda, S. (1994) 'Filmar en el tiempo: Arturo Ripstein y Paz Alicia Garcíadiego', *Revista Dicine*, 58: 13–17.

Maciel, D. R. (1992) 'The Cinematic Renaissance of Contemporary Mexico: 1985–1992', *Spectator*, 13(1): 71–85.

—— (1997) 'Serpientes y Escaleras: The Contemporary Cinema of Mexico, 1976–1994' in Martin, M. T. (ed.) *New Latin American Cinema, Volume Two: Studies of National Cinemas*, Detroit: Wayne State University Press.

—— (1999) 'Cinema and the State in Contemporary Mexico, 1970–1999', in Maciel, D. R and Hershfield, J. (eds) *Mexico's Cinema: A Century of Film and Filmmakers*, Wilmington, DE: S. R. Books.

Maciel, D. R. and García-Acevedo, M. R. (1998) 'The Celluloid Immigrant', in Maciel, D. R. and Herrera-Sobeck, M. (eds), *Culture Across Borders: Mexican Immigration and Popular Culture*, Tuscon: University of Arizona Press.

Maciel, D. R. and Herrera-Sobek, M. (eds) (1998) *Culture Across Borders: Mexican Immigration and Popular Culture*, Tucson: University of Arizona Press.

Mahfouz, N. ([1956] 1995) *Palace Walk*, trans. Hutchins, W. M. and Kenny, O. E., London: Black Swan.

Maltby, D. and Craven, I. (1995) *Hollywood Cinema: An Introduction*, Oxford: Blackwell.

Mancillas, A., Wallen, R. and Waller, M. R. (1999) 'Making Art, Making Citizens: Las Comadres and Postnational Aesthetics', in Bloom L. (ed.) *With Other Eyes: Looking at Race and Gender in Visual Culture*, Minneapolis and London: University of Minnesota Press.

Margulies, I. (ed.) (2003) *Rites of Realism: Essays on Corporeal Cinema*, Durham, NC: Duke University Press.

Marks, L. U. (2000) *The Skin of the Film: Intercultural Cinema, Embodiment and the Senses*, Durham, NC: Duke University Press.

Martin, M. T. (1997) *New Latin American Cinema, Volume One: Theory, Practices, and Transcontinental Articulations*, Michigan: Wayne State University Press.

—— (1997) *New Latin American Cinema, Volume Two: Studies of National Cinemas,* Michigan: Wayne State University Press.

Martín-Barbero, J. (1987) *De los medios a las mediaciones: Comunicación, cultura y hegemonía,* Mexico City and Barcelona: Ediciones G. Gili.

Mato, D. (1999) 'Telenovelas: transnacionalización de la industria y transformaciones del género', in García Canclini, N. and Achugar, H. (eds) *Las industrias culturales en la integración latinoamericana,* Buenos Aires: EUDEBA/Secretaría Permanente del Sistema Econonómico Latinoamericano.

Mayne, J. (1993) *Cinema and Spectatorship,* London: Routledge.

McClennan, S. (2002) '(De)Signing Women: Mexican Women Directors and Feminist Film', *Revista de Estudios Hispáncios,* 36.

Medina de la Serna, R. (1995) 'Sorrows and Glories of Comedy' in Paranaguá, P. A. (ed.) *Mexican Cinema,* London: BFI.

Melhuus, M. (1996) 'Power, Value and the Ambiguous Meanings of Gender', in Melhuus, M. and Stølen, K. A. (eds) *Machos, Mistresses, Madonnas: Contesting the Power of Latin American Gender Imagery,* London: Verso.

Melhuus, M. and Stolen, K. A. (eds) (1996) *Machos, Mistresses and Madonnas: Contesting the Power of Latin American Gender Imagery,* London: Verso.

Messinger Cypess, S. (1991) *La Malinche in Mexican Literature: From History to Myth,* Austin: University of Texas Press.

Meyer, M. C. and Beezley, W. H. (eds) (2000) *The Oxford History of Mexico,* Oxford: Oxford University Press.

Mignolo, W. D. (2000) *Local Histories/Global Designs: Coloniality, Subaltern Knowledges, and Border Thinking,* Princeton, IL: Princeton University Press.

Miquel, A. (1997) *Salvador Toscano,* Mexico: Universidad de Guadalajara/Gobierno del estado de Puebla, Secretaría de Cultura/Universidad Veracruzana/Dirección General de Actividades Cinematográficas UNAM.

Mirandé, A. (1998) *Hombres y Machos: Masculinity and Latino Culture,* California: Westview Press.

Mistron, D. E. (1983) 'The Role of Pancho Villa in the Mexican and the American Cinema', *Studies in Latin American Popular Culture,* 2: 1–13.

—— (1984) 'A Hybrid Subgenre: The Revolutionary Melodrama in the Mexican Cinema', *Studies in Latin American Popular Culture,* 3: 47–56.

Mitchell, W. J. T. (2002) 'Showing Seeing: A Critique of Visual Culture', *Journal of Visual Culture,* 1(2): 165–81.

Monnet, J. (1995) *Usos e imágenes del centro histórico de la Ciudad de México,* Mexico City: Departamento del Distrito Federal/Centro de Estudios Mexicanos y Centro-americanos.

Monsiváis, C. (1981a) 'Notas sobre la historia de la fotografía en México', *Revista de la Universidad de México,* 35.

—— (1981b) *Escenas de pudor y liviandad,* Mexico City: Grijalbo.

—— (1990) 'El matrimonio de la butaca y la pantalla', *Artes de México,* 10.

—— (1992) 'Las mitologías del cine mexicano', *Intermedios,* 20.

—— (1993) 'Mexican Cinema: Of Myths and Demystifications', in King, J., López, A. M. and Alvarado, M. (eds) *Mediating Two Worlds: Cinematic Encounters in the Americas,* London: BFI.

—— (1994a) 'Notas sobre la cultura mexicana en el siglo xx', in *Historia general de México, Vol. 2,* Mexico City: El colegio de México, Centro de Estudios Históricos.

—— (1994b) 'Se sufre, pero se aprende. (El melodrama y las reglas de la falta de límites)', *Archivos de la Filmoteca*, 16.

—— (1995) 'All the People Came and Did Not Fit onto the Screen: Notes on the Cinema Audience in Mexico', in Paulo Antonio Paranaguá (ed.) *Mexican Cinema*, London: BFI.

—— (1997a) *Mexican Postcards*, trans. Kraniauskus, J., London: Verso.

—— (1997b) 'Cultural Relations between the United States and Mexico', in Rodríguez O., Jaime, E. and Vincent K. (eds) *Common Border, Uncommon Paths: Race, Culture, and National identity in U.S.–Mexican Relations*, Wilmington, DE: Scholarly Resources.

—— (1999) 'Cantinflas and Tin Tan: Mexico's Greatest Comedians', in Hershfield, J. and Maciel, D. R. (eds) *Mexico's Cinema: A Century of Film and Filmmakers*, Wilmington, DE: S. R. Books.

—— (2000) *Aires de familia: Cultura y sociedad en América Latina*, Barcelona: Anagrama.

Monsiváis, C. and Bonfil, C. (1994) *A través del espejo: El cine mexicano y su público*, Mexico City: Ediciones El Milagro/Instituto Mexicano de Cinematografía.

Monteagudo, L. and Bucich, V. (2001) *Carlos Gardel y el primer cine sonoro argentine*, Huesca: Filmoteca de Andalucía/Chicago Latino Film Festival/Festival de Cine de Huesca.

Mora, C. J. ([1982] 1989) *Mexican Cinema: Reflections of a Society: 1896–1988*, Berkeley, CA: University of California Press.

Mraz, J. (1996) 'Lo gringo en el cine mexicano y la ideología alemanista', in Durán, I., Trujillo, I. and Verea, M. (eds) *México–Estados Unidos: Encuentros y desencuentros en el cine*, Mexico City: Filmoteca de la UNAM/IMCINE/CISAN.

—— (1999) 'The Revolution Is History: Filming the Past in Mexico and Cuba', *Film-Historia*, 9(2): 147–67.

—— (2003) *Nacho López: Mexican Photographer*, Minneapolis: University of Minnesota Press.

Murray, S. O. (ed.) (1995) *Latin American Homosexualities*, Albuquerque: University of New Mexico Press.

NACLA (1995), Anti-Immigration Backlash Issue, Nov.–Dec.

Navarrete, G. (1994) 'María Novaro reaparece en el panorama de los festivales internacionales de cine', *El heraldo*, 31 August: 31.

Nead, L. (1992) *The Female Nude: Art, Obscenity and Sexuality*, London: Routledge.

Nesbet, A. (2003) *Savage Junctures: Sergei Eisenstein and the Shape of Thinking*, London: I. B. Tauris.

Nesvig, M. (2001) 'The Complicated Terrain of Latin American Homosexuality', *Hispanic American Historical Review*, 81(3–4): 689–729.

Niblo, S. R. (1999) *Mexico in the 1940s: Modernity, Politics, and Corruption*, Wilmington, DE: S. R. Books.

Nichols, B. (1994) *Blurred Boundaries: Questions of Meaning in Contemporary Culture*, Bloomington: Indiana University Press.

—— (2001) 'Documentary Film and the Modernist Avant-Garde', *Critical Inquiry*, 27(4): 580–610.

Noble, A. (1998a) 'Photography and Vision in Porfirian Mexico', *Estudios interdisciplinarios de América Latina y el Caribe*, 9(1): 122–31.

—— (1998b) '*Zapatistas en Sanborns* (1914): Women at the Bar', *History of Photgraphy*, 22(4): 366–70.

—— (2000) *Tina Modotti: Image, Texture, Photography*, Albuquerque: University of New Mexico Press.

—— (2001a) 'If Looks Could Kill: Image Wars in *María Candelaria*', *Screen*, 42(1): 77–91.

—— (2001b) 'Yéndose por la tangente: The Border in María Novaro's *El Jardín del Edén*', *Journal of Iberian and Latin American Studies*, 7(2): 191–202.

—— (2003) 'Sexuality and Space in Jorge Fons' *El Callejón de los Milagros*', *Framework*, 44(1): 22–35.

—— (2004) 'Photography–Memory–Disavowal: The Casasola Archive' in Anderman, J. and Rowe, W. (eds) *Images of Power: Iconography, Culture and the State in Latin America*, Oxford: Berghahn Books.

Noriega, C. A. (ed.) (2000) *Visible Nations: Latin American Cinema and Video*, Minneapolis: University of Minnesota Press.

Noriega, C. A. and Ricci, S. (1994) *The Mexican Cinema Project*, Los Angeles: UCLA Film and Television Archive.

O'Malley, I. (1986) *The Myth of the Revolution: Hero Cults and the Institutionalization of the Mexican State: 1920–1940*, New York: Greenwood Press.

Oroz, S. (1995) *Melodrama: El cine de lágrimas de América Latina*, Mexico City: UNAM, Dirección General de Actividades Cinemátograficas.

Ortiz Monasterio, P., Hamill, P., Arroyo, S. R. and Casanova, R. (2002) *Mirada y memoria: Archivo fotográfico Casasola, México: 1900–1940*, Madrid: Turner/Mexico City: Consejo Nacional para la Cultura y las Artes/INAH.

Ortner, S. B. (1996) *Making Gender: The Politics and Erotics of Culture*, Boston, MA: Beacon Press.

Paranaguá, P. A. (ed.) (1995) *Mexican Cinema*, López, A. M., London: BFI in association with IMCINE.

—— (1997) *Arturo Ripstein: la espiral de la identidad*, Madrid: Cátedra/Filmoteca Española.

—— (1998) 'Of Periodizations and Paradigms: The Fifties in Comparative Perspective', *Nuevo Texto Crítico*, 10(21/22): 31–44.

—— (1999) 'María Félix: Imagen, mito y enigma', *Archivos de la Filmoteca*, 31: 76–87.

Paz, O. ([1950] 1988) *El laberinto de la soledad*, Mexico City: Fondo de Cultura Económica.

—— (1967) *The Labyrinth of Solitude: Life and Thought in Mexico*, trans. Kemp, L., London: Penguin.

Peña, M. (1994) 'Resultados desiguales en la primera cinta internacional de María Novaro', *El heraldo*, 6 September.

Pérez Montfort, R. (1994) *Estampas de nacionalismo popular mexicano: Ensayos sobre cultura popular y nacionalismo*, Mexico City: CIESAS.

—— (2000) *Avatares del nacionalismo cultural: Cinco ensayos*, Mexico City: CIESAS/CIDHEM.

Pick, Z. (1993) *The New Latin American Cinema: A Continental Project*, Austin: University of Texas Press.

—— (2000) 'A Romance with Mexico: The Epic Spectacle of the Revolution', *Canadian Journal of Film Studies*, 9(2): 3–22.

Pilcher, J. M. (2001) *Cantinflas and the Chaos of Mexican Modernity*, Wilmington, DE: S. R. Books.

Podalsky, L. (1993a) 'Disjointed Frames: Melodrama, Naturalism and Representation in 1940s Mexico', *Studies in Latin American Popular Culture*, 15.

—— (1993b) 'Patterns of the Primitive: Sergei Eisenstein's *¡Qué viva México!*' in King, J., López, A. M. and Alvarado, M. (eds) *Mediating Two Worlds: Cinematic Encounters in the Americas*, London: BFI.

—— (2000) 'Fulfilling Fantasies, Diverting Pleasures: Ana Carolina and *Das tripas coração*', in Noriega, C. A. (ed.), *Visible Nations: Latin American Cinema and Video*, Minneapolis: University of Minnesota Press.

—— (2003) 'Affecting Legacies: Historical Memory and Contemporary Structures of Feeling in *Madagascar* and *Amores Perros*', *Screen*, 44(3): 277–94.

Pollock, G. (1996) 'Gleaning in History or Coming after/behind the Reapers' in Pollock, G. (ed.) *Generations and Geographies in the Visual Arts: Feminist Readings*, London: Routledge.

Preston, J. and Dillon, S. (2004) *Opening Mexico: The Making of a Democracy*, New York: Farrar, Straus & Giroux.

Quiroz Arroyo, M. (1995) 'El cine de María Novaro, un guiño femenino', *Revista cine premier*, 3 October: 29.

Radstone, S. (2000) 'Screening Trauma: *Forrest Gump*, Film and Memory' in S. Radstone (ed.) *Memory and Methodology*, Oxford: Berg.

Ramírez Berg, C. (1989) 'Cracks in the *Macho* Monolith: *Machismo*, Man, and Mexico in Recent Mexican Cinema', *New Orleans Review*, 16: 1.

—— (1992a) *Cinema of Solitude: A Critical Study of Mexican Film, 1967–1983*, Austin: University of Texas Press.

—— (1992b) 'Figueroa's Skies and Oblique Perspective: Notes on the Development of the Classical Mexican Style', *Spectator*, 13(1): 25–41.

—— (1999) 'Every Picture Tells a Story: José Guadalupe Posada's Protocinematic Graphic Art' in Miller, T. and Stam, R. (eds) *A Companion to Film Theory*, Oxford: Blackwell.

—— (2000) '*El automóvil gris* and the Advent of Mexican Classicism', in C. Noriega (ed.) *Visible Nations: Latin American Cinema and Video*, Minneapolis: University of Minnesota Press.

—— (2002) *Latino Images in Film: Stereotypes, Subversion, Resistance*, Austin: University of Texas Press.

Ramírez Pimienta, J. C. (1997) 'Del rancho al arrabal: guías para ayudar a formar un estado-nación en el cine mexicano de la época de oro', *Nuevo Texto Crítico*, 10, (19/20): 211–21.

Ramos, S. (1962) *Profile of Man and Culture in Mexico*, trans. Earle, P. G., Austin: University of Texas Press.

Ranucci, K. and Feldman, J. (1998) *A Guide to Latin American, Caribbean, and U.S. Latino made Film and Video*, Lanham, MD: Scarecrow Press.

Rashkin, E. (2001) *Women Filmmakers in Mexico: The Country of Which We Dream*, Austin: University of Texas Press.

'Revisión del cine mexicano', (1990) special issue of *Artes de México*, 10.

Reyes, A. (1960) *Obras completas de Alfonso Reyes*, vol. XI, Mexcio City: Fondo de Cultura Económica.

Rodríguez Cruz, O. (ed.) (2000) *El 68 en el cine mexicano*, Puebla: Universidad Iberoamericana.

Romero, R. J. (1993) 'Border of Fear, Border of Desire', *Borderlines*, 1(1): 36–70.

Rowe, W. and Schelling, V. (1991) *Memory and Modernity: Popular Culture in Latin America*, London: Verso.

Rozado, A. (1991) *Cine y realidad social en México: Una lectura de la obra de Emilio Fernández*, Guadalajara: Universidad de Guadalajara/Centro de Investigación y Enseñanza Cinematográficas.

213

Rubenstein, A. (1998a) *Bad Language, Naked Ladies, and Other Threats to the Nation*, Durham, NC: Duke University Press.

—— (1998b) 'Raised Voices in the Cine Montecarlo: Sex Education, Mass Media and Oppositional Politics in Mexico', *Journal of Family History*, 23: 3.

—— (2000) 'Mass Media and Popular Culture in the Post Revolutionary Era', in Meyer, M. C. and Beezley, W. H., *The Oxford History of Mexico*, Oxford: Oxford University Press.

—— (2001) 'Bodies, Cities, Cinema: Pedro Infante's Death as Political Spectacle', in Joseph, G., Rubenstein, A. and Zolov, E. (eds) *Fragments of a Golden Age: The Politics of Culture in Mexico since 1940*, Durham, NC: Duke University Press.

—— (2002) 'El Santo's Strange Career', in Joseph, G. M. and Henderson T. J. (eds) *The Mexico Reader: History, Culture, Politics*, Durham, NC: Duke University Press.

Russell, C. (1999) *Experimental Ethnography: The Work of Film in the Age of Video*, Durham, NC: Duke University Press.

Ruy Sánchez, A. (1990) 'Introduction to an Enquiry', *Artes de México*, 10: 83.

Sánchez, F. (2001) *Luz en la oscuridad: Crónica del cine mexicano, 1896–2002*, Mexico City: CONACULTA: Cineteca Nacional: Casa Juan Pablos.

Santaolalla, I. *et al.* (2004) *Buñuel, Siglo XXI*, Zaragoza: Prensas Universitarias de Zaragoza.

Schaefer, C. (2003) *Bored to Distraction: Cinema of Excess in End-of-the-Century Mexico and Spain*, Albany, NY: State University of New York Press.

Schelling, V. (ed.) (2000) *Through the Kaleidoscope: the Experience of Modernity in Latin America*, New York: Verso.

Schlesinger, P. (2000) 'The Sociological Scope of "National Cinema"', in Hjort, M. and Mackenzie, S. (eds) *Cinema and Nation*, London: Routledge.

Schnitman, J. (1984) *Film Industries in Latin America: Dependency and Development*, Norwood, NJ: Ablex.

Shaw, L. (2003) 'The Brazilian *Chanchada* and Hollywood Paradigms (1930–1959), *Framework: The Journal of Cinema and Media*, 44(1): 70–83.

Sherman, J. W. (2000) 'The Mexican "Miracle" and its Collapse', in Meyer, M. C. and Beezley, W. H. (eds) *The Oxford History of Mexico*, Oxford: Oxford University Press.

Shohat, E. and Stam, R. (1994) *Unthinking Eurocentrism: Multiculturalism and the Media*, London: Routledge.

Sklar, R. (1993) *Film: An International History of the Medium*, London: Thames & Hudson.

Smith, M. (1995) *Engaging Characters: Fiction, Emotion, and the Cinema*, Oxford: Clarendon Press.

Smith, P. J. (2002) 'Heaven's Mouth', *Sight and Sound*, 4: 16–19.

—— (2003a) 'Transatlantic Traffic in Recent Mexican Films', *Journal of Latin American Cultural Studies*, 12: 389–400.

—— (2003b) *Amores Perros: Modern Classic*, London: BFI.

Solomon-Godeau, A. (1997) *Male Trouble: A Crisis in Representation*, London: Thames & Hudson.

Stam, R. (1997) *Tropical Multiculturalism: A Comparative History of Race in Brazilian Cinema and Culture*, Durham, NC: Duke University Press.

—— (2000a) *Film Theory: An Introduction*, Oxford: Blackwell.

—— (2000b) 'Film Theory and Spectatorship in the Age of the 'Posts'', in Gledhill, C. and Williams, L. (eds) *Reinventing Film Studies*, London: Arnold.

Stavans, I. (1998) *The Riddle of Cantinflas: Essays on Hispanic Popular Culture*, Albuquerque: University of New Mexico Press.

Stevens, D. F. (ed.) (1997) *Based on a True Story: Latin American History at the Movies*, Wilmington, DE: S.R. Books.

Stokes, M. and Maltby, R. (1999) *Identifying Hollywood's Audiences: Cultural Identity and the Movies*, London: BFI.

Taibo, P. I. (1991) *La Doña*, Mexico City: Planeta Mexicana.

Tobing Rony, F. (1996) *The Third Eye: Race, Cinema, and Ethnographic Spectacle*, Durham, NC: Duke University Press.

Torgovnick, M. (1990) *Gone Primitive: Savage Intellects, Modern Lives*, Chicago: University of Chicago Press.

Torrents, N. (1993) 'Mexican Cinema Comes Alive' in King, J., López, A. M. and Alvarado, M. (eds) *Mediating Two Worlds: Cinematic Encounters in the Americas*, London: BFI.

Trelles Plazaola, L. (1991) *Cine y mujer en América Latina: Directoras de largometrajes de ficción*, Puerto Rico: Universidad de Puerto Rico.

Tuñón, J. (1987) *Mujeres en México: Recordando una histora*, Mexico City: Conaculta.

—— (1993) 'Between the Nation and Utopia: The Image of Mexico in the Films of Emilio "Indio" Fernández', *Studies in Latin American Popular Culture*, 12.

—— (1995) 'Emilio Fernández: A Look Behind the Bars', in Paranaguá, P. A. (ed.), *Mexican Cinema*, London: BFI.

—— (1998) *Mujeres de luz y sombra en el cine mexicano: La construcción de una imagen*, 1939–1952, Mexico City: El Colegio de México/Instituto Mexicano de Cinematografía.

—— (2002) 'Domando la naturaleza: La violencia hacia las mujeres en el cine de Emilio Fernández', in De Diego, F. and Schwartz, A. (eds) *Repensando la violencia y el patriarcado frente al nuevo milenio: Nuevas perspectivas en el mundo hispánico y germánico*, Ottawa: University of Ottawa.

Turim, M. C. (1989) *Flashbacks in Film: Memory and History*, London: Routledge.

Turner, G. (ed.) (2002) *The Film Cultures Reader*, London: Routledge.

Valenzuela Arce, J. M. (1999) *Impecable y diamantina: La desconstrucción del discurso nacional*, Tijuana: El Colegio de la Frontera Norte/Instituto Tecnológico y de Estudios Superiores de Occidente.

Vasey, R. (1997) *The World According to Hollywood, 1918–1939*, Madison: University of Wisconsin Press.

Vásquez Mantecón, A. (1998) 'No se olvida . . .', *Estudios interdisciplinarios de América Latina y el Caribe*, 9: 1.

Vaughan, M. K. (2001) 'Transnational Processes and the Rise and Fall of the Mexican State: Notes from the Past', in Joseph, G., Rubenstein, A. and Zolov, E. (eds) *Fragments of a Golden Age: The Politics of Culture in Mexico since 1940*, Durham, NC: Duke University Press.

Vidrio, M. (2001) *El goce de las lágrimas: El melodrama en el cine mexicano de los años treinta*, Guadalajara: Universidad de Guadalajara.

Virilio, P. (1989) *War and Cinema: The Logistics of Perception*, trans. Camiller, P., London: Verso.

Wallace, E. R. (1983) *Freud and Anthropology: A History and Reappraisal*, New York: International Universities Press.

Wallis, B. (1994) 'Selling Nations: International Exhibitions and Cultural Diplomacy', in

215

Sherman, D. J. and Rogoff, I. (eds) *Museum Culture: Histories, Discourses, Spectacles*, London: Routledge.

Waslin, M. (2001) 'Immigration Policy in Flux', *NACLA Report on the Americas*, 35: 3.

West, D. (1977) 'Castle of Machismo: A Meditation on Arturo Ripstein's Film *El castillo de la pureza*', *Revista de la literatura hispánica*, 5–6.

Widdifield, S. G. (1996) *The Embodiment of the National in Late Nineteenth-Century Mexican Painting*, Tucson: University of Arizona Press.

Williams, L. (ed.) (1994) *Viewing Positions: Ways of Seeing Films*, New Brunswick: Rutgers University Press.

Wilt, D. E. (2003) *The Mexican Filmography: 1916 through 2001*, Jefferson: Macfarland & Co.

Woldenberg, J. (1995) 'El Tapado', in Florescano, E. (ed.) *Mitos mexicanos*, Mexico City: Aguilar/Nuevo Siglo.

Wollen, P. (1970) *Signs and Meanings in the Cinema*, London: Thames & Hudson.

Womack, J. (1968) *Zapata and the Mexican Revolution*, London: Thames & Hudson.

Wood, N. (1999) *Vectors of Memory: Legacies of Trauma in Postwar Europe*, Oxford: Berg.

Xavier, I. (1997) *Allegories of Underdevelopment: Aesthetics and Politics in Modern Brazilian Cinema*, Minneapolis: University of Minnesota Press.

—— (1999) 'Historical Allegory', in Miller, T. and Stam, R. (eds) *A Companion to Film Theory*, Oxford: Blackwell.

Yankelevich, P. (ed.) (2002) 'México, país de Refugio', *La experiencia de los exilios en el siglo XX*, Mexico City: INAH-Plaza y Valdés.

Yúdice, G. (1992) 'Postmodernity and Transnational Capitalism', in Yúdice, G. and Flores, J. (eds) *On Edge: The Crisis of Contemporary Latin American Culture*, Minneapolis: University of Minnesota Press.

Zavala, L. (1994) *Permanencia voluntaria: el cine y su espectador*, Xalapa, Ver. Universidad Veracruzana/Universidad Autónoma Metropolitana-Xochimilco.

Zolov, E. (1999) *Refried Elvis: The Rise of the Mexican Counter Culture*, Berkeley, CA: University of California Press.

Zúñiga, A. (1994) 'De la madre en el melodrama mexicano. (*Nosotros los pobres*, 1948)', *Archivos de la Filmoteca*, 16.

WEBSITE RESOURCES

The first two sites listed opposite – one in Spanish and one in English – are excellent starting points to carry out web searches for more sites related to the Mexican cinema. In addition to information about films, directors, stars and critical literature, both sites contain links to the key film institutions in Mexico, including the Filmoteca de la Universidad Autónoma de México (UNAM, Mexico City), Centro de Investigación en Estudios Cinematográficos (Universidad de Guadalajara), and the major film schools, studios and producers. LAVA is a useful site that facilitates the location and purchase of Latin American and US Latino made film and video.

Más de cien años de cine mexicano
http://cinemexicano.mty.itesm.mx/front.html

The Mexican Film Resource Page
http://www.wam.umd.edu/~dwilt/mfb.html

LAVA (Latin American Video Archives)
www.latinamericanvideo.org

INDEX

Related titles from Routledge

Chinese National Cinema
Yingjin Zhang

What does it mean to be 'Chinese'? This controversial question has sparked off a never-ending process of image-making in Chinese-speaking communities throughout the twentieth century. This introduction to Chinese national cinema covers three 'Chinas': mainland China, Hong Kong and Taiwan. Historical and comparative perspectives bring out the parallel developments in these three Chinas, while critical analysis explores thematic and stylistic changes over time. As well as exploring artistic achievements and ideological debates, Yingjin Zhang examines how - despite the pressures placed on the industry from state control and rigid censorship - Chinese national cinema remains incapable of projecting a single unified picture, but rather portrays many different Chinas.

Hb: 0-415-17289-6
Pb: 0-415-17290-X

Available at all good bookshops
For ordering and further information please visit:
www.routledge.com

Related titles from Routledge

Cinema & Nation
Mette Hjort & Scott Mackenzie

Ideas of national identity, nationalism and transnationalism are now a central
feature of contemporary film studies, as well as primary concerns for filmmakers themselves. Embracing a range of national cinemas including
Scotland, Poland, France, Turkey, Indonesia, India, Germany and America,
Cinema and Nation considers the ways in which film production and
reception are shaped by ideas of national belonging and examines the
implications of globalisation for the concept of national cinema. In the first
three Parts, contributors explore sociological approaches to nationalism,
challenge the established definitions of 'national cinema', and consider the
ways in which states - from the old Soviet Union to contemporary Scotland
- aim to create a national culture through cinema. The final two Parts
address the diverse strategies involved in the production of national cinema
and consider how images of the nation are used and understood by
audiences both at home and abroad.

Hb: 0-415-20862-9
Pb: 0-415-20863-7

Available at all good bookshops
For ordering and further information please visit:
www.routledge.com

Related titles from Routledge

Cinema Studies: The Key Concepts
Second Edition
Susan Hayward

This is the essential guide for anyone interested in film. Now in its second edition, the text has been completely revised and expanded to meet the needs of today's students and film enthusiasts. Some 150 key genres, movements, theories and production terms are explained and analyzed with depth and clarity. Entries include:

- auteur theory
- Blaxploitation
- British New Wave
- feminist film theory
- intertextuality
- method acting
- pornography
- Third World Cinema
- Vampire movies.

A bibliography of essential writings in cinema studies completes an authoritative yet accessible guide to what is at once a fascinating area of study and arguably the greatest art form of modern times.

Hb: 0-415-22739-9
Pb: 0-415-22740-2

Available at all good bookshops
For ordering and further information please visit:
www.routledge.com

Related titles from Routledge

Spanish National Cinema
Núria Triana-Toribio

A nation is nothing without the stories it tells about itself. In *Spanish National Cinema*, Núria Triana-Toribio studies some of the stories told through film, as well as the demands made on Spanish cinema to provide new stories to contribute to the formation of the nation. She also examines the changing national qualities of Spanish cinema, such as the 'Spanishness' of its filmmakers, while taking issue with studies of national cinemas that focus on 'important moments'.

Núria Triana-Toribio's insightful study examines the discourses of nationalism as they intersected or clashed with Spanish film production from its inception to the present. While the book addresses the discourses around filmmakers such as Almodóvar and Medem, whose work has achieved international recognition, Spanish National Cinema is particularly novel in its treatment of a whole range of popular cinema rarely touched on in studies of Spanish cinema. Using accounts of films, popular film magazines and documents not readily available to an English-speaking audience, as well as case studies focusing on the key issues of each epoch, this volume illuminates the complex and changing relationship between cinema and Spanish national identity.

Hb: 0-415-22059-9
Pb: 0-415-22060-2

Available at all good bookshops
For ordering and further information please visit:
www.routledge.com